The Works

A History of Rippers Joinery M
of Castle and Sible H

by

by Pam and Adrian Corder-Birch
with photographic restoration by Christine Walker

A 1909 view of the works from the Colne Valley and Halstead Railway showing joinery in trucks on Ripper's siding

Dedication:
To everyone employed at The Works who played a part in its history

Front Cover: Employees in 1907 and an aerial view of 'The Works', housing and railway at Sible Hedingham in 1929

Back Cover: Drawings of a former warehouse and maltings in Castle Lane, Castle Hedingham used by Ripper Brothers for storage and workshops during the late 1890s.

Published by: Adrian Corder-Birch, D.L., (in conjunction with Pam)
Rustlings
Howe Drive
Halstead
Essex CO9 2QL

Email: corder-birch@lineone.net

Printed by The Lavenham Press Limited
Arbons House
47 Water Street
Lavenham
Suffolk
CO10 9RN

ISBN 978-0-9567219-2-1

Further copies of this book are available from the Authors/Publishers as above

Price £14.95 plus P&P
Cheques and postal orders in English Pounds Sterling, payable to either
Mr A Corder-Birch or Mrs P Corder-Birch.

CONTENTS

AUTHOR'S PREFACE

In September 2013 an exhibition called 'Rippers and the Hedinghams' took place at Sible Hedingham Village Hall when over six hundred people including twenty seven members of the Ripper and related families attended. It was held as a tribute to the late Stephen Ripper who had built up a collection of documents, photographs and other memorabilia relating to his family and their joinery works. The interest was so great that it was decided to compile this book to record further information about the family and their businesses, which flourished in the Hedinghams and became the largest employer.

The joinery factory was always known by the family and employees as "The Works" and therefore this was chosen as the title for this book and is referred to as such in the text. The earliest joinery workshops were located in Castle Hedingham during the 1880s and 1890s but when the business moved to Station Road, Sible Hedingham in 1899 it was decided to retain the Castle Hedingham address. This remained on all stationery, catalogues and other documentation for many decades.

The first business in Castle Hedingham was in the name of 'E & T Ripper, Carpenters and Joiners'. The second business, which also originated in Castle Hedingham was in the name of their youngest brother 'W. C. Ripper' and remained in his name following the move to Sible Hedingham. In 1908 the three brothers went into partnership and traded as Ripper Brothers. In 1915 a private company Rippers Limited was incorporated, which was converted into a public company in 1933 and continued until taken over by Bowater in 1973 when it became Bowater Ripper Limited. This book is principally about Ripper Brothers and Rippers Limited but to avoid repetition this has largely been abbreviated to Rippers.

Rippers had three associated companies namely George Evans & Sons Limited later Evans Bellhouse Limited of Thornton Heath, Manchester, William Kay (Bolton) Limited and The Sible Hedingham Red Brick Company Limited. This book includes chapters about George Evans & Sons Limited, which became Evans Bellhouse Limited and William Kay (Bolton) Limited. However The Sible Hedingham Red Brick Company Limited is not included in detail because a comprehensive history of this company appears in the book, "Bricks, Buildings and Transport, A history of Mark Gentry, the Hedingham red brick industry, buildings, road and rail transport", published 2013.

During 1946 and 1947 Tucker Ripper wrote a book, which he had privately printed in 1948. It is titled 'Recollections of an old Woodpecker', which is principally his autobiography but contains much information about other members of the Ripper family, their homes, the village of Castle Hedingham and its residents. This book, which is now very scarce, contained some information about early business ventures but this was mainly saved for a second book, which he wrote about 1950 and was never published. The title for this book would have been 'With Chisel, Saw and Plane – The story of an East Anglian Village Industry'. The second book was thought to be missing for nearly sixty years but fortunately it was found and both books have been a valuable source of information about the family and the works up to 1950. However the history has been continued until the takeovers of Evans Bellhouse and Rippers in 1971 and 1973 respectively.

This book is not intended to be a complete history of the Ripper family. It mainly concentrates upon those members of the family who were closely associated with the four companies. These companies employed several hundred people but unfortunately it has not been possible to include all employees, although many are featured in various chapters and in appendix one.

Many products were supplied during a period of nearly one hundred years, the majority of which are recorded in this book, together with details of buildings in which they were incorporated. Space does not allow all products and buildings to be detailed and therefore those referred to in chapter eleven have mainly been restricted to Essex. This provides useful examples of the type of work undertaken in a variety of buildings. However a list of work undertaken in buildings outside Essex is contained in appendix two.

PAM and ADRIAN CORDER-BIRCH
18th April 2014

ACKNOWLEDGEMENTS

The Ripper family
While we have researched and written this book, it would be very unfair to take all the credit as many members of the Ripper family have helped us enormously with information and photographs.

Over the years the late Stephen Ripper created his own archive of Ripper material and when his wife Frances knew about the exhibition held in September 2013 and later about plans to write this book, everything Stephen had collected was immediately made available to us to borrow or copy. Fran was an inspiration to us both, always willing to help and generous with her time and we are deeply saddened that she passed away shortly before this book was finished.

Stephen and Fran's daughter Anne Shellim contributed a number of 'boards' for the exhibition and very kindly allowed us to extract information contained on them. We know that some of the subjects Anne tackled, such as buildings where Rippers joinery was used, took many hours of patient research as she contacted various company archives for information and photographs. Anne also researched patents granted to her great grandfather, Tucker Ripper. We are extremely grateful for her hard work and for the encouragement, interest and support that we have received from both Anne and her sister Cathy Malone.

Julian Ripper has kindly made available a large amount of documents and photographs from his late father, Norman Ripper's collection of memorabilia, including some very useful historical notes and photographs.

Christopher Ripper and his sister Judy Ford have also contributed much useful information, especially about their late father Jim Ripper, a bomber pilot during the Second World War.

Sheila Ripper, a member of the 'Manchester' branch of the family also loaned many useful company records not only relating to Evans Bellhouse but also to Rippers Limited. When attending the exhibition she kindly produced the draft of Tucker Ripper's second book, which was never published. Interestingly the illustrations, which Tucker intended to use, were in Stephen's collection and some have been used in this book, by kind permission of the family. This includes the three drawings in chapter two, which were drawn by Margaret Smith, twin sister of Kate Smith, the wife of John Wilkin Porkess.

Jill Yates and Roger Porkess, John and Kate's grandchildren provided valuable information about William Kay (Bolton) Limited, a company taken over by Rippers in 1943. They also supplied photographs of the Porkess family and Kay's timber yard which enhanced this chapter.

Michael Ripper, the last surviving former director of Rippers Limited, readily answered numerous questions and loaned photographs, documents and newspaper cuttings of events which occurred during his years as managing director. Although hard to reproduce we have included some of these pictures in the book as they are informative and interesting.

Other relations including Ian Finch, Holly Ripper, Michael Ripper (of Manchester), Malcolm Wearing, Christine Weight formerly Porkess and Allyn Weight gave material which helped with both the exhibition and the book.

We thank the family for supporting this publication, and for their help which is much appreciated.

Other acknowledgements
The majority of illustrations have been copied, enhanced and restored by Christine Walker using her very able photographic and computer skills. We know this is very time consuming and precise work, and we are extremely grateful for her continued support and interest. A few of many photographs taken by her husband, Phil Walker at the exhibition have also been included.

Angela Weatherley and Nick Ellis carried out much work in connection with the exhibition and have made the results of their research and 'boards' available, which have been most useful.

The authors would like to thank the following for their generous help with the loan of documents, photographs and publications, and for providing information for the 2013 exhibition much of which has been included in this book.

George Argent	Jackie Hart	Dawn Pilgrim
Delyss Barber	Mary Hart	Leslie Pilgrim
Anne and Sean Bambrick	Owen Hawkes	Doreen Potts
Mike Brown	Jane Haycock	Derek Pratt
Lawrence Chatten	James Hewlett	Darren Prentice
Valerie Chase	Brian Hoadley	Julie Rawson
Jean Cock	Colin and Katherine Hoye	Glen Rawlinson
David Colthorpe	Graham Hume	The late Bill Raynham
Peter Cook	Heather King	Marcel Rayner
Jean Cooper	Sally Kinsman	John Redgewell
Dorothy Cornell	Gillian Lamb	Derek Reeve
Pat Dakin	Andrew Lynch	Thomas Ruffle
Brian Day	Marjorie McAleese	The late Arthur Ruffle
Joan Denham	Noreen Metson	Shirley Seaman
Claire Evans	Harry and Marie Morrell	Peter Smith
Malcolm Firman	Sandra Mortimer	Derek and Gladys Smith
David Gambell	Monica Nash	Professor Richard Smith
John Garwood	Roger Oliver	Barry Sparke
Linda Halls	Joyce Palmer	The late Peter Steward
Audrey and Bob Hardy	Nigel Palmer	Eileen Tobitt
Keith Harrington	Keith and Laura Pilgrim	Percy Wiseman

Research has also been carried out at a number of locations including the Essex Record Office and the National Archive Office. Jim Davis, the archivist and curator of Halstead and District Local History Society collection has been most helpful especially with the production of old copies of the Halstead Gazette newspapers.

The late Stephen Ripper collected together many photographs and documents, which were displayed in the exhibition and used in this publication, from the following:

Bert Ambrose	Margaret Judd	Miss. Dorothy Raymond
Sybil Amey	The late Leslie Ling	The late Cyril Smith
The late Phyllis Cox	John Moles	The late Fred Wells
The late Gordon Faiers	The late Maurice Nash	The late Jean Whiting
Brian Fleming	Monica Nash	The late Maurice Wiseman
The late Bertram Hogarth	Doreen Potts	Jack Woolveridge

It was Jack Woolveridge who took many photographs of the works for Stephen Ripper during the 1960s and early 1970s, a few of which have been used in this book.

The late Bertram Hogarth also took many photographs of the works over a period of forty years. These, together with his meticulous drawings and detailed notes have also proved invaluable.

Anne Shellim read the proofs and suggested improvements, which have been readily included.

Finally, we should like to thank Anne Shellim and Cathy Malone, for writing the joint Foreword.

PAM and ADRIAN CORDER-BIRCH
11th May 2014

FOREWORD

by

Anne Shellim (nee Ripper) and Catherine Malone (nee Ripper)

It was a great honour to be asked to write the Foreword to a book about the joinery business started by our great grandfather and his two brothers nearly 125 years ago in the late nineteenth century.

However this book is not just about the Ripper family, it is also about the many men and women who worked there and helped to build the business from its early beginnings in a workshop in Castle Hedingham, into the large nationally-known company it later became.

'The Works' was the largest employer in the area and therefore played an important part in the life of the Hedinghams and surrounding villages. With business rapidly expanding after the First World War housing for employees became a problem. To attract the necessary workforce they developed a housing scheme of their own and over three years built 94 houses. In 1924 they introduced paid holidays for employees earning themselves a good reputation as an employer. The local volunteer fire service was manned by Rippers workers who were seen cycling through the workshops when the siren went. The business supported many sports and social clubs and provided lorries for the annual village carnival floats. As a local once remarked, "All roads lead to Rippers".

It should also be mentioned that Rippers owned two other businesses in the north; George Evans & Sons Limited (later known as Evans Bellhouse Limited) in Manchester and William Kay (Bolton) Limited. Both companies were timber merchants and joinery manufacturers and were managed by members of the Ripper family.

In his retirement our father, Stephen Ripper, started a collection of photographs of the companies. It was this collection which inspired the organisers and became the basis of the Ripper Exhibition held in Sible Hedingham Village Hall in September 2013. Our only sadness was that our father was not alive to see the exhibition – he would have been thrilled to see the interest it generated and the former employees of Rippers meeting up again after many years and sharing their stories; at times the atmosphere in the Village Hall felt more like a social club gathering.

Following the overwhelming success of the exhibition, the family was delighted when Pam and Adrian Corder-Birch decided to write this history of 'The Works' using some of the information gathered for the exhibition, but they have also utilised records from many other sources and found much new material as well. They are to be congratulated having carried out a magnificent job and as a result have provided a record of information that would have otherwise been dispersed and lost over the coming years.

Anne Shellim and Catherine Malone
10th May 2014

The Hedingham Branch of the Ripper family

Descendants of John Ripper

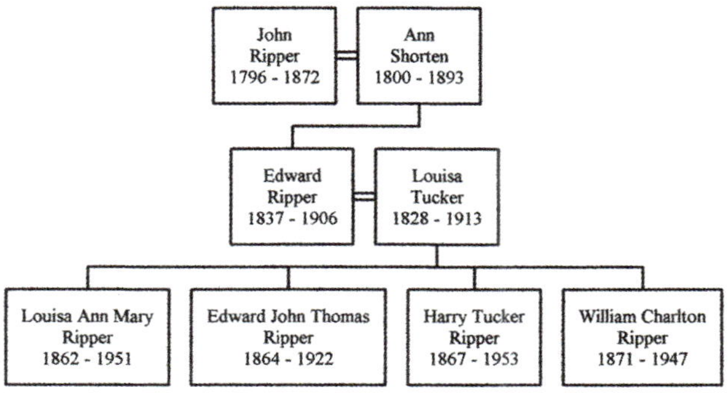

Descendants of Edward John Thomas Ripper

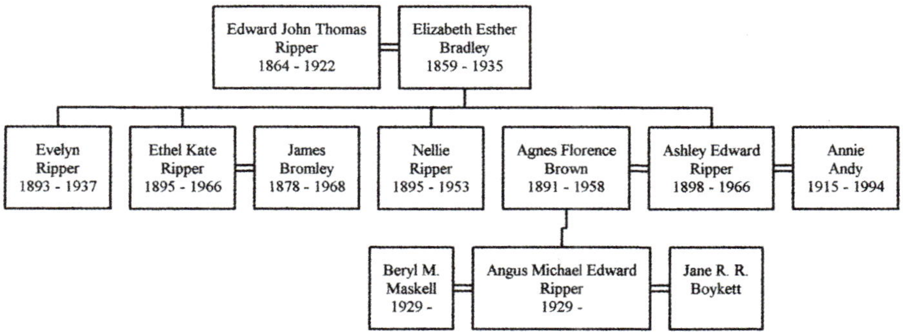

Descendants of Harry Tucker Ripper

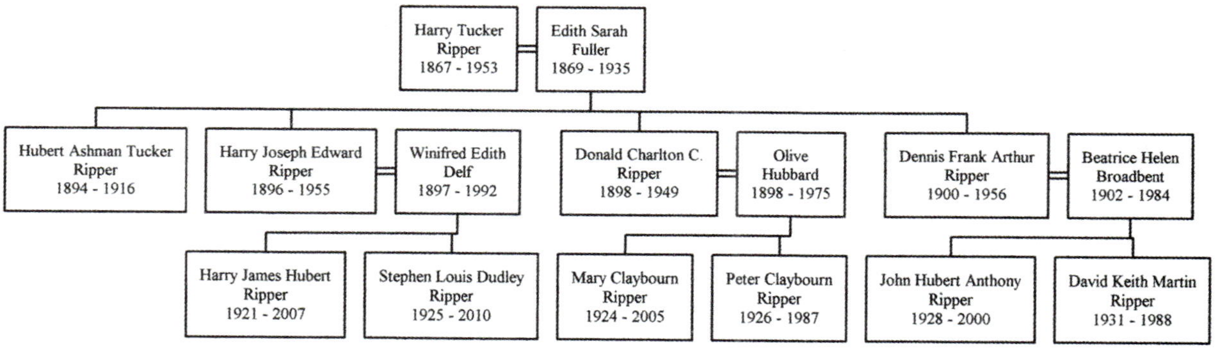

Descendants of William Charlton Ripper

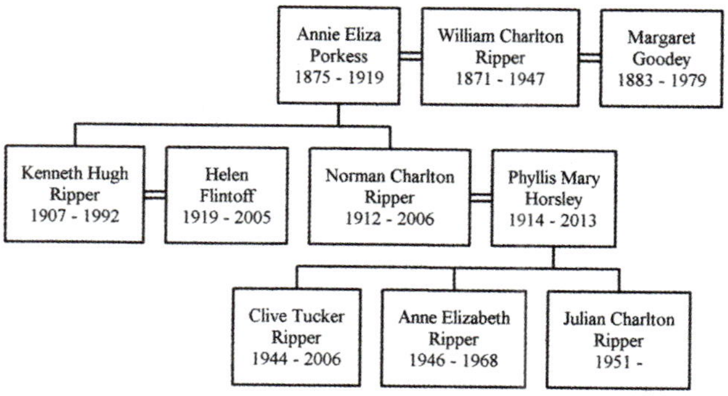

Chapter 1

The Ripper Family

Edward Ripper was born on the 11th April 1837, the son of John and Ann Ripper, formerly Shorten. John and Ann had at least ten children between circa 1821 and circa 1845. They lived on a farm at Terrington St. John, near Kings Lynn, Norfolk until around 1841 when they moved to the High Road, where John was a publican. John and Ann moved to Kings Lynn when John retired as both a farmer and publican; John died in 1872 and Ann in 1893.

In 1851 Edward Ripper was apprenticed to his brother Thomas who had a grocer and draper's shop in Terrington St. John. When Edward completed his apprenticeship he worked in a shop in Tottenham Court Road, London before he found employment in Halstead. Edward Ripper married Louisa Tucker on 30th July 1861 at St. Giles Church, Great Maplestead. Edward met Louisa when she was a regular customer at his shop and gradually romance blossomed. Louisa's father, Thomas, was brought up on a farm at Castle Hedingham by his grandfather Thomas Tucker, as his father, Sergeant Thomas Tucker was killed at the Battle of Vittoria in 1813.

Before Edward married Louisa, he moved to Castle Hedingham and worked in Daniel Harvey's grocery and drapery shop. Following their marriage Edward and Louisa lived in Great Maplestead where their daughter Louisa Ann Mary was born in 1862. When Louisa was three years old the family moved to Castle Hedingham and lived in different properties around the village. Edward and Louisa's son, Edward John Thomas (Ted) was born in 1864, followed by Harry Tucker (Tucker) born in 1867 in a cottage at Pye Corner and William Charlton (Charlton) who was born in 1871 in a house in Nunnery Street. In 1889 Edward and Louisa moved next door into the attached house, known as Cherry Lawn. This property had been vacated by their friends, the Reverend James Burgess and his family who had moved into the Manse. However Edward and Louisa did not remain at Cherry Lawn for long as they moved again in 1893 into one of three houses, which their sons had built in St. James Street where they remained for the rest of their lives.

Edward and Louisa Ripper with their four children Ted standing at the back, with left to right, Louisa, Louisa (senior), Charlton, Edward and Tucker

Edward was a kindly man who loved music and sang in the Chapel choir. He was instrumental in starting music classes in the village and occasionally played the violin. To augment his meagre salary he turned his hand to many things in his spare time, which included buying and selling harmoniums and pianos. During the 1870s Edward was in business on his own account as a linen draper in Castle Hedingham. Edward and Louisa also took in lodgers to help their financial situation, and in later life Edward was assistant overseer for Castle Hedingham and responsible for collecting the poor rates. He was clerk to Castle Hedingham Parish Council and Burial Board, including the administration of the cemetery. Many people in the village sought Edward's advice and he was well known for assisting villagers when they wished to make a will. When necessary he would consult his nephew who was chief clerk in a solicitor's office in Chelmsford to clarify legal points. Much amusement was caused when the reply came addressed to: "Mr. Edward Ripper, Parish Lawyer"! One will prepared by Edward was for William Parr, the landlord of the Eleven Elms Beer House at Crouch Green, Castle Hedingham, which was made on 18th June 1903 and witnessed by Edward Ripper and Robert Corder. Some years earlier when William Parr was a carter, Edward Ripper asked him to remove a heap of earth and rubble. He later sent his account as follows:

"Edward Ripper to William Parr – Moving the earth - 4s 6d".

Edward and Louisa Ripper and their family
Tucker standing, middle row: Ted and Louisa (senior), front row: Charlton, Edward and Louisa

Edward died on the 15th January 1906 and Louisa on the 24th December 1913.

1. Louisa Ann Mary Ripper later Finch and family

Louisa Ann Mary Ripper who was born in 1862 was the eldest child and only daughter of Edward and Louisa. She was well educated and passed her school certificate examination which she sat in London, with 'honours'. Louisa taught at the local school in Castle Hedingham until she secured a teaching position in Bedford, but returned home when her mother was unwell and remained with the family until she married Lewis Finch in 1889. Following their marriage Lewis and Louisa moved to Cambridge where Lewis opened a prosperous ironmongery business.

They had two children, Elsie born on the 16th September 1890 and Stanley Keith born on the 26th November 1900.

In 1917 Lewis Finch joined the staff of Rippers with responsibility for ironmongery at the works. He remained connected with the company until his death on the 19th April 1940. Louisa died in 1951.

Descendants of Lewis Finch

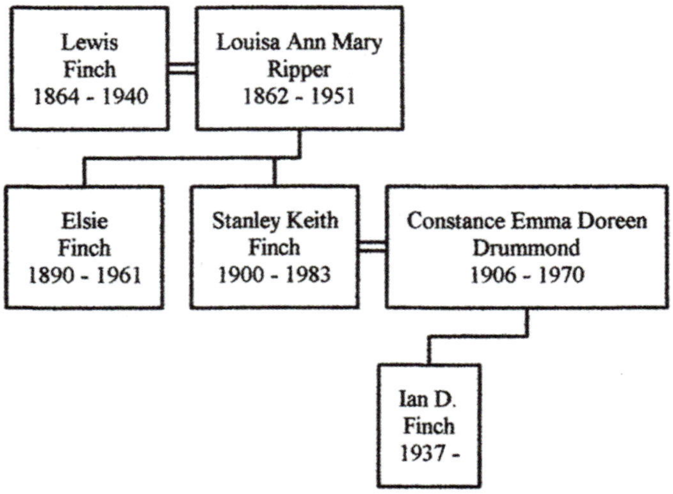

1. (i) Elsie Finch studied at the Royal Academy of Music in London where she became a sub-professor and later elected as Associate of the Academy. She returned to Castle Hedingham to look after her mother and used her musical talents to help young aspiring musicians in the village to achieve success. Elsie did not marry and died in 1961 aged 70 years.

1. (ii) Stanley Keith Finch was born in 1900 at Chesterton, Cambridgeshire. He was educated at Perse School, Cambridge and read Greek at university. Stanley worked for the Cubitt Motor Company at Aylesbury, Buckinghamshire before his parents moved to Castle Hedingham and he joined Rippers in 1925. He married Constance Emma Doreen Drummond, known as Doreen or Drummie, on the 28th September 1935. Drummie who was the daughter of William and Bertha Drummond of Thornton Heath, Surrey was born in 1906. She had moved to Halstead and was matron at the Cottage Hospital, before she married Stanley. Following their marriage Stanley and Drummie lived at Tokat House, Sible Hedingham and had one son, Ian, born in 1937.

Stanley was particularly interested in stock joinery, especially when Rippers built a workshop and designed and produced their own products. In 1939 Stanley became joint managing director of Rippers Limited with his cousins Harry and Ashley Ripper, and during the Second World War, he was appointed joint parish food organiser with Harry.

By 1963 Stanley held the position of company secretary until 1966 when he was elected as chairman. In 1969 he became honorary life president and retired as a director in 1970. He was also a director of Evans Bellhouse Limited and of The Sible Hedingham Red Brick Company Limited until its closure in the 1950s.

Stanley was president of The English Joiners Association and also president of The British Woodwork Manufacturers Association from 1964 to 1966. He was a governor of both Hedingham School and Braintree College of Further Education.

The Finch family circa 1938
Left to right, back row: Elsie, Lewis, and Louisa
Front row: Stanley and Doreen with their son, Ian

Stanley Finch 1900-1983

Drummie died in March 1970 and Stanley remained at Tokat house until he moved to Rose Cottage, Castle Hedingham where he died in 1983.

1. (2). Edward John Thomas Ripper and his family

Edward Ripper, known as Ted, was born in 1864 the eldest son of Edward and Louisa. With his brothers Tucker and Charlton, Ted was one of the founder members of Rippers Brothers, later Rippers Limited of the Station Joinery Works.

Ted married Elizabeth Esther Bradley (Lizzie) in 1892. Lizzie was the eldest daughter of William, a builder and Esther Bradley of Cockfosters (Village), Middlesex.

Following their marriage Ted and Lizzie lived at 'Palmers' in Queen Street, Castle Hedingham and they had four children; Evelyn born in 1893, Ethel Kate and Nell, who were twins, born in 1895 and a son, Ashley Edward born in 1898.

Ted took an active role in the Congregational Church and was a deacon and acted as Church secretary. He was always interested in the welfare of the villagers and although not a well man for many years, he was personally involved with the construction and building of the Castle Hedingham Women's Institute wooden hall, which was erected behind the tennis courts in St. James Street.

Ted who looked after the plant and offices died on the 12th October 1922, when he was the senior director at Rippers. Lizzie died 13 years later on the 10th February 1935.

Ted and Lizzie Ripper with their family

1. (2). (i) Evelyn Ripper who was born in 1893, worked as a domestic science teacher in Bath, Somerset for several years. She remained a spinster and died in a London nursing home on the 30th July 1937 aged 53 years.

1. (2). (ii) Ethel Kate Ripper who was born in 1895 resided from at least the mid 1930s in London and lived for several years at 109 Charlburt Court, Marylebone. Ethel married Dr. James (Jim) Bromley, (born 1878) of The Meadows, Castle Hedingham in Marylebone in 1958, following the death of his first wife, Blanche. Ethel died in 1966 and Jim died in 1968 aged 89 years.

1. (2). (iii) Nell Ripper known as Nellie, lived with her twin sister Ethel in Marylebone in the early 1950s and died in a nursing home on the 24th August 1953 aged 58 years.

1. (2). (iv) Ashley Edward Ripper who was born on the 30th November 1898, was the only son of Ted and Lizzie. He was educated at Earls Colne Grammar School and started at the works in 1914. He enlisted in 1917 and served in France where he was wounded and returned home in spring 1918 suffering from shell shock.

Ashley eventually returned to work at Rippers and was employed in the office. He was in charge of the company accounts and was a director of Rippers Limited, Evans Bellhouse Limited and The Sible Hedingham Red Brick Company Limited. In 1939 he became joint managing director of Rippers with Harry Ripper and Stanley Finch.

Ashley married Agnes Florence Brown, known as Tom, in 1922 at Cowes on the Isle of Wight. Tom was born in 1891 and was the daughter of David Brown, a master mariner on the island. She trained as a nurse and was at Kings House College, Wiltshire in 1911. Following their marriage Ashley and Tom lived at Crossways, Sible Hedingham and had a son, Angus Michael Edward, who was born in 1929.

During the Second World War, Ashley was actively involved with Civil Defence. He was always interested in sport and in his younger days played football for the Hedinghams United and later became president of the club. Both Ashley and Tom were keen golfers and practiced their shots daily, having erected a large 'practice' net in the garden of Crossways. Tom was involved with the running of the Castle Hedingham Branch of the Women's Institute and its president for a number of years.

Ashley was appointed a magistrate in 1957 and sat on the Hedingham Bench. He was very musical and played both the piano and organ and as an accomplished organist played at services held in St. Nicholas's Parish Church, where he was Church Warden and at the Congregational Church, both located in Castle Hedingham. He conducted the Hedingham Choral Society and was a member of the Bach Choir, he was also a great supporter of the Chelmsford Choral Society.

Ashley and Agnes (Tom) Ripper

Agnes (Tom) died in 1958 aged 67 years. The canopy over the pulpit in St. Nicholas Church was made at Rippers and given in her memory.

Ashley married secondly Annie Andy, known as Anne (born 1915) in 1958. Ashley died in 1966 and Anne moved to Godmanchester, Huntingdonshire where she died in 1994.

1. (2). (iv) (i) Angus Michael Edward Ripper, M.B.I.M.

Angus Michael Edward Ripper, known as Michael, was born in 1929 the only son of Ashley and Agnes Ripper. He joined Rippers in 1946 as an apprentice carpenter and joiner and passed his City and Guilds. He then went on the road as a representative and became a junior sales manager, when sales were the responsibility of Harry Ripper. However Michael's interest lay in the technical and production side of joinery and although promoted to sales manager, he left the company and joined Killby & Gayford, a building company, with a joinery works near Liverpool Street Station in London, which made wooden fittings for Westminster Banks, (now Nat West Banks) in the London area. Michael built a new joinery factory for Killby & Gayford at Billericay and remained with them for five years. He then joined the board of John Williams in Cornwall, a building company that also had a joinery works, which was a subsidiary of English China

Clays Limited. In 1969 Michael returned to Rippers as managing director and remained in this position until the takeover by Bowater in 1973. He then worked in Bowater Building Products Limited's office in West Stockwell Street, Colchester. Whilst managing director of Rippers he lived at Tilbury Court, Tilbury Juxta Clare. Michael was later head hunted by Sir Arthur Norman, chairman of De La Rue, for the position of chief executive when he instigated drastic changes to enable the company to grow.

Michael's philosophy has always been: "Production from Consultation". In 2007 he joined the board of Abbeyfield UK and now lives in retirement on the Isle of Wight. He has the distinction of being the last surviving former director of Rippers Limited.

Michael married Beryl Maskell in 1952, they were divorced and he married secondly Jane Boykett in 1964. Apart from boats, one of which was an 1891, 42 foot yawl, one of Michael's interests was in the mechanics of producing power. He recalled one of the early gas engines in the power house at Rippers with a large fly wheel about ten feet in diameter.

1. (3). Harry Tucker Ripper and family

Harry Tucker Ripper was born in 1867, the second son of Edward and Louisa. Tucker left school in 1881 and with his elder brother Ted was apprenticed to Walter Mason, a builder in Haverhill; the two lads sharing lodgings in Haverhill.

Tucker married Edith Sarah Fuller on the 29th April 1893 at Hills Road Methodist Church, Cambridge and they spent their honeymoon in Paignton, Devon. Edith, who was known as Edie, was the second daughter of Joseph Adams Fuller and his wife Rachel formerly Claybourn. Joseph was an engineer with his own business who also taught engineering at the Leys School, Cambridge. Tucker and Edie had four sons, Hubert born in 1894, Harry 1896, Donald 1898 and Dennis in 1900. All the children attended the Manse School at Castle Hedingham for their early education.

The Hedingham descendants of Harry Tucker Ripper

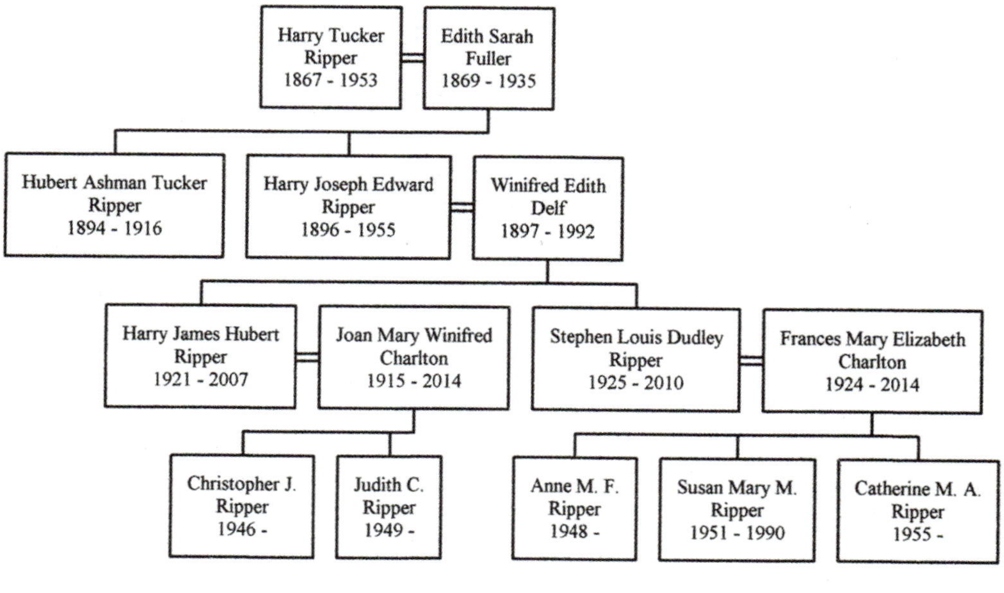

In the 1920s Rippers and Evans Bellhouse flourished and expanded under Tucker's chairmanship which was due to his practical ability, technical knowledge and business acumen. He kept in touch with large building contractors and conducted Ripper's affairs with the London banks.

Tucker made many trips by sea to both America and Canada and was instrumental in importing foreign woods to the United Kingdom.

Tucker and Edie Ripper with their four sons. Left to right: Hubert, Dennis, Harry and Donald

Tucker was a popular gentleman with a pleasant personality who took an active interest in village life and for a number of years ran the Choral Society in Castle Hedingham. He was a devoted supporter of the Congregational Church and was its choirmaster and superintendent. Edie was well respected and had a large number of friends. She was involved with many good works in the village and was always ready to lend a hand. With Beatrice Powell, Edie founded the Girls Club and for many years was one of the organisers who provided tea for the cricket club matches. She was vice president of the Women's Institute and was interested in the social activities at the Congregational Church.

Edie's parents, Joseph and Rachel Fuller, left Cambridge and built a retirement bungalow in Swan Street, Sible Hedingham at the junction with Alexandra Road, shortly after 1901, which they named 'Downfield'.

Tucker was chairman and managing director of Rippers Limited until 1939 when he continued as chairman. He was then succeeded by Harry and Ashley Ripper and Stanley Finch.

On Sunday 31st March 1935, Edie who suffered from health problems walked to the Congregational Church instead of taking the 'motor car'. During the service she became unwell, collapsed and died. Tucker's niece Nellie, whose mother Lizzie had also recently died, went to Cherry Lawn and took over the running of the Ripper household for a while. Later Joan Fuller, Tucker's sister in law, took over the role and moved into the house. Joan remained with Tucker who enjoyed relatively good health until his death on the 12th November 1953. When he died Tucker owned shares in Rippers Limited, Evans Bellhouse Limited, William Kay (Bolton) Limited and The Sible Hedingham Red Brick Company Limited.

1. (3). (i) Hubert Ashman Tucker Ripper was born on the 31st March 1894. When he was nine years old he left the Manse School and attended the Earls Colne Grammar School until 1910, when he left and started at the works. Hubert worked in the various departments at Rippers and assisted the workmen with building work, carpentry and joinery which often meant travelling to other parts of the country. He worked for some time in London and while there he joined the Westbourne Park Church Choir. Hubert enlisted at the start of the First World War and died while on active service at Pas de Calais on the 23rd February 1916. Had he survived Hubert had been recommended for a commission, which he would have accepted and probably joined one of the Engineering Battalions.

1. (3). (ii) Harry Joseph Edward Ripper was born on the 18th September 1896 and after attending the local school he too was educated at Earls Colne Grammar School. He started his training at the works in 1912 and enlisted in 1914 having volunteered for the Royal Flying Corps and served in East Africa. When the war ended Harry returned to the works and became a director of Rippers and Evans Bellhouse.

Harry married Winifred Edith Delf, known as Winnie, in 1920 who was the youngest daughter of Louis and Ellen Delf of Bowyers, Great Yeldham. Louis Delf was the Registrar of Births and Deaths for the Halstead Registration District.

Harry and Winnie had two sons, Harry James Hubert born in 1921 and Stephen Louis Dudley born in 1925. Harry, Winnie and family lived in Castle Lane, Castle Hedingham before they moved to The Bays, Swan Street, Sible Hedingham in 1935.

Harry devoted his life to the joinery trade and was a prominent member of the English Joinery Manufacturers Association and the Joinery and Woodwork Employers Federation. He also served on a number of committees connected with the work of the British Standards Institution.

A photograph of Harry Ripper taken during the 1930s

During the Second World War Harry was actively associated with Civil Defence in the district. In 1947 he was appointed a Justice of the Peace and sat on the Hedingham Bench. He was a founder member of the Hedinghams and District Branch of the British Legion and its treasurer. A keen sportsman, Harry played football for Hedingham's United and was later president of the club. He also played cricket for Castle Hedingham Cricket Club and was a member of their committee. Harry took a keen interest in the village and at one time was a councillor and served on Castle Hedingham Parish Council. He was a member of the Parochial Church Council of St. Peter's Church and manager of St. Peter's Primary School. He also supported the scout and guide movement and was a member of the committee.

Harry became a director of Rippers Limited in 1920 and in 1939 became joint managing director with Ashley Ripper and Stanley Finch. Harry was senior director when he died on the 25th August

1955. Following Harry's death Winnie moved to a house at High Street Green. However she could not settle and missed Swan Street so when Hill House, which was next to The Bays became available she moved into it. She later resided at School Road and died at Applegate's Nursing Home, Great Yeldham in 1992.

1. (3). (ii) (i) Harry James Hubert Ripper, known as Jim, was born on the 4th December 1921. He was educated at Framlingham College in Suffolk, and in 1940 volunteered for the Royal Air Force and was sent to Swift Current in Canada to train. Jim was a bomber pilot when he met Joan Johnstone, the widow of Pilot Officer Ian Johnstone. As Joan was 'non commissioned' and it was frowned upon to fraternise with the ranks, Jim and Joan's courting days were a covert operation, sneaking past the guardhouse and off on Jim's motor bike to the local public house! Jim married Joan who was the second daughter of the Honourable Mrs. Charlton and the late George Charlton of Woodford Lodge, Kettering, Northamptonshire, on the 27th November 1945.

After the war Jim and Joan moved to Grays Hall, Sible Hedingham and had two children, Christopher and Judith. Jim joined the family business and trained in the English timber trade. As a timber buyer he travelled around the Eastern Counties which he enjoyed. He was in charge of the saw-mill until 1960 when he transferred to the purchasing department and in 1969 became personnel director.

Following the sale of Rippers in 1973, Jim, his brother Stephen and work colleague John Moles set up a specialist joinery company, JSR Joinery Limited, where he worked until ill health forced early retirement. However his love of joinery continued and for several years he made toast tongs for Harrods of London in his workshop at home. Jim died on the 14th May 2007 and Joan on the 23rd February 2014.

1. (3). (ii) (i) (i) Christopher Ripper was not actively involved with the company but during his school holidays worked in the factory as an assistant timber selector under Harry Hewlett.

1. (3). (ii) (ii) Stephen Louis Dudley Ripper was born on the 6th August 1925. Stephen attended Gosfield School where he enjoyed scouting activities, swimming in Gosfield Lake in the summer and skating on it during the cold winter months. As a teenager Stephen attended Framlingham College and left when he was 17 years old. He volunteered for the Air Force but was turned down on medical grounds so he joined the Home Guard and worked in their office at Hilton House, Sible Hedingham.

Stephen started at the works in 1944 and was an apprentice on the bench under Frank Westrop who taught him the skills of the trade. In 1945 he transferred to Evans Bellhouse where he spent six months working at their timber store at Rudyark Lake, outside Manchester, before he returned to Rippers and worked his way through various departments to gain experience.

In 1947 Stephen married Frances Charlton, sister of Joan his brother's wife, and they had three daughters, Anne, Susan and Catherine. Stephen eventually joined the estimating department and later became the sales director, supervising the representatives. He was a member of Sible Hedingham Parish Council and chairman from 1961 to 1964. Both Stephen and Jim were hard working members of the fund raising committee for the new village hall. They also organised the annual Hedingham Carnival for many years when Rippers lorries would be used as floats in the processions. With Stephen's retirement drawing near JSR Joinery Limited was sold, although he continued to work for the new owners for a few days a week until he retired. Stephen was always interested in the history of Ripper Brothers and Rippers Limited and its development and collected memorabilia until he died on the 25th July 2010. Frances died on the 14 March 2014.

The Manchester descendants of Harry Tucker Ripper

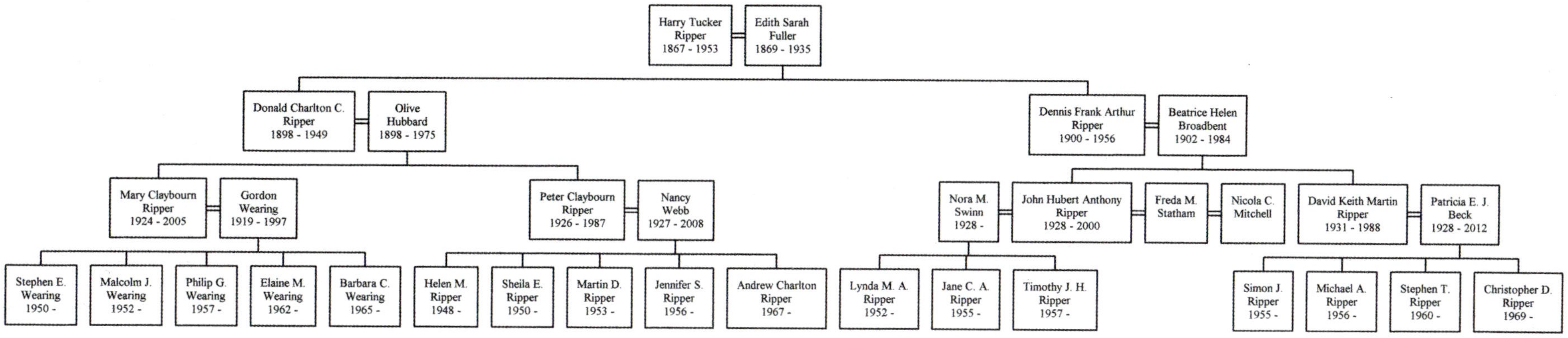

1. (3). (iii) Donald Charlton Claybourn Ripper and family

Donald Charlton Claybourn Ripper was born on the 10th October 1898 and started at the works in 1914 of which he later became a director. He left in 1922 when he moved to Manchester to run the newly acquired company, George Evans and Sons Limited and its successor company Evans Bellhouse Limited. He married Olive Hubbard on the 18th April 1923, the daughter of William Hubbard of Naughton, Suffolk and they had two children, Mary Claybourn born in 1924, and Peter Claybourn in 1926. Donald was president of the Manchester Timber Trades Association and senior managing director at Evans Bellhouse, Manchester when he died on the 2nd November 1949.

1. (3). (iii) (i) Mary Claybourn Ripper, who was born in 1924 married Malcolm Wearing 1919-1997 and they had three sons and two daughters; Stephen, Malcolm, Philip, Elaine and Barbara.

1. (3). (iii) (ii) Peter Claybourn Ripper, the son of Donald and Olive was born in 1926. He was a boarder at Framlingham School, before he left circa 1938/1939 and attended King's School, Macclesfield. It was as a schoolboy on the train travelling between Poynton and Macclesfield that Peter met his future wife, Nancy Webb, who was a pupil at Macclesfield High School and young Peter would share his sweets with her! Peter left school around 1941/1942 and joined the army. He was in the Royal Armoured Corps, but was too young to see active service although after VE Day he was in Antwerp, Belgium in 1945 and Austria in 1946. He married Nancy in May 1948 and returned to Evans Bellhouse in 1949 to fill his late father's position.

Peter was president of the Manchester Timber Trades Association 1958-1959 when he was only 32 years of age and thought to be one of the youngest men to hold that office.

Peter and Nancy had five children; Helen born in 1948, Sheila 1950, Martin 1953, Jennifer 1956 and Andrew in 1967. Peter died in 1987 and Nancy in 2008.

DIRECTORATE:

(1) Mr. H. T. Ripper, *Chairman.*
(2) Mr. W. C. Ripper. (3) Mr. J. W. Porkess. (4) Mr. H. J. E. Ripper.
(5) Mr. A. E. Ripper. (6) Mr. D. C. C. Ripper. (7) Mr. S. K. Finch.
(8) Mr. D. F. A. Ripper.

The directors of Rippers in 1929

1. (3). (iv) Dennis Frank Arthur Ripper and family

Dennis Frank Arthur Ripper was born on the 15th November 1900. He was educated at Earls Colne Grammar School and Perse School, Cambridge. He started at the works in 1918 where he stayed until 1922 when he joined George Evans & Sons Limited. He was appointed a director of both companies in 1925. He joined the board of William Kay (Bolton) Limited in 1943 and became joint managing director of Evans Bellhouse Limited in 1944.

Dennis married Beatrice Broadbent in 1926 and they had two sons, John Hubert Anthony, who was born in 1928 and David Keith Martin born in 1931. Dennis was a keen snooker player and had a snooker room at the office. He had a warm and friendly personality and fought ill health for almost eight years before he died in 1956 at his home named 'Hedingham' in Wilmslow, he was 55 years of age.

1. (3). (iv) (i) John Hubert Anthony Ripper known as Tony, was born in 1928 and educated at Giggleswick School, Yorkshire. He joined Evans Bellhouse in 1945, left for National Service and rejoined again in 1950. He remained with Evans Bellhouse for some years after his younger brother, David, left. Tony married his first wife Nora Swinn in 1951 and they had three children, Lynda, Jane and Timothy. Tony died in 2000 on Anglesey where he was living with his fourth wife.

1. (3). (iv) (ii) David Keith Martin Ripper was born in 1931 and married Patricia Beck in 1954. They had four sons, Simon, Michael, Stephen and Christopher. David was associated with both Evans Bellhouse Limited and with Rippers Limited. He started with Evans Bellhouse in 1950 and after leaving started his own successful joinery business. He was appointed as northern sales director of Rippers Limited on 1st April 1969 when action was taken to extend the sales of standard joinery in areas not previously covered. He resigned with effect from the 20th August 1970 when the policy for the northern sales area was re-appraised and consequently, by mutual arrangement David left the company. He died in 1988.

Tony and David Ripper in the late 1940s

1. (4). William Charlton Ripper and family

William Charlton Ripper, known as Charlton, who was the youngest son of Edward and Louisa was born in 1871. He left school early and in 1879 helped his brothers Ted and Tucker when they started their carpentry business. Charlton married Annie Eliza Porkess on the 19th July 1906 and they moved into Willowbrook, Station Road, Sible Hedingham, a house which Charlton had built. Annie, who was born in 1875, was the eldest daughter of Uriah and Eliza Jane Porkess, a builder from Grimsby. Charlton and Annie had two children Kenneth Hugh born in 1907 and Norman Charlton in 1912.

Charlton and Annie Ripper with their children
Left to right: Norman, Annie, Ken and Charlton

Annie died on the 23rd May 1919 and Charlton married secondly on 22nd September 1921, Margaret Goodey (born 1883) who lived at Earls Court, London. They did not have issue.

Charlton, who was affectionately known as Mr. Charlton within the timber industry, was a director of Rippers Limited, The Sible Hedingham Red Brick Company Limited, Evans Bellhouse Limited and William Kay (Bolton) Limited. He specialised in buying and selecting timber for the Hedingham Company and spent a great deal of time in the timber yard; his particular interest being the hard wood section. Ill health forced him to retire from active work at the company in 1937 although he returned in 1939 at the outbreak of the Second World War and remained until he suffered a stroke in 1945.

Charlton was a deacon at the Congregational Church, Castle Hedingham and was the church and Sunday School secretary. He never recovered from the stroke he suffered and died on 15th June 1947. Margaret who was known as 'Granny Ripper', eventually moved into a residential home in Spring Lane, Colchester and died in 1979.

1. (4). (i) Kenneth Hugh Ripper known as Ken, was born at Willowbrook, on 2nd December 1907. He started at the works in 1926 and later moved to Evans Bellhouse. He married Helen Flintoff, known as Tanny who was born in 1919, the youngest daughter of the late Thomas and Marion Flintoff of Kersal, Manchester on the 16th February 1944. He had become a director of Rippers by 1933. He resigned from the board in 1937 but rejoined in 1938. Ken was appointed joint managing director of Evans Bellhouse in 1949 and remained with the company until he retired in 1971 at the time of the takeover by Tower Investments. He ceased to be a director of Rippers Limited on 20th December 1971. Ken died in 1992 and Helen died in 2005. They did not have any children.

1. (4). (ii) Norman Charlton Ripper was born at Willowbrook on the 12th July 1912 and in 1916/1917 he was sent to Grimsby to live with his maternal grandparents and aunt, where he attended school. He returned to Sible Hedingham after the death of his mother in 1919 and attended Halstead Grammar School. At the age of fourteen he was a pupil at Stanley House School, Clifton Ville, Margate, Kent. Norman started at the works in 1929 and was a director by 1937.

He married Phyllis Mary Horsley, known as Phyl in 1937, who was the daughter of Harold and Ida Horsley of Hill Farm, Barnardiston, Suffolk and they had three children, Clive Tucker born 1944, Anne Elizabeth 1946 and Julian Charlton 1951.

Norman who served in the Royal Artillery during the Second World War concentrated on the soft wood side of the business. He was managing director until 1969 when he was succeeded by Michael Ripper. Norman continued as a director and after the Bowater takeover was appointed timber purchasing director and retired shortly afterwards. He died on 18th November 2006 aged 94 years and Phyl died on 19th February 2013 aged 98 years.

1. (4). (ii) (i) Clive Tucker Ripper was born on the 25th May 1944 and educated at Bloxham School. He joined Rippers Limited and following service with the company and later Bowater Ripper Limited, where he worked as their timber purchasing manager, Clive was the last member of the family associated with the works. He then worked for Wheelers Limited, timber merchants of Sudbury, Suffolk for a short time around 1981. During November 1982 he formed his own company, C.R. Timber Limited, which operated from the former airfield at Earls Colne and specialised in wooden roof trusses. Clive died on 25th June 2006 aged 62 years.

1. (4). (ii) (ii) Anne Elizabeth Ripper, known as Liz, married Noel le Chevalier Scott Agazarian (born 1942) in 1966. Sadly they were both killed in a car accident in France in 1968.

1. (4). (ii) (iii) Julian Charlton Ripper was not actively involved with the company, but did work there during his school holidays. From the age of 14 Julian would drive a tractor and trailer around the factory, and after he passed his driving test at 17, he graduated to lorries, occasionally making local deliveries. His first wife Jane, formerly Frost, was secretary to Michael Ripper at the Hedingham office. Julian now lives in Castle Hedingham with his second wife Julie.

A young Clive helping his father Norman with the stock taking

Norman and Phyl Ripper in 1975

Clive Ripper in 1969

Julian Ripper in 1969

1. (5). John Wilkin Porkess and family

John Wilkin Porkess who was born in 1879, was the son of Uriah and Eliza Jane Porkess, formerly Wilkin. Uriah was a builder and the family lived in Grimsby.

All-in-One Tree of Uriah Porkess

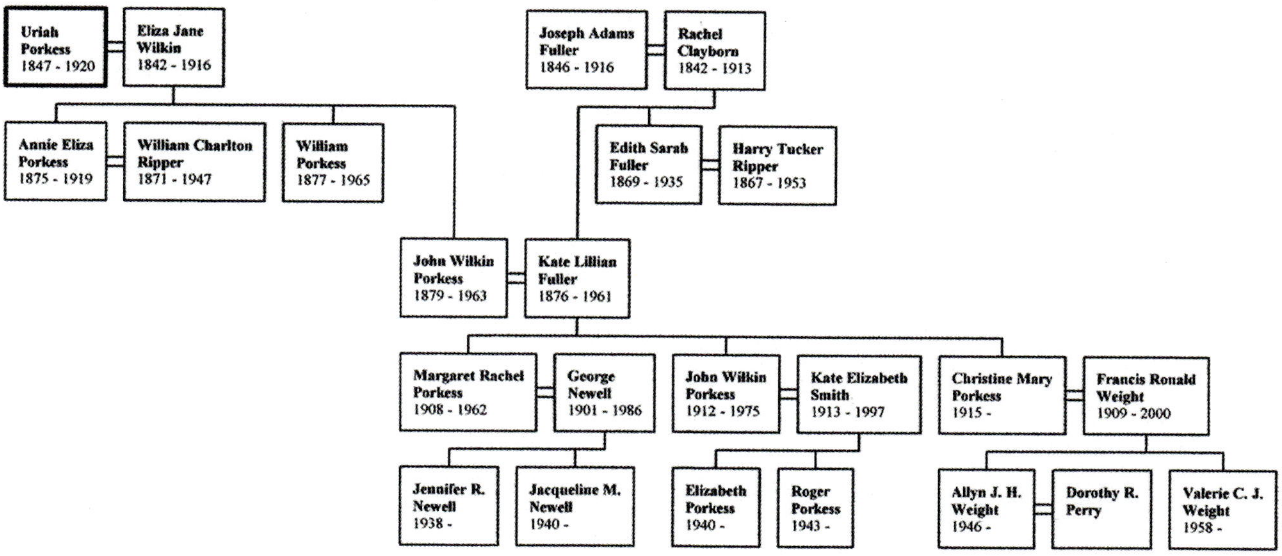

The above family tree shows the double relationship between the Porkess and Ripper families. Kate's sister Edith married Tucker Ripper and John was the brother of Annie Eliza Porkess who married Charlton Ripper.

Kate who was born in 1876 was the daughter of Joseph Adams Fuller, an engineer from Cambridge and Rachel Fuller formerly Claybourn. In 1891 Kate was apprenticed to Walter Smith, a draper who specialised in fancy goods and lived with the family in Hitchin, Hertfordshire. By 1901 she had returned to Grimsby and lived in lodgings while working as a draper's assistant. Kate married John Wilkin Porkess in 1905, and they moved to Cleethorpes, Lincolnshire where their children were born, Margaret Rachel in 1908, John Wilkin (junior) in 1912 and Christine Mary in 1915. John was employed as a timber merchant's assistant traveller.

John served in the Motor Transport Company of the army during the First World War and saw active service in France. He received his discharge in order to act as cashier at Rippers in 1919 and in 1922 following the death of Ted Ripper he joined the board and became company secretary. He also purchased the company's soft wood. John and his family moved into Brook House, Sible Hedingham, which was situated close to one of the main entrances to the works.

John who was a director of both Rippers Limited and Evans Bellhouse Limited was keenly interested in local government. He was elected to Halstead Rural District Council in 1922 and served on the council until he retired in 1961. He also served on the Halstead Board of Guardians and Sible Hedingham Parish Council and in 1937 was president of the Building Trade Employer's Federation. John was company secretary of The Sible Hedingham Red Brick Company Limited from its incorporation in 1919 until its closure in the 1950s.

He was a staunch Congregationalist and during his later years was a life deacon of Castle Hedingham

Congregational Church. Kate died in 1961 and John died on 12th November 1963 at Eastcote, Great Maplestead, the home of his daughter Christine.

John Wilkin and Kate Porkess

1. (5). (i) Margaret Rachel Porkess who was born in 1909 spent her childhood at Brook House, which then had a fairly large garden with a stream running through it. She trained and worked as a teacher. She married George Newell L.R.I.B.A. (1901-1986) in 1934 at St. Peter's Church, Sible Hedingham and the reception was held at Brook House. Following their marriage they lived at Hatfield Hertfordshire where George was employed at the County Council Offices in the Architectural Department. They had two daughters, Jennifer and Jacquie. Margaret died in 1962 aged 54 years.

1. (5). (ii) John Wilkin Porkess known as Jack, was born 10th March 1912. Jack started at the works in 1929 and was appointed a director in 1937. He married Kate Elizabeth Smith, known as Betty, on the 24th June 1939 and while on honeymoon he was called to join up. Jack and Betty had two children Elizabeth Jill, known as Jill born on 16th May 1940 and Roger John Edward born on 23rd June 1943. Following the takeover by Evans Bellhouse of Kays of Bolton, Jack was released from military service to take control of the business and moved to Bolton where they remained for many years. Jack resigned as a director of Rippers on 17th August 1971. Following his retirement from Evans Bellhouse, Jack and Betty sailed to the Mediterranean on their boat. They bought an old farmhouse in Mallorca and it was while Jack was working in the garden that he suffered a heart attack and died on the 22nd March 1975. Betty died in 1997 at Nuffield, Oxfordshire.

1. (5). (iii) Christine Mary Porkess who was born in 1915 was one of two lady members* of the family to be employed in the office at Rippers where she worked for her father. Chrisitne married Second Lieutenant Francis Weight, R.A.S.C. (1909-2000) in 1941 at the Congregational Church, Castle Hedingham. Christine now lives in Oban, Scotland.

*Jane Frost, later Ripper was the other lady family member to be employed as a secretary at the works when she worked for Michael Ripper, when he was managing director.

A family gathering to celebrate the Golden Wedding of John and Kate Porkess
Left to right, back row: Betty Porkess, Elsie Finch, Jennifer Newell, Ronald Weight, Jacquie Newell, Jill Porkess and Roger Porkess
Front row: Allyn Weight (standing), George Newell, Margaret Newell, John Porkess, Kate Porkess, Jack Porkess and Christine Weight

Jack and Betty Porkess on board their boat

Portrait of Harry Tucker Ripper by Edward Hartley Mooney, 1937

Edward Hartley Mooney (1878-1938) lived at Newton Heath, Manchester the same location as Evans Bellhouse. He specialised in portraits, landscapes and still life and exhibited between 1926 and 1932 at the Walker Art Gallery Liverpool, Manchester City Art Gallery and the Royal Cambrian Academy. Many of his paintings are now in art galleries and museums particularly in Manchester and Salford. The portrait of Tucker hung in the entrance to Ripper's Hedingham offices for many years and is now in the care of one of his great grandsons.

Chapter 2

Ripper Brothers at Castle Hedingham and Cambridge

During 1879 and 1880 Ted the eldest son of Edward and Louisa Ripper trained with Henry Wright, a local carpenter in Great Maplestead and acquired a good knowledge in rough woodwork. Determined to improve his carpentry skills Ted became apprenticed to Walter Mason, a master builder and carpenter in Haverhill, Suffolk. Ted was described as an improver when Tucker followed him into the carpentry trade and was also apprenticed to Walter Mason. The two brothers, who shared lodgings in Haverhill, returned home at weekends until Ted left Mason's as a fully trained craftsman.

Ted started his own business in Castle Hedingham and soon required an assistant. Tucker meanwhile had not completed his apprenticeship but wanted to join Ted. Walter Mason had no desire to release Tucker from his agreement but eventually a compromise was reached, and Tucker was released from his indenture, providing he paid Walter Mason 10 shillings a week for the unexpired term of his apprenticeship.

Tucker worked as Ted's assistant until 1885 when they started their own 'jobbing' business in Castle Hedingham trading as E. & T. Ripper, carpenters and joiners. They took on their younger brother Charlton as an un-indentured apprentice carpenter and used some disused buildings behind their parent's house in Nunnery Street from which to run the business. As well as carpentry jobs the brothers took on building work including brickwork, painting, glazing and when necessary carved inscriptions on gravestones.

The three Ripper brothers standing outside their workshop
Left to right: Charlton, Edward (Ted) and Tucker

One of the first contracts was to make coffins for the Halstead Union Workhouse which they acquired when Joe Newman, a carpenter who had worked for the family, became too old to make them and died in early 1888. The Workhouse which was situated in Hedingham Road, Halstead, was built in 1838 and capable of holding 500 inmates. The Union comprised sixteen parishes including Halstead, the Hedinghams and Yeldhams. There were undoubtedly a number of deaths in the Workhouse, which kept the brothers in regular work. They maintained a small stock of oak and elm boards for making coffins. The brothers were also kept busy with the usual village calls; repairing broken sash cords, chairs, tables and wheelbarrows, as well as making new kneading troughs.

When Edward and Louisa moved into the house next door called Cherry Lawn, the three brothers were forced to find new premises and were fortunate enough to secure an old shop and yard known as Smith's Yard in Nunnery Street, formerly owned by William Smith, a builder, carpenter and undertaker who had recently died. He was also estate carpenter and gamekeeper for the Hedingham Castle Estate.

Following the farming depression work was not plentiful and Tucker went to London to gain extra experience and to ease the monetary situation. He obtained work with John Oldrey & Son, but was happy to return home when there was an upsurge in work. On returning to Castle Hedingham he met Edith Fuller who was visiting the Reverend James Burgess and his family at the Manse. By the time Edith was due to return home to Cambridge, Tucker had found employment in the city so that he could continue his friendship with her. Tucker returned to Castle Hedingham after two years to help his brothers, but left again to start his own business as a builder and undertaker, hiring a small yard and workshop in Russell Road, Cambridge.

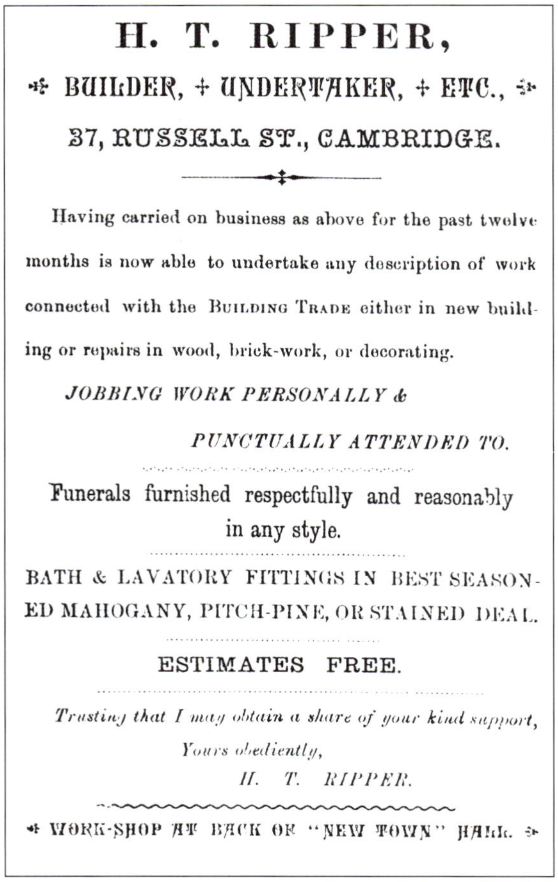
H. T. RIPPER,

BUILDER, + UNDERTAKER, + ETC.,

37, RUSSELL ST., CAMBRIDGE.

Having carried on business as above for the past twelve months is now able to undertake any description of work connected with the BUILDING TRADE either in new building or repairs in wood, brick-work, or decorating.

JOBBING WORK PERSONALLY & PUNCTUALLY ATTENDED TO.

Funerals furnished respectfully and reasonably in any style.

BATH & LAVATORY FITTINGS IN BEST SEASONED MAHOGANY, PITCH-PINE, OR STAINED DEAL.

ESTIMATES FREE.

Trusting that I may obtain a share of your kind support,
Yours obediently,
H. T. RIPPER.

WORK-SHOP AT BACK OF "NEW TOWN" HALL.

A leaflet distributed by Tucker Ripper

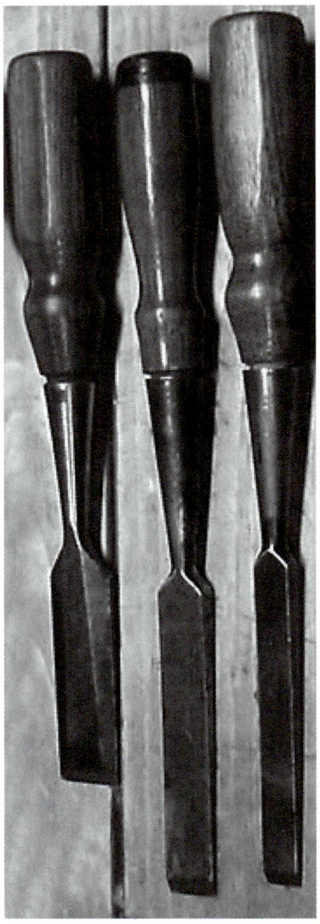

Carpenters chisels

By 1890 Ted was trading on his own account at Castle Hedingham as a carpenter and builder. On the 6th February 1888 he bought 'Palmers', a house in Queen Street. When it was advertised for sale by the Trustees of Richard Dodson Cheveley, it included the description "Small yard in rear in which are buildings extending to Back Lane, capable of forming warehouses, stables, etc., ...". The property was occupied by Miss. Catherine Brown until Michaelmas 1890, when Ted Ripper went into occupation. When the business moved into the buildings behind the house (in Back Lane now Church Lane) it took on more employees. A new two storey workshop was built around 1892 at the rear of Ted's first workshop. The upper floor was a joiner's shop and the lower one a wood store and later a machine room. When it was being constructed some inquisitive people enquired, "What is it going to be used for?" With tongue in cheek the answer was a "Wesleyan Chapel". The two businesses were linked for supplies and when Tucker was very busy some of his work was handled by the Castle Hedingham business which was not doing so well, and Charlton would help Tucker in Cambridge. In 1893 the brothers built a drying shed for William Rayner & Son at Maiden Ley Brick Works, Castle Hedingham. They invited William John Rayner, the son, to join them in partnership but he declined.

The Ripper Brother's premises in Back Lane, Castle Hedingham circa 1890s

In 1893 Tucker married Edith and they moved into Cherry Lawn as Edward, Louisa and Charlton had moved into a house in St. James Street. Unfortunately nine months later, because of the brothers lack of commercial knowledge and the sharp dealing practises of backers in the housing market, the Cambridge business collapsed and Edward and Tucker were declared bankrupt. However, the Committee of Inspection who assessed the brother's assets were prepared to let them keep the Castle Hedingham business, on condition that the valuation sum was paid. Family and friends rallied round and the money was paid, although Ted and Tucker were left in debt to their guarantors.

As bankrupts, Ted and Tucker could no longer own a business, so from 1894 they traded under Charlton's name as W. C. Ripper. In 1895 he was listed as a builder and in 1899 as a joinery manufacturer. They carried on working in the yard and workshops attached to Ted's house and gradually built up a good work force of craftsmen. During the 1890s they also used a brick shed at the rear of their parent's garden in St. James's Street for storage purposes. One early employee was Charles Ling who was born in Horseheath, Cambridgeshire, and was a skilled carpenter and joiner working on the roof timbers in the University Library at Caius College, Cambridge when he met Tucker. They became friends and after Tucker returned to Castle Hedingham he persuaded Charles to join him and his brothers as foreman of their joinery business in Back Lane. They worked together for several years until Charles set up his own business as builder, ironmonger and undertaker. Printing was a hobby and he started this business in a very small way. Both businesses progressed well until the First World War when his men were taken for war work. Charles made the lych gate for the cemetery in Sheepcot Road, and built two flat roof houses in Queen Street where he lived. He sold his printing business to the Shearcroft Printing Company in Braintree and retired in 1924. Charles returned to Horseheath for fourteen years where he was Churchwarden and School Manager. He returned to Castle Hedingham in 1938 and lived at "Restleigh" until his death in 1958.

The business of W. C. Ripper grew and eventually a dozen men were employed. From using hand power and machinery in the form of a saw bench and morticer, the brothers purchased a third hand vertical boiler with a six horse power steam engine, which when new had acted as auxiliary power at the old windmill, on Sudbury Hill owned by John Ruffle. This was followed by many years in a turner's establishment in Halstead, which was probably that of Henry Cocksedge and Son. The old boiler was nicknamed "the coffee pot" and served the brothers well until it became too costly to operate and finished up on the scrap heap. With limited financial resources the brothers could not afford new machinery and therefore purchased a few second hand machines, including the casting of a single-spindle moulding machine and an old hand-power saw-bench, which was converted into a power-driven machine.

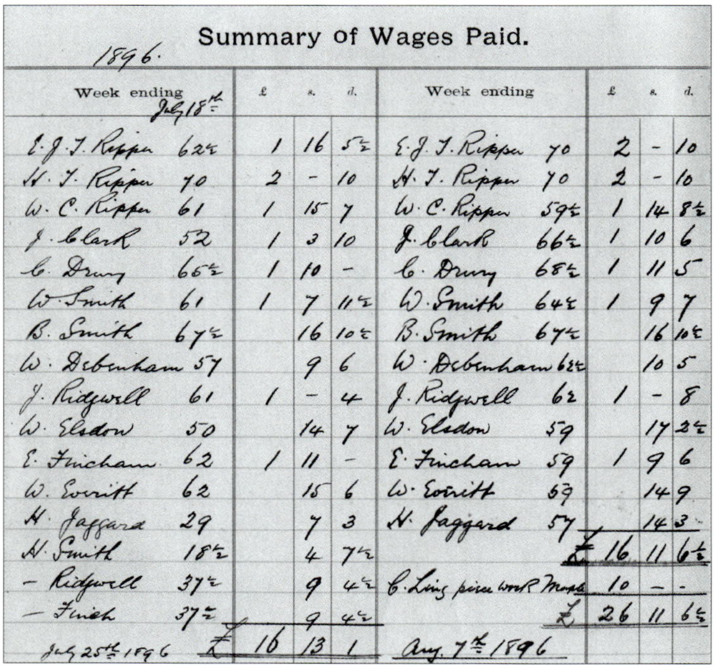

Summary of Wages Paid.

1896.

Week ending July 18th		£	s.	d.	Week ending		£	s.	d.
E. J. T. Ripper	62½	1	16	5½	E. J. T. Ripper	70	2	-	10
H. T. Ripper	70	2	-	10	H. T. Ripper	70	2	-	10
W. C. Ripper	61	1	15	7	W. C. Ripper	59½	1	14	8½
J. Clark	52	1	3	10	J. Clark	66½	1	10	6
C. Drury	65½	1	10	-	C. Drury	68½	1	11	5
W. Smith	61	1	7	11½	W. Smith	64½	1	9	7
B. Smith	67½		16	10½	B. Smith	67½		16	10½
W. Debenham	57		9	6	W. Debenham	62½		10	5
J. Ridgwell	61	1	-	4	J. Ridgwell	62	1	-	8
W. Elsdon	50		14	7	W. Elsdon	59		17	2½
E. Fincham	62	1	11	-	E. Fincham	59	1	9	6
W. Everitt	62		15	6	W. Everitt	59		14	9
H. Jaggard	29		7	3	H. Jaggard	57		14	3
H. Smith	18½		4	7½		£	16	11	6½
– Ridgwell	37½		9	4½	C. Ling piece work Mouldings		10	-	-
– Finch	37½		9	4½		£	26	11	6½
July 25th 1896	£	16	13	1	Aug. 7th 1896				

Extract from wages book dated July 1896

By 1898 further machinery and equipment was needed and extra space was required so a disused malting in Castle Lane was hired for storage and an additional assembly shop. When this malting was advertised for sale in 1888 it was described as substantially brick built with kiln, malt shop and three working floors with a street frontage of about 100 feet. The top storey of the old malting was eventually removed and later became part of the former Youth Hostel; it is now residential. Also in 1898, a two storey warehouse on the opposite side of Castle Lane was hired for a workshop and storage. When it was sold in 1888 it was described as a “range of brick built warehouses in five compartments containing storage capacity for many hundred quarters of grain and other commodities”. This building was demolished many years ago.

Maltings in Castle Lane used for storage in 1898

Warehouse in Castle Lane opposite the Maltings used for storage and workshops in 1898

Workmen outside Ripper Brothers workshop in Back Lane, Castle Hedingham circa 1897

The interior of the joiner's workshop in Back Lane, Castle Hedingham circa 1897
Left to right front row: Charles Ling, Bennett Smith and unknown
Back row: Charlie Drury, John Clarke, unknown, unknown, George Smith and Alfred Mulley

When the business outgrew its various premises in Castle Hedingham it was decided in 1899 to move to a larger site in Sible Hedingham. The two storey shop at Back Lane was dismantled and re-erected, to form an addition to the new machine shop, which continued to be known as the Wesleyan Chapel.

Chapter 3

A brief history of Ripper's Joinery Works

(Many of the events and subjects below are featured in more detail in their respective chapters).

On 29th September 1896 a 99 year lease was secured on 1½ acres of land close to the Colne Valley and Halstead Railway Station in Sible Hedingham. The land was leased in Charlton's name and the business was known as W.C. Ripper, Joinery Manufacturer. Although the factory was based in Sible Hedingham the postal address always remained as Castle Hedingham. No doubt confusing the unwary newcomer!

Prior to 1899 only a sawpit and shed existed on the land adjacent to the railway station

The Boer War caused normal working conditions to be disrupted and with large contractors requiring manufactured woodwork for South Africa, Rippers work force worked at full stretch. With a covered storage area desperately needed and no funding available, Rippers leased and erected, a large marquee which was used as both a storage area and workshop. Unfortunately when the weather was bad the area became a quagmire and with no heating it was an extremely cold place to work in.

During the War in South Africa, sectional timbered buildings were required for the Congo, Transvaal and Cape Colony which Ripper Brothers were able to provide. These shipments enhanced their reputation as they gained experience with overseas documentation and shipping. This enabled the company to obtain further contracts to later export products to Europe, South Africa and Bolivia.

Rippers' reputation for providing good work was growing and there was a steady expansion of the business. Two plots of land at Crosspath, (Crosspath Field) were purchased, again in Charlton Ripper's name, which secured any future development plans for expansion. The business also expanded, on the Station Yard site and made use of the railway siding.

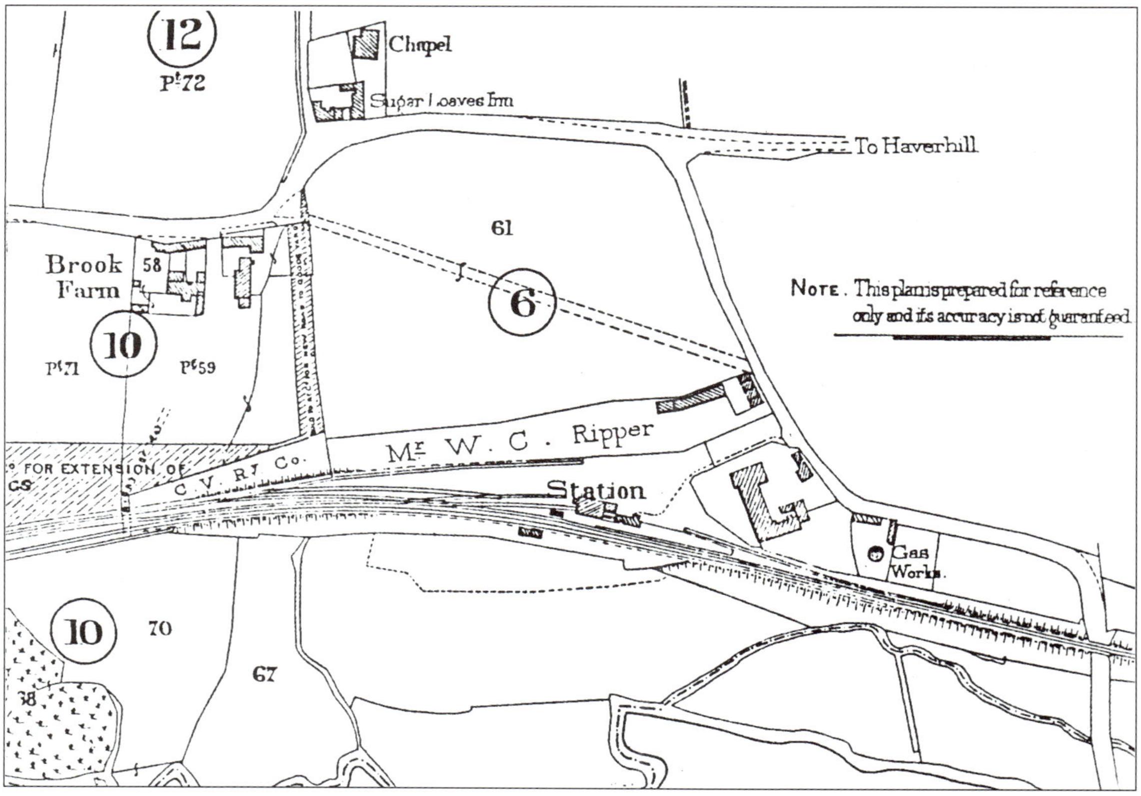

Map from the sale particulars of Brook Farm showing the narrow strip of land leased to William Charlton Ripper in 1896 and lot 6, being Crosspath field, which he purchased in 1901

In 1904 Charlton Ripper purchased the freehold of the land which he held on a 99 year lease and in 1905 Ted and Tucker were discharged from bankruptcy.

In 1908 Ted, Tucker and Charlton formalized their partnership and the necessary agreements were drawn up by solicitors Surridge and Smith, (later Smith, Morton & Long and now Birkett Long), and they traded under the name of Ripper Brothers, manufacturing joiners. The London and County Banking Company Limited in Halstead handled the partner's affairs, and the value of the stock and goodwill was put at £7,500.

Following the voluntary liquidation of Crompton and Fawkes Limited of Chelmsford in 1912, Rippers acquired more contracts and work including the Roman Catholic Cathedral in Westminster.

With the outbreak of the First World War in 1914 the pattern of trade soon altered. The work force was greatly depleted as young men volunteered to fight for King and Country. Therefore older men had to be employed, and for the first time Rippers employed women! The type of work carried out at the works also changed as Rippers undertook jobs to help the war effort.

Surrounded by wooden products and wood waste 'fire' was inevitably a hazard and during 1914 a fire in a building used to store sawdust and wood shavings extracted from "B" Mill caused damage to the building.

In 1915 the partnership was converted into a private limited liability company known as Rippers Limited, with a registered capital of £25,000.

In 1917 the Government called for additional war work from Rippers and they started to make aeroplane parts and laminated propellers.

Ted Ripper (left) with workmen early 1900s

Building an early extension to the works in rough weather

This building was at the rear of the four red brick houses in Station Road and on the right hand side of the approach to the Railway Station. Parts of the old maltings can be seen in the background. The 'new' building is on the right of the photograph at the top of page 38.

Many of the earlier buildings were of timber framed construction as shown in the above photographs. Some of them had corrugated metal roofs and wooden walls. However from 1917 some large buildings were constructed of red brick including 'The Brick Shop', which was used for war work. These were substantial buildings with slate roofs.

Sible and Castle Hedingham Railway Station and Goods Shed are in the centre background of this busy scene during the Edwardian era. The large building on the right is part of Ripper's works and on the left is the malting of Thomas Bradridge & Co., which was purchased by Rippers in 1926.

In 1918 the remaining part of Brook Farm was purchased to allow for future expansion. When war ended in November 1918 it meant that Rippers could return to more normal work, this was in spite of the Office of Works quotas to prevent unemployment, which caused difficulties finding enough work for everyone. Short time was introduced to avoid as much unemployment as possible, however, when possible, overtime was worked to make up for the lost hours. Gradually there was a surge in expansion across the country and in 1920 Rippers set up a permanent London office to help secure contracts in the area and, to provide a service to their customers in the Home Counties.

A large quantity of standard joinery was produced to local Hedingham builder's specifications and specialized individual orders were processed using the finest woods available; these orders included staircases and house paneling.

The Sible Hedingham Red Brick Company Limited was incorporated in 1919. It continued the business of brick manufacturers formerly carried on by Eli Cornish at Purls Hill and Mark Gentry at Highfield, Sible Hedingham. The first directors were Tucker Ripper, Charlton Ripper, Eli Cornish and Reuben Hunt of Earls Colne. The company secretary was John Wilkin Porkess who was also company secretary of Rippers Limited. In later years Ashley Ripper and Stanley Finch became directors of the brick company. Rippers Brick Works, as it was known, had a siding onto the Colne Valley and Halstead Railway upon which coal was delivered to fire the kilns and bricks were transported away. Bricks were made by hand and with a 'Berry' brickmaking machine. There were five downdraught kilns operating at various times. Manufacture ceased in 1954 and was the last of the numerous brickworks, which once existed in the Hedinghams, to close. Stocks of bricks continued to be sold until at least 1956 and the company was eventually wound up in 1960 when the property reverted to Rippers Limited. Among buildings erected with 'Hedingham reds' was Hedingham School, which was built between 1937 and 1939 on land which had been sold by Rippers Limited to Essex County Council.

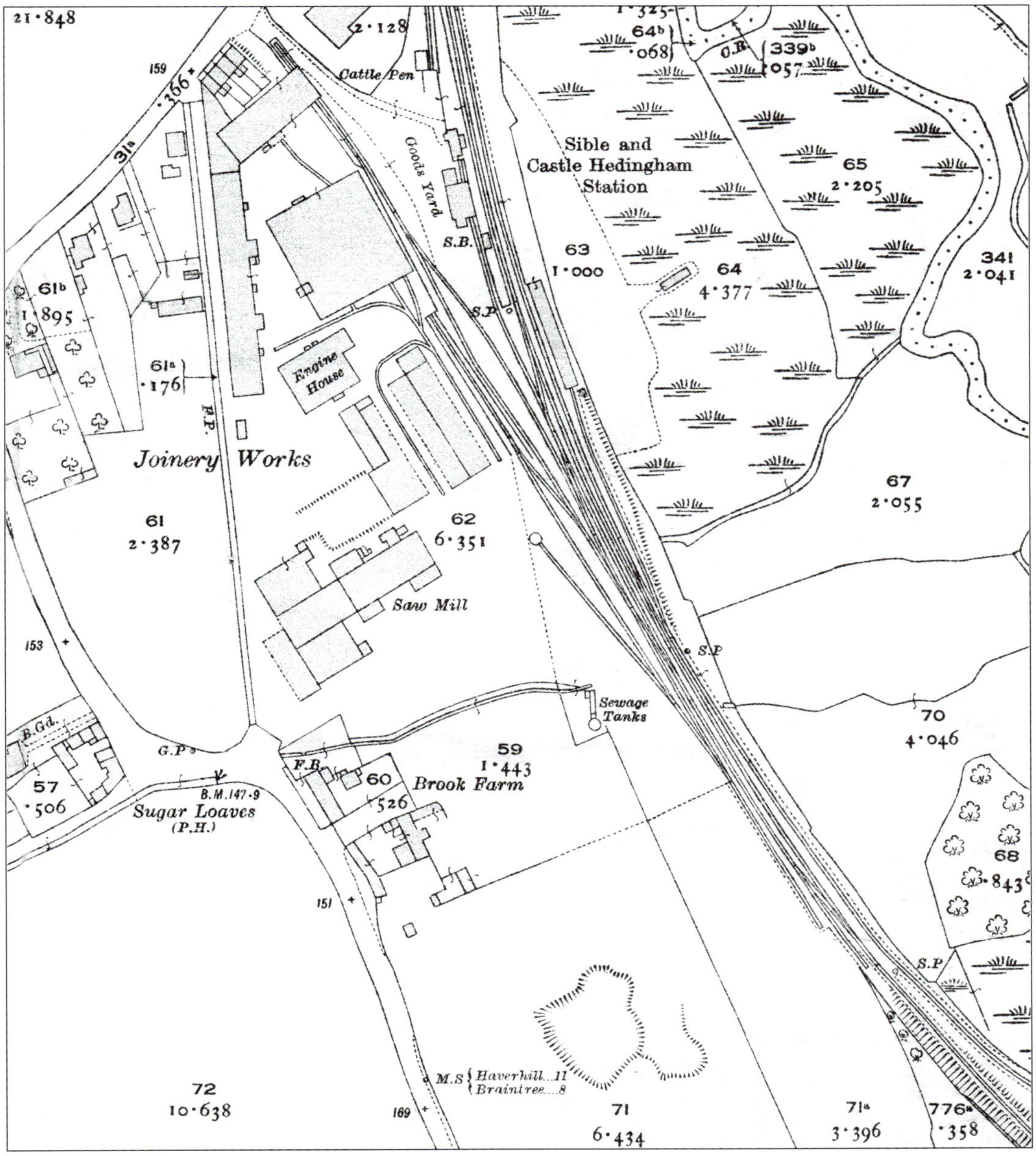

The works from the 25 inch to one mile Ordnance Survey map of 1922

In 1919 to help with the shortage of housing, fourteen wooden bungalows were erected near Brook House, from surplus army hut parts. In 1920 five red brick houses were purchased in Nunnery Street, Castle Hedingham, also to house employees.

In 1919 John Wilkin Porkess joined the Company to assist Ted Ripper who was in poor health. Ted died in 1922 shortly after Rippers Limited acquired George Evans and Sons Limited, timber importers and joinery manufacturers at Newton Heath, Manchester. Standard joinery started to be made at Rippers in 1923 and separate mills were used for bulk and special orders. Rippers earned the accolade of a 'good firm to work for', as in 1924 they introduced paid holidays for their employees.

Between 1924 and 1927 Rippers built 94 houses in two large housing estates. (See chapter 16) During the General Strike of 1926 the works closed except for staff who, unloaded trucks and carried out other necessary work.

A view of the works during the early 1920s with the engine house (centre) and the brick shop (left). The fencing in the foreground was along both sides of Crosspath

A 1920s photograph, of the sawmill. This was located north of Brook Farm House

The works circa 1928 showing the water tower, which was constructed over a 200 foot deep bore hole in 1927. The large building in the centre was a sawmill and in front is a jib to move logs. Brook Farm House, then the home of John Wilkin Porkess is on the right

The works viewed from the south in 1929. This shows all the new housing in Brook Terrace, Swan Street, Yeldham Road, Station Road and Crosspath. It also includes the 14 huts in the centre, and the railway on the right

Telephone: 9 Castle Hedingham — Telegrams: Rippers, Castle Hedingham

JOINERY

FOR HOUSING, COMMERCIAL BUILDINGS, HOSPITALS, BANKS

RIPPERS LIMITED CASTLE HEDINGHAM ESSEX

STANDARD CATALOGUE SENT ON APPLICATION

Sole distributing Agents for the North and Northern Midlands

GEO. EVANS & SONS LTD.

Saw Mills, Newton Heath, MANCHESTER

A Rippers Limited and George Evans & Sons Limited, advertisement from 'The Architect and Building News' dated 24th December 1926

During 1926 Rippers purchased the Maltings and in 1931 received a visit from the Essex Branch of the Chartered Surveyors' Institution. In 1931 the associate company of George Evans & Sons Limited, Manchester amalgamated with J. & W. Bellhouse Limited and the name of the company was changed to Evans Bellhouse Limited, which by 1934 was completely owned by Rippers. In 1933 Rippers Limited went Public in order to provide the necessary finance to support the level of new buildings, production and equipment that the company required to expand. In London building work was extensive with new office blocks and housing being erected; Rippers joinery was in demand. In 1933 Princess Marie Louise made a tour of the factory.

During late 1939 and early 1940, a large amount of work was carried out by the provision of A.R.P. protection for the works and involved the company in considerable expenditure. This included the erection of air raid shelters for employees, a fire watcher's hut and a garage for the works wartime fire engine trailer pump. The Second World War caused a great influx of older craftsmen as the younger ones enlisted at both Rippers and Evans Bellhouse. These older men were nicknamed "the saw-hatchet brigade". Women were once again employed in the factory and a vast variety of timber products were made. The works narrowly missed being hit by bombs on several occasions although the factory did take a direct hit in 1941.

Between 1941 and 1945 the directors of Rippers and Evans Bellhouse tried to keep their two factories operating smoothly and held business meetings at the Ram Jam Hotel on the A1 at Stretton, north of Stamford, which was about half way between the two companies. In spring 1943 William Kay (Bolton) Limited was taken over by Evans Bellhouse Limited and in 1945 Jack Porkess took over the running of "Kays". In 1947 Charlton Ripper died and in 1953 Tucker Ripper, the last of the three founding brothers died.

Following the war years, in 1946 and 1947 timber could only be bought 'on licence', which did not end until March 1951. Therefore it was necessary to obtain supplies from any available source which once included buying tent poles from the Government Surplus Stores by tender, to complete a job undertaken in Gibraltar. In 1951 the company made a large quantity of joinery for the Festival of Britain including doors, windows, clock cases, television cabinets and radiator casings.

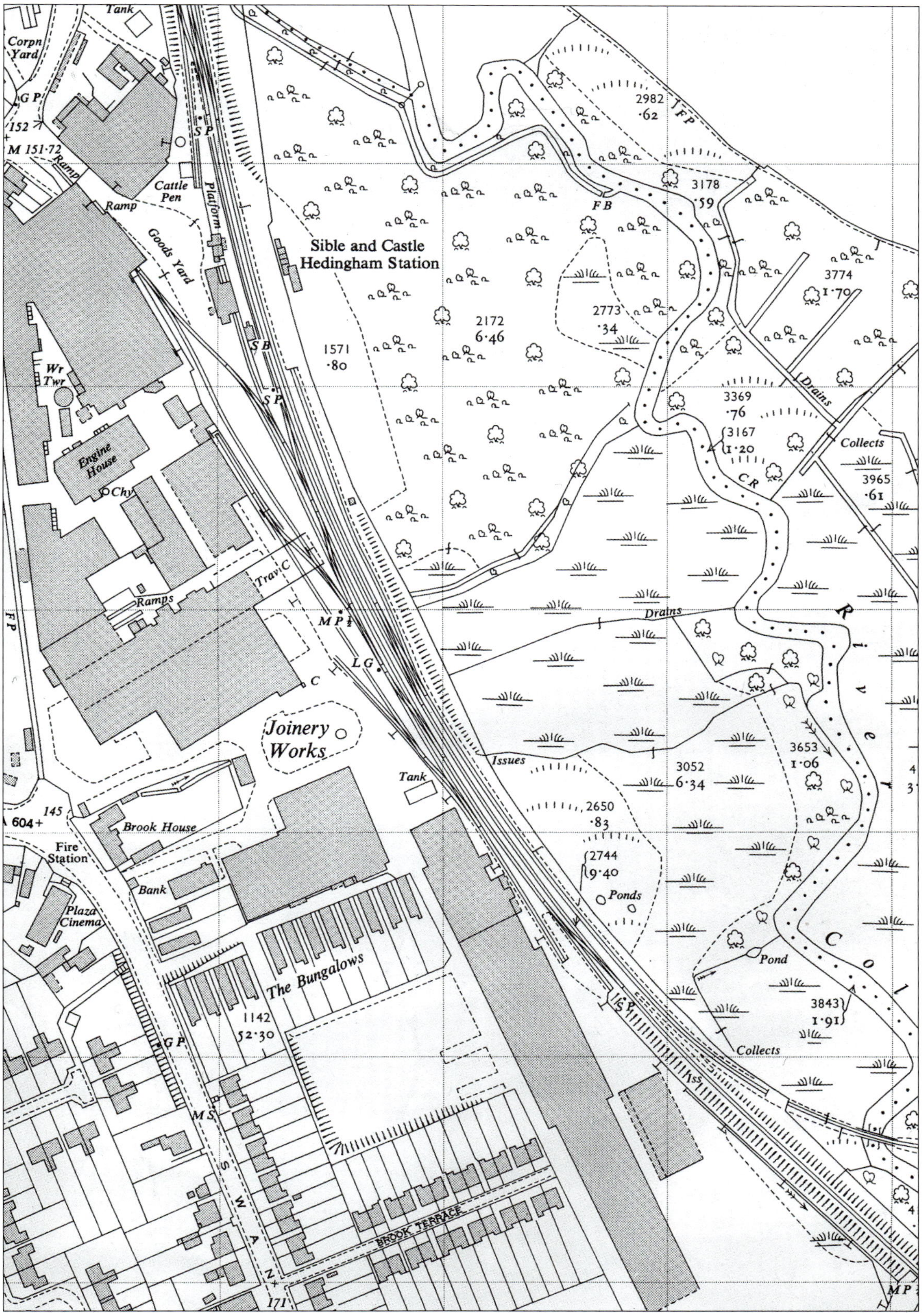

Map of the works in 1953 from the 25inch to one mile Ordnance Survey map

In November 1962 a fire at the Maltings in Station Road completely destroyed the building. The area was quickly cleared of debris, a new building was erected and by June 1963 they were back in production.

The works during the mid 1960s with Crossways, then the home of Ashley Ripper, left background, the old fire engine shed, centre foreground and Crosspath, in the centre

In 1965 the company employed over 680 people and was one of the major employers in the area. In 1971 Rippers found employment for some Ugandan Asians who had left Uganda having been expelled by Idi Amin. They were housed in former RAF buildings at Stradishall and travelled to and from Hedingham by bus. It was in 1971 that Rippers sold its stock of over 90 industrial houses to finance improvements to the factory, and the same year sold Evans Bellhouse Limited to the Tower Group. Unfortunately, the industrial climate was changing and by the early 1970s smaller companies in the United Kingdom struggled. It became very difficult for Rippers to compete or operate as it wished, especially as the cost of raw materials continued to soar.

In March 1973, eleven executives from the Canadian joinery industry visited Rippers as part of a study tour of European joinery manufacturers. Their visit, arranged by the Canadian government, also included similar plants in Italy, West Germany and France. They studied advanced manufacturing techniques, raw materials utilization, product innovation and marketing methods to be used by the Canadian industry to increase productivity.

Towards the end of 1973 when disputes led to three day weeks, paralyzing industry in Britain involving coal mines, railways and power stations, Rippers was more fortunate than most because, they were able to generate much of their own power from wood waste. They also brought standby generators into use and avoided closing down and short time, although production was still affected.

In 1973 to assure the future of the company, the Bowater Corporation, an International Company took over Rippers, and for a short time some of the Ripper family remained with the new company of Bowater Ripper Limited. Following further sales and takeovers, production ceased in 2009.

Chapter 4

Other Directors and Company Secretary

The majority of directors of Rippers Limited were members of the Ripper family and their relations including the Finch and Porkess families. However a few directors were appointed who were not members of the family. They are detailed below in chronological order:

Frank Maitland May (1874-1938)
Frank Maitland May, born 1874, was a son of Frank May a builder and contractor of 21 Gloucester Square, London. Frank junior also became a builder and contractor at 31 Gloucester Terrace, Hyde Park, London and lived at "Abbotswood", Godalming, Surrey. He married Sybil Harris Miles and they had two daughters, Barbara Maitland May and Jocelyn Mary Maitland May. In 1928 Barbara married Sergius Ivan Chermayeff (1900-1996), who initially worked as an interior designer for Waring and Gillow. He later became an architect and his work included the De La Warr Pavilion in Bexhill-on-Sea. Barbara and Sergius later moved to the USA. Jocelyn married Georges Lebrun in 1930. Frank May was appointed a director of Rippers Limited by 1933 and died in 1938 aged 63.

Bertram Helmuth Whewell Hogarth, M.I.E.C., (1907-2001)
Bertram Helmuth Whewell Hogarth, born 1907 at Morecambe, Lancashire, was the second son of Dr. Bertram Whewell Hogarth, M.D., F.R.C.S., L.R.C.P., J.P., Following service in the Kings Own Royal Lancaster Regiment and the Palestine Police, Bertram junior joined Evans Bellhouse Limited, which was Rippers associate company in Manchester as plant engineer. However his services were required by Rippers and he moved to Hedingham in 1933, where he became plant engineer and works manager. Bertram married Mary Somers in 1935 at Morecambe, the daughter of Edith and Arthur Caton Somers, a Bradford wool merchant. Following their marriage they moved into a bungalow in Alexandra Road and later to Romany Tan a house in Station Road. Bertram served in the Observer Corps during the Second World War at the Castle Hedingham Post. He was appointed as works director of Rippers Limited in 1961 and for some years remained as the only director who was not related to the Ripper family. When he retired as a director in 1972, he continued as a consultant. Bertram had been responsible for technology and all major projects in plant and equipment since 1933 and designed and supervised to completion the machine shop. Bertram and Mary had a daughter Pam who married Adrian Corder-Birch in 1994.

(How did Bertram come to work for Evans Bellhouse? In 1929 Tucker Ripper was aboard the Flandre sailing to the Pacific Coast of the USA and Canada. Two of his dinner companions were Mrs Ellen Hogarth and Miss Hill, her companion on the voyage. The three soon became good friends and sometime on the trip Ellen mentioned that her son Bertram was about to return from Palestine and would be seeking a career in engineering. Tucker suggested that Bertram should contact Evans Bellhouse and the rest as they say, 'is history')!

Robert Alexander Burnet, C.A., (1923-1983)
Robert Burnet who originated from Scotland, moved to Beaconsfield and then to Littlefields, Prayors Hill, Sible Hedingham to become Ripper's accountant. He was appointed as financial director on 1st December 1969. Following the takeover in 1973 he remained with Bowater Ripper Limited and later transferred to Bowater's head office at Knightsbridge.

Peter Stewart Lane, F.C.A., later Lord Lane of Horsell (1925-2009)
Peter Lane of Woking, Surrey served as a Lieutenant in the Royal Navy during the Second World War. He later joined his father's accountancy firm, Lane Scotton, which became part of Binder Hamlyn of which he was senior partner from 1979 to 1992. He was appointed as a director of Rippers on 1st January 1970, when he also became chairman of the board. He also chaired

Opperman Holdings, KMPH Advertising, British Electronic Controls, Brent International, Elswick, Automated Security and Attwoods (succeeding Sir Denis Thatcher). He was a confidant of Margaret Thatcher and highly influential in the Conservative Party. He was knighted in 1984 and created a life peer in 1990.

Eric Thomas Judd (1932-2006)
Eric Judd joined Rippers in 1962 as a junior manager in charge of planning. In November 1969 he was promoted to production manager, was appointed as production director in August 1970 and remained with Rippers and its successors until about 1982. He then joined John Sadd & Sons Limited, timber merchants and joinery manufacturers of Maldon. He originally lived in Braintree, later moving to Sible Hedingham and became a member of Sible Hedingham Parish Council and chairman from 1993 to 2001.

David Lyon Geaves (1938-2004)
David Geaves of Burnham on Crouch joined the company in November 1969 as sales manager for the area north of the Thames. In May 1970 he was appointed marketing manager for all company products and in August 1970 became marketing director. He resigned in February 1971.

Company Secretary - Maurice Bernard Nash (1927-2008)
Maurice Nash was born in Toppesfield where he attended the village school. He joined Rippers in 1942 at the age of 14 years with the intention of becoming an electrician under Fred Craven. He was considered too young to become an apprentice and therefore went to work in the office, which he enjoyed. When 18 years of age he commenced National Service in the RAF and served in Egypt and Italy. Upon being demobbed in 1948 he returned to Ripper's and in 1953 married Monica Pettit who was also employed in the offices. He succeeded Stanley Finch as company secretary in 1966 and remained with successor companies until he retired on 31st July 1992 following 50 years service. He was latterly credit controller for Crosby Sarek Limited. He was variously churchwarden, treasurer, organist, choirmaster and bellringer at Castle Hedingham Church.

Bertram Hogarth (1907-2001)

Robert Burnet (1923-1983)

Peter Lane (1925-2009)

Eric Judd (1932-2006)

David Geaves (1938-2004)

Maurice Nash (1927-2008)

A view of Rippers joinery works and Brook House from Brook Meadow circa 1928

The Sugar Loaves Public House is on the left and sawn planks in stick in Rippers yard on the right. In the centre background is a meadow used by Rippers for the storage of logs, which is now the site of Graysmead housing estate

Chapter 5

Industrial Buildings

In September 1896 when the brothers acquired 1½ acres of land close to the Colne Valley and Halstead Railway in Sible Hedingham, it was a bare piece of ground except for an old shed and a saw pit. During 1897 a main machine room, an engine room with assembly shop adjoining and rough sheds to store timber were built. In addition they built four red brick cottages on part of the land facing Station Road for key employees and to help with security. The great advantage of the new site was the use of the railway sidings. In 1899 when Ripper Brothers moved from Castle to Sible Hedingham, their business prospects had improved, although working conditions were rather tough. The prefabricated building constructed at Castle Hedingham was moved to the new site at Sible Hedingham and continued to be known as the 'Wesleyan Chapel' and was later used as a store shed. At this time they employed 38 men, the concern continued to grow and workshops were added to house machinery for the assembly of products.

The initial workshops constructed between 1899 and 1901
These were eventually widened and lengthened and became "B" Mill, the main machining mill

From 1900 to 1914 steady expansion was maintained, necessitating additional storage and assembly space to balance the increase of machinery and power plant. On 4th March 1901 "Cross Path Field" containing an area of about 8a 2r 9p, which was part of Brook Farm, was purchased in the name of Charlton Ripper. It was effectively divided into two plots by a public footpath from Swan Street to Station Road, which still exists. One part of it adjacent to the original premises allowed for expansion as far as the footpath. The second part between the footpath and the main road was later used for residential development and the works canteen. It was on part of this second plot that Charlton Ripper built his house known as Willowbrook in 1905-06. This was followed by four houses in Station Road and Crossways in Swan Street where Ashley Ripper later lived. Many years later the remaining part of this plot was used for the storage of logs and a factory building.

The erection of a large additional shop and store in 1904 enabled the brothers to use the original assembly area to double the machine room. At the same time adequate timber sheds were built for storing a larger volume of dry material undercover; both hardwood and softwood. In 1904 the freehold was purchased of the land on which the works was constructed, which had previously been held on the 99 year lease.

In 1909 a boiler house and chimney were erected which burnt all the wood waste and produced power to run the machinery, lighting and heating. This meant that they did not have to rely on any outside sources of power and therefore remained independent. By 1909 electric lighting, generated on site, was installed in all the buildings. A three storey building with a Belfast roof was built behind the Station Road employees cottages. This building provided offices, a workshop and a loading dock. It overlooked the Colne Valley and Halstead Railway, with access to the siding and was an ideal place to store the assembled joinery prior to the loading and despatching of completed orders. The joiner's shop extended to 50 feet by 120 feet. In 1909 there were about 30 skilled men here but in time of pressure there was ample accommodation for over 50 men. The office was on the same floor and beneath were the stores, consisting of two specially constructed floors for holding timber. The lower floor was devoted to heavier timber and hardwood such as oak, mahogany and teak whilst the next floor contained lighter timber for making mouldings and panels. These timber stores measured 30 feet by 165 feet. At that time the painting and polishing was carried out in the stores, which also housed finished fittings ready for delivery to customers. This building was later used as the 'Setting Out Department' and offices, with a polishing department on the top floor. The sawmills, which were in existence by 1909, consisted of two shops, one of about 30 feet by 100 feet and the other 60 feet by 80 feet. The stores, sawmill and joiners shops were connected by tram lines, with trolleys to facilitate the transport of timber around the works. There was also a packing shop where finished goods were packed ready for transportation. These goods were loaded on railway trucks, which ran under the loading shed, connected with the packing shop by a gangway. All the heavy loading was carried out by an overhead crane.

Throughout 1916 the works was filled to capacity when the Munitions Works Board requested that additional work was undertaken, which would involve a large extension to the buildings and machinery. This was approved and in 1917 building commenced of brick workshops, a large sawmill, eight drying kilns and a power plant as no public supply existed except for gas lighting. The two storey brick built joiners assembly shop was built parallel to Crosspath as well as a mess and recreation room. A large brick power house with a gas producer unit and sawdust extraction ducts and cyclones over the plant was constructed, as well as a large sawmill with drying kilns and a saw doctor's shop. The sawmill was used for converting logs, both home grown and imported, into planks. In order to fulfil the obligation to the Government a complete re-casting of the works took place, whilst maintaining output of current work of urgent importance to the war effort. New types of work was added some of which was aeronautical such as wooden propeller blades. The "Brick" shop was used in the Second World War for making wooden parts for aircraft, as well as storm boats for commandos and ammunition boxes. It was afterwards used for special joinery assembly and kitchen fittings on the ground floor and spraying of kitchen units on the first floor.

In June 1918 an additional 23 acres of land was purchased at Brook Farm and a new bore hole was drilled to provide a better water supply and a water tower was designed which held 7,500 gallons of water. In 1918 a temporary sawing outfit was constructed near Brook House by the old back road to the Station Yard. The saw belt was driven by a steam engine loaned to the company by George Bishop of Alderford Street. This sawing outfit was used for cutting trees into scantlings for use in the construction of more new buildings. During the First World War, George Bishop had carried out extensive timber hauling for the Government with his traction engines.

The temporary sawing outfit on 6th April 1918, with Brook House in the background

The first water tower is in the centre and in the foreground a new bore hole is being drilled

On 23rd March 1919 the three Ripper Brothers conveyed Sale Field to Rippers Limited.

When standard joinery started to be made in 1923 separate mills were constructed and used for bulk and special orders. A second water tower was constructed about 1924-25 and was known locally as 'The Sible Hedingham Castle'! It was said that the tower was constructed too quickly and that the joints leaked, a fault that was quickly rectified. Water was supplied from the works' own artesian well. The tank on top of the tower held 100,000 gallons and was constructed over a 200 foot deep bore hole. The tested supply volume was 10,000 gallons per hour. It supplied water for the works, together with all the Rippers houses and latterly for other dwellings in Christmas Field. In fact it continued to supply water for houses in Christmas Field long after the other houses were connected to the mains water supply.

In 1926 'The Maltings', a building which ran alongside the entrance to the railway station and fronting onto Station Road together with two cottages was purchased. These maltings were originally owned by Vero William Taylor when they were known as 'Halfway House Maltings' and later as the 'Station Maltings'. He sold them on 2nd September 1908 for £900 to Thomas Bradridge and Edward Ruggles-Brise (later Col. Sir Edward Ruggles-Brise, Bt., M.C., T.D., D.L., J.P., M.P.,) who traded as Thomas Bradridge & Co., maltsters, corn, seed and coal merchants. Under their ownership they continued to be known as 'Station Maltings'. They were constructed of brick, timber and slate and comprised three drying floors, two kilns, two malt stores and a barley store. The whole area was 1a 0r 9p including the two cottages. When sold to Rippers, the maltings were converted into workshops and a wooden extension was added to form an additional workshop. These workshops continued to be known as 'The Maltings' and were initially used for machine and assembly shops, for producing folding chairs, lockers for the army, clock faces and paint spraying.

Timber storage sheds constructed by Bert Corder for Rippers Limited during 1927-28

During 1927 and 1928 timber sheds were built by Bert Corder, a Sible Hedingham builder and contractor, on land at Brook Farm. He had been employed by Rippers as a joiner during the early 1900s prior to establishing his own business in 1924. These covered timber sheds were used for storing softwood and hardwood. By 1929 there were over ten acres of sheds and stock grounds for raw materials including hardwood logs in stick. The sawn logs "in stick" were air dried for customer or company use.

The hardwood timber sheds on the left on two floors with walkway on the top floor. The chimney on the right was the first factory chimney for the boilers and drying kilns alongside the sawmill

This view shows the second factory chimney with the power house behind. The second water tower is on the left and the first in the centre. On the right are cyclones which received wood waste for burning to provide power.

On 17th November 1927, John Wilkin Porkess, as company secretary, submitted plans to the former Halstead RDC for a small bank building. The plans were for a 'lock up room to be used one or two days per week as a Sub Bank'. The proposed building was to be 12 foot wide by 14 foot deep of wooden construction, with tiled roof to be erected on brick or concrete foundations. Its location was on the south side of Brook House facing Swan Street. Approval was given, the building was erected and it still survives. It was a sub branch of the former Westminster Bank Limited and was open on Tuesdays and Fridays from 10.30am to 1.30pm only. The bank was built on land owned by Rippers and was principally used by them for employees wages and other transactions.

In 1929-30 "C" Department, was built which ran roughly from the 1917 brick shops, to the sawmill. This was followed by a store building with a segmented 'Lamella' roof of German design. Timber sheds were erected with a 60 foot span and Belfast trusses. The only level ground large enough to assemble the sheds was on the goods section of the railway lines between trains! The timber drying ground was extended to the south east towards the River Colne, where the Riverside Way estate now stands. Being situated in such close proximity to the railway was a great advantage to the business. Frequent trips were made to Liverpool to attend the timber auctions where exotic woods were available for purchase with easy delivery to Hedingham. A railway siding was fitted with a gantry crane which was used to load and unload logs. The crane could also lift and take logs into the sawmill for cutting on the band saw. The top floor of "C" Department was added in 1933-34 and a lift was installed which was used to bring machined joinery parts up from the ground floor for special joinery assembly. During the Second World War this building was used for the assembly of Bailey Bridge support floats. It was later used for special joinery and up and over garage door assembly.

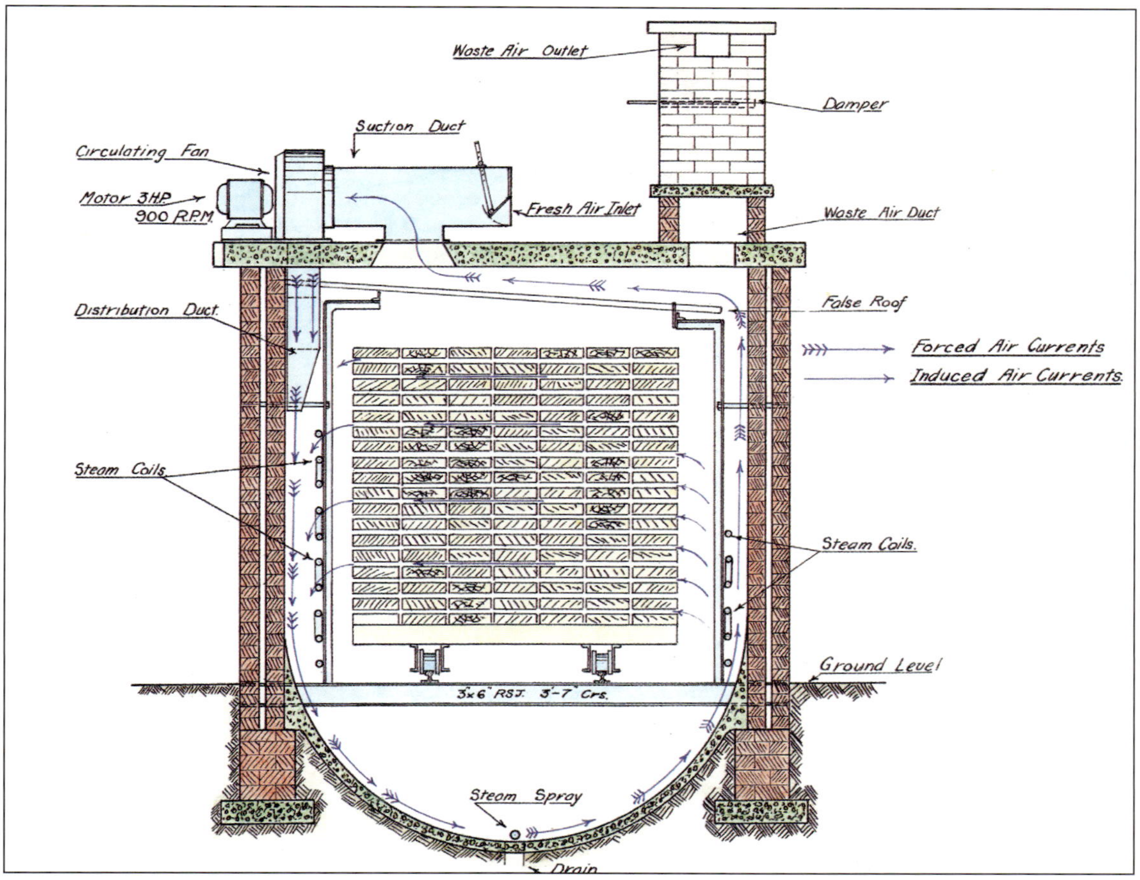

A cross section of a Goodall drying kiln drawn by Bertram Hogarth in 1934

Timber at the entrance to the Goodall drying kiln after its construction in 1934

By the end of the First World War drying kilns were constructed to artificially season wood. In 1934 a Goodall Drying Kiln was built by (Arthur) Frank Gibson for £172 17s 6d for labour and materials excluding bricks, which were supplied by The Sible Hedingham Red Brick Company Limited for £66 5s 0d. By the Second World War there were eight drying kilns in operation. Rippers also undertook kiln drying of logs and sawing for other companies such as for William Oliver and Sons of London. They were founded in 1799 at Clerkenwell and in 1899 acquired a site in East Ferry Road, Millwall close to the West India Docks where the majority of tropical hardwoods they used were imported. Whilst the East Ferry Road site was their main yard, they also rented storage space at Rippers Works at Castle Hedingham.

The 'old' canteen was a former army hut that had been used as sleeping quarters for Ripper's men employed at Cranwell. Upon completion the former army hut was dismantled and transported to the works where it became the canteen. The 'new' Rippers Canteen was built of red brick supplied by The Sible Hedingham Red Brick Company during the late 1930s. It was constructed on the south side of the 'old' canteen, which became known as the 'Mess and Recreation Room' and was later used by apprentices. On the south side of the 'new' canteen was the First Aid Room. During 2009 the canteen was thoroughly renovated internally and opened by the late Stephen Ripper as the Hedingham Social Club and Ripper Hall.

In 1938 the installation of the new power plant took place. Boilers which used woodchip and wood-waste were used to create steam to operate the turbine and replaced the old gas engines which had produced electricity for the works. Diesel engines provided back up.

During November 1938 Rippers applied for permission for a loading dock extension to 'The Maltings', which was then used as a joiner's shop and approval was granted on 20th January 1939. This loading dock was at the north west corner of the Maltings close to the road and was clearly for vehicular and not railway use. (Another loading dock existed on the opposite side of the roadway to the Station).

In 1939 air raid shelters, a fire watcher's hut and a garage to house the works fire engine were built. The latter was a brick building near the bottom gates to the left of Crosspath when faced from Swan Street. The fire watcher's hut was a wooden hut located along Crosspath on the Station Road side of Ripper's Canteen. Air raid shelters were strategically located around the works; one being between 'The Maltings' and Station Road and another near the Colne Valley Railway Goods Yard.

The building, which became the "Cutting Out" Department, was built 1941-42. During the Second World War it was used to crate up jeeps, motorcycles and R.A.F. Beacons for shipping overseas.

In 1948 when Harold Wilson was the Secretary of the Board of Trade, a new shop, "D" Department was built, with its unique 'umbrella' roof. This was for standard joinery and in particular for the assembly of standard windows and frames. In January 1949 the company purchased just over four acres of land from The British Railways Board for £2,350, which was surplus to railway requirements. This land was on the west side of the goods yard and included the former access to it from Swan Street, immediately north of Brook House.

In 1958 the T2 Hangar was erected on the old pit site, which was once used to supply sand and gravel to several local builders including Bert Corder, George Elsdon, Frank Gibson and Percy Parr. The former pit was located between the huts and Brook Terrace with vehicular access being between the huts. T2 (type two) Hangars were erected on airfields during the Second World War to house aeroplanes and when Rippers purchased an old airfield hangar to extend the factory, it was used variously as the stair assembly department, sash dipping line, standard joinery machined parts and assembled frame and sash store.

In November 1962 a fire at the Maltings off Station Road completely destroyed the building. The area was quickly cleared and a new workshop erected by June 1963. The replacement was mainly used for making and finishing wooden television cabinets.

Preparing the site for a new factory building on Sale Field in 1964 for which the contractors were Pudney and Son, builders of Colne Engaine

In 1964 a new building was erected on Sale Field, between Crosspath and Crossways, which had provision for a 3 ton lift from the roof. This building and the parking area in front of it occupied land extending to about 1.5 acres. The building was 11,800 sq. ft. and its covered loading bay 2,875 sq. ft. making a total of about 14,675 sq. ft. It was of steel portal frame construction with brick and wired glass panelled walls and an asbestos sheet and glazed panelled roof. It had a concrete floor and wooden sliding doors providing access for vehicles. Bewick Court houses and flats now occupy the site of this building and parking area.

On 18th February 1965 George Henry Rayner of Maiden Ley Farm, Castle Hedingham sold nearly three acres of land on the south side of Station Road and west of the River Colne to Rippers and on 18th March 1965 the company purchased a former Osier Ground of 2r 23p from Ernest White, which was situated on the south side of Station Road on the east side of the railway embankment. On 6th June 1969 Rippers sold a small piece of both parcels of land to Essex County Council for road widening, which never happened. On 6th November 2013 this land was conveyed to Sible Hedingham Parish Council and will form part of the Hedingham Riverside Walk.

Following closure of the railway, the company purchased for £13,000, further land from The British Railways Board extending to about six acres. This included the former Sible and Castle Hedingham Railway Station, the roadway to Station Road, the goods shed, the former sidings area and the site of the main line from the bridge abutments at the northern and southern extremities, from Station Road in the north to the River Colne in the south.

The former abutment on the south side of Station Road was later demolished but the southern abutment on the north side of the River Colne partly remains. The purchase by Rippers was completed on 11th March 1966 and the site of the former Station was later allocated for extensions to the factory.

Ripper's petrol pumps and garage workshops in former Nissan huts

The majority, if not all, of the buildings erected between 1933 and 1972 were constructed under the supervision of Bertram Hogarth. On his retirement in 1972 Michael Ripper, then managing director, stated, "Without his efforts and skills we would have little of what we have today". His retirement coincided with the completion and opening of a new 12,000 square feet machine shop, which increased the total machining area to 100,000 square feet. The building was designed by the company's architects, The Norwich Partnership and built by Duncan Cameron & Hutchinson. The site was cleared, the building erected and the latest machinery installed within seven months at a cost of £200,000. It was claimed that this machinery, when worked to full capacity, could produce enough standard window components in one year, which, if placed end to end, would stretch from Rippers to Moscow and back. At the same time more new plant was introduced in the factory and the opening ceremony was performed by the Rt. Hon. Ray Gunter, P.C., M.P., Minister of Labour.

In 1972 the cutting out shed was expanded and in 1973 a timber shed was built on the site of the old hardwood shed. During the late 1970s, following removal of 'the Huts', further extensions to the factory took place, but under the ownership of Bowater Ripper Limited.

As indicated in this chapter, buildings were used for different purposes at various times. For example the original office later became the 'Setting Out Department' known as "S" Mill. Later the new "S" Mill building included a machine shop and router operation for television cabinet parts together with stair assembly before the latter moved to the T2 Hangar. "B" Mill was the main shop for machining timber to profiles ready for assembly and "D" Department was for the assembly of standard window and door frames. A Nissan hut near "D" Department was used for storage of machined parts for standard windows and door frames. The original "Hut" Department was where wooden huts for the services were made during the Second World War and was conveniently situated close to the Colne Valley Railway to facilitate transportation of sections. The "Hut" Department was later used for fitting sash and fasteners to standard window frames. For the Power House and associated maintenance buildings please see chapter six.

Aerial photograph taken on 3rd April 1929 looking from south to north

Aerial photograph taken on 5th May 1948 looking from north to south

Key to 1929 aerial photograph

A	Company houses built 1926-27 on Christmas Field, Yeldham Road
B	Willowbrook, Station Road, the home of Charlton Ripper built 1905
C	Company houses built 1926-1927 on Christmas Field, Station Road
D	Company offices
E	Four cottages built by Ripper Bros, circa 1899
F	Workshops and storage with loading bay for railway
G	The former Maltings used since 1926 for assembly and machining
H	"B" Mill, the main machining mill
I	Small brick water tower
J	Main water tower
K	Two storey brick assembly shop
L	Original canteen or mess hall
M	Electricians' shop
N	Power House
O	Gas producing buildings for Power House gas engines
P	Railway Station
Q	Timber sheds
R	"S" Mill Machine Shop
S	Assembly Shop
T	Timber Sheds
U	Sawmill
V	Saw Doctor's Shop
W	Kilns for drying sawn hardwoods
X	Timber storage, mainly planked hardwood "in stick"
Y	Hardwood Timber Sheds
Z	Logs to be sawn in Sawmill

AA Brook Meadow
BB Brook House
CC Westminster Bank and shop
DD Softwood Timber Sheds
EE Wooden bungalows, known as “The Huts”
FF Hardwood timber “in stick”, air drying
GG More wooden bungalows
HH More hardwood timber “in stick”

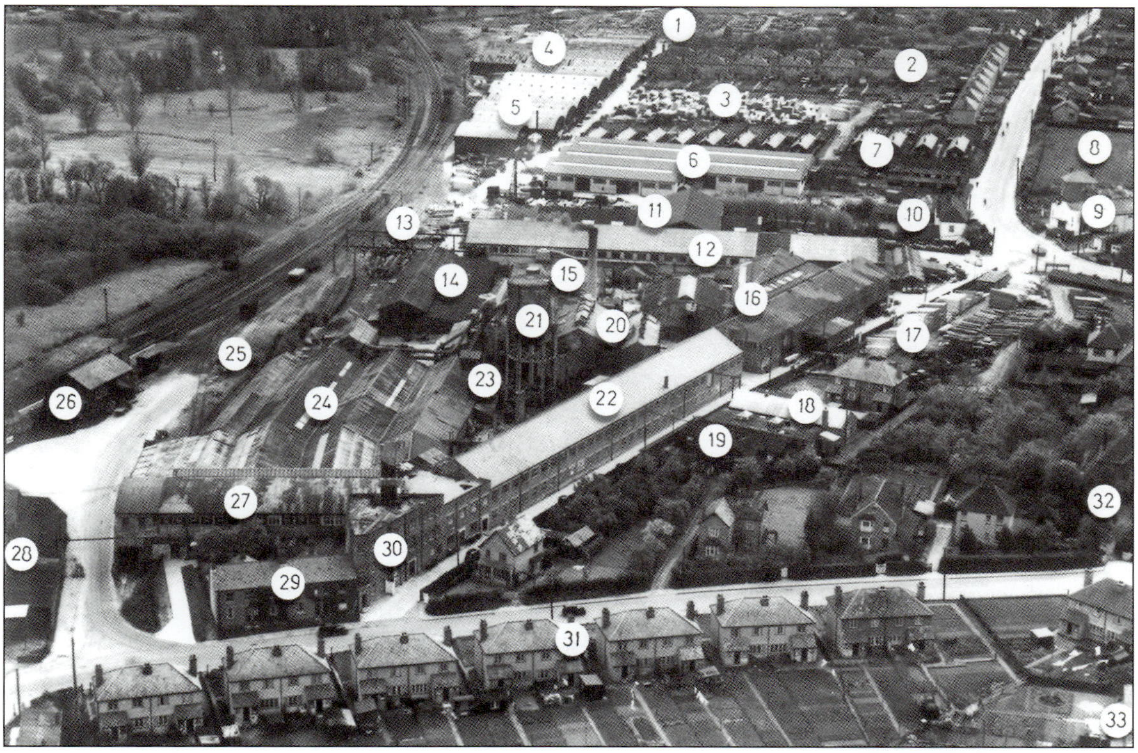

Key to 1948 aerial photograph

1 Sawn logs “in stick” air drying
2 Company houses in Swan Street and Brook Terrace built 1924-26
3 Imported sawn softwood
4 Covered timber sheds for softwood and hardwood
5 The “Hut” Department
6 “D” Department built 1947-48 for the assembly of standard windows and frames
7 Wooden bungalows, known as “The Huts”
8 Brook Meadow
9 Plaza Cinema
10 Brook House
11 “Cutting Out” Department built 1941-42
12 Sawmill for converting logs, home-grown or imported, into planks
13 Gantry crane rails
14 Sawn timber storage shed

15 "S" Mill
16 "C" Department
17 Timber storage, softwood and hardwood
18 Canteen
19 Original canteen called the "Mess Hut", later used by apprentices
20 Power House
21 Water Tower
22 "Brick" Shop
23 Original Water Tower
24 "B" Mill
25 Station Yard sidings
26 Sible and Castle Hedingham Railway Station
27 One of the earliest buildings used as an assembly shop, polishing shop, setting out department and offices
28 The Maltings machine and assembly shop
29 Four brick cottages for employees of which, two became offices and the board room
30 Main office block
31 Houses in Station Road built 1926-27
32 Willowbrook House, Station Road, the home of Charlton Ripper
33 Houses in Christmas Field, Yeldham Road, built 1926-27

The Power House buildings photographed after the removal of the dust extraction cyclones and ducts. The section of building in the centre was the fitter's engineering workshop where jigs and assembly compressed air clamps were built. This shop also housed a blacksmiths forge and cutter grinding shop. The water towers are in the right background.

Chapter 6

The Power House and Plant

Following the purchase of land in Sible Hedingham, Rippers required buildings and a new power plant. They bought firstly a second hand horizontal 15hp steam engine together with a Cornish boiler. By 1909 a 14hp and a 20hp engine were in use and Rippers generated their own electricity. An electric generator and storage plant were installed to produce lighting which took the place of the oil burning lamps which were a potential fire hazard.

From the early 1900s expansion in the factory was maintained, and increased machinery was required in the power plant, therefore the 15hp steam engine was augmented by a 30 hp semi-portable boiler and engine. After a few years an 80hp gas engine with suction gas plant which burnt anthracite coal was installed and the 15hp horizontal and 30hp semi portable were scrapped.

Eventually a wood gas producing plant was put in place to convert the large volume of wood waste which was a by-product from the manufacture of joinery. Unfortunately it proved to be uneconomic as the plant required too many men to run it. There was also a problem with the disposal of the liquid effluent that the plant produced which was originally drained into a large disused gravel pit on site. However when larger power units were installed the problem escalated and effluent seeped into the River Colne causing serious pollution. After complaints from fishermen and the local authorities it was decided to abandon the whole wood gas plant.

By 1928 the wood waste, shavings and chippings were drawn up from the machinery workshops and mills and discharged by large fans to cyclones on the power house roof where it dropped by gravity on to the 'firing floor'. Here the waste was manually fed into the four 'hoppers' of the suction gas producers situated on the ground floor below. These were fired to drive off the wood gas through 'cleaning scrubbers' and 'tar extractors' and on to the gas engines which on each suction stroke activated the process of gas generation.

The gas producers were liable to blow back causing a water seal at the base to be blown out, or gas to be ignited at the top on the firing floor; the former resulted in tar water being ejected over everything, and the latter could result in a fire spreading over the firing floor and seriously burning a stoker. Should a fire occur there were two hand-operated, five-a-side hand pumps which were used to extinguish the fires; Nunn Schooling was in charge of this process. Apparently the men manning these pumps were 'refreshed' by ale supplied by the management!

At this time there were five gas engines of various size and manufacture:

a) Ruston 4 cylinder horizontal 450 hp engine which was housed in a separate building. In the main engine room there were four other gas engines:

b) National 2 cylinder horizontal 350 hp engine.

c) Crossley single cylinder horizontal 200 hp engine.

d) Stockport single cylinder horizontal 150 hp engine.

e) National single cylinder horizontal 100 hp engine. This engine was called 'the Little 'Un'!

These four engines had open cranks and this together with the noise and racing drive belts gave an impression of great power and added visual excitement for an onlooker, unlike the present totally enclosed units of today. A small 'National' engine was bought to charge the starting bottles.

There were also two diesel engines with a unique history. Originally they were ex German Submarine propulsion engines (air blast injection), which after the First World War were put into the Southend Municipal Power House before they came to Rippers to supplement the gas engine plant.

The smaller of the two engines had a vibration problem and to correct this, the 'taper end' shaft was removed; this took a relay of Power House electricians several days to saw through the 5 inch diameter steel causing severely blistered hands. The sawn off steel stub became something of a trophy and was used on the workshop bench as a useful hammering anvil for many years.

These submarine engines had no speed governors and load sharing could only be accomplished by adjusting the engine throttles. The larger engine always backfired extremely loudly and would startle an unwary observer. All the power generated by these gas and diesel engines was direct current at 250 volts and was distributed by many massive overhead cables to the various mills. Some cables passed over the top of the mills and terminated at the Old Maltings, which had been converted into a large carpenters shop.

Power House gas engines 1929/30
The German submarine engine in the far background was used for auxiliary power supply

The power generated by the engines was transferred to dynamos, which converted mechanical into electric energy by electric induction. Each dynamo was belt driven, the largest being about fifteen inches wide. All belts were enclosed between guard railings along the bottom run of the belts. Electric power was then distributed from a large switchboard situated in the power house. Bill Raynham was an apprentice electrician during this time and worked for Freddie Ridgewell for five years and, assisted with operating the switchboard, overhauling of the lighting, overhead cranes, saws and moulding machines.

In the 1930s alternating current woodworking machines began to be used at Rippers and to accommodate these a direct current driven alternator was obtained from Crompton Parkinson Limited.

Circa 1932 the National 2 cylinder horizontal engine was replaced by a new Ruston Hornsby engine. The flywheel was made in two halves, split across the diameter, bolted together at the hub and secured at the outer circumference by two large steel rings shrunk into the flywheel outer face.

Circa 1934 the old Ruston 4 cylinder horizontal engine, which was housed in a separate building was replaced by a new vertical Ruston Hornsby.

With no spare parts available for the German ex submarine engines which were not built to last and were always burning out their pistons, and the other engines not starting due to tar in the gas, work in the machine shops could be halted for hours due to lack of power. Therefore in the mid 1930s it was decided to replace the gas engines.

A new power plant was established between 1936 and 1938 and the following machinery was installed:

a) Metropolitan Vickers 650 kilowatt pass out steam turbine.
b) 2 x Babcock and Wilcox water tube boilers.
c) Neckar water softening plant
d) Small Greenwood and Batley turbine to run at night and weekends to produce power for the drying kilns.

The Power House 1938/39
The boilers are left background and the compressed air plant is centre foreground. In the right background are the two standby diesel generators. The furthest one is a First World War German submarine engine.

As well as being more efficient the new plant was operated by three men in 1937 whereas the old plant had required eleven men.

Two Allen Airless Injection Oil engines at 250 hp each were installed for use in place of the ex German submarine diesel engines, which were retained for auxiliary power. The Allen Injection Oil engines were bought cheaply from the Essex Brick Company Limited of Little Warley, when it shut down at the beginning of the Second World War.

They were originally supplied new to its predecessor Essex Brick and Tile Works Limited, which was incorporated in 1927. In 1944 a new Fraser 10 water tube boiler was installed.

The power plant was required to be serviced regularly and maintenance work had to be performed when the factory was closed. Therefore during the two week annual holiday period and the Christmas and Easter breaks the men who worked in power house and turbine room were overhauling the engines. Immediate repair work would take place at weekends.

Power House steam turbine 1939/40
The turbines were fired using wood waste. The steam created was used to run a turbine and produce electricity for the factory, lighting for the offices and heating for the employees.

Cyclones over the power house roof receiving wood waste

The cooling tower for the power house engines was situated nearby and close to the large water tower.

Plant and Maintenance staff 1971/1972 included: Aubrey Ince, G. Webb, Miss J. Tolliday, G. Tarbin, F. Williams, Charlie Rippingale, R. Everitt and J. Elkins.

At least one of the former First World War German submarine engines remained in the power house until the 1970s. Although it was very rarely used in later years, it was available to provide power in the event of failure by any of the other engines.

As previously stated, wood waste was used to produce heat and power to run all machinery, keeping the works independent of other sources of power. This applied throughout the history of Rippers, and worked well for many decades. However Bowater scrapped the process, which ultimately proved a very costly mistake by them because their replacement system was not successful. The maxim "If it ain't broke, don't fix it" certainly applied here.

The plant was situated towards the centre of the factory and as well as the turbine and power house, there were several shops where various work took place. There were a blacksmiths, fitters, electricians, maintenance and saw doctor's shops as well as the stores. When Rippers suffered a direct hit by a German bomb in 1941, the original saw doctor's shop was completely demolished and had to be rebuilt.

Before a grinding shop was built next to the fitter's shop every machinist at Rippers had to grind his own cutters on an ancient wheel grinder, so the new grinding shop, when it was built, was a welcome addition with its modern plane iron grinders and bolinders.

Saw doctor's shop where saws were set and sharpened for all departments
Left to right: Douglas Hasler, Austin Beckwith and Herbert Everitt

In 1939 joinery was machined and assembled by hand with few extra aids. There was one vertical door press and one small horizontal press. All other work was done by joiners using their own tools on the benches. There was no compressed air system so therefore no compressed air cylinders, drills, sprays or sanders and no welding equipment. At the start of the Second World War, Rippers managed to purchase a Reavell compressor, the only one left in stock, which was made for road breaking. After getting a fly wheel cast at the Tortoise Foundry in Halstead and fitting a motor, Rippers ran compressed air pipes through the factory. This enabled the workers to use compressed air tools for the first time, such as Desoutter drills. The company also built its own blacksmiths forge and purchased a Murex Electric Arc Welder.

Between 1944 and 1945 the fitters shop was used to make Rippers own presses and assembly jigs. Rippers purchased a 4ft radial arm motorised drill from Vickers of Barrow in Furness for £150 and a Kerns horizontal borer from Rolls Royce, Glasgow for £250. They bought 4 tons of 6 inch by 6 inch by 3 foot angle iron and a further 3 tons of angle iron about 6 foot long, ex Morrison and Anderson shelters from a scrap yard, which cost the company very little as the material was considered 'to be of no use to anyone'! The angle iron was successfully used in the fitters shop for making, sash hanging jigs and for drying trolleys for sprayed kitchen unit sides.

In around 1960 Rippers gave an old, redundant Second World War portable steam boiler made by Marshall & Sons of Gainsborough (plate number 90913) to Cyril Philp, a local farmer who lived at Kirby Hall Farm, Castle Hedingham. Cyril was interested in anything connected with steam and the boiler was placed in a corner of his yard next to the granary where it remained for many years. Following his death the boiler was included in an auction conducted by Cheffins Grain & Comins, auctioneers of Saffron Walden on 24th June 1995 at Kirby Hall Farm.

The Marshall steam boiler at Kirby Hall Farm, Castle Hedingham in 1995

Chapter 7

The War Years

Rippers helped the war efforts during the Boer War and the First and Second World Wars.

During the Boer War from 1899 to 1902 Rippers was kept very busy with orders from large contractors for manufactured woodwork for buildings and equipment. The products, which included sectional buildings were required for shipment to South Africa where some of them were used by the Royal Navy. These orders kept the company operating at full capacity and as a result they ran out of covered storage space, so a very large marquee was erected for their immediate needs. Eventually further orders inundated Rippers with too much work and they were forced to seek outside help. This meant that several local builders whose normal work was curtailed by the War were once again busy. Rippers continued to work under pressure for another eighteen months with serious storage problems arising when shipping orders were delayed. To ease the situation Rippers hired barns from neighbouring farmers for storage purposes. Before the goods left the works various War Office inspectors visited the factory to approve the shipments. It was partly through these men that Rippers gained a good reputation for their high class work; the inspectors considered Rippers work to be far superior to several of the companies who sub-contracted work out to them.

At the outbreak of the First World War, Rippers supplied special buildings and fittings to house equipment for use against German raiders in the Caribbean. With war came the inevitable increase in the variety of wooden products the company was required to manufacture. These included wooden propellers and instrument panels for aeroplanes, made from walnut and Honduras mahogany, plus all kinds of equipment for use in the munitions factories which were situated around the country. With so many young men enlisting, Rippers employed older men and, for the first time, a number of women; many of the women were involved in the manufacture of the wooden parts for aeroplanes. The dispersal of the women aircraft workers took place in March 1919.

Women aircraft workers employed at Rippers during the First World War
Left to right: Ethel Underwood (later Redgewell), May Corder, Dolly Banks (later Smith), unknown and Elsie Harper

Women workers at Rippers during the First World War
Left to right: Ethel Underwood (later Redgewell), Jane Elliot (daughter of the Reverend Henry Elliot, Vicar of St. Catherine's Church, Gosfield) and Hilda Gatwood

Douglas fir trees were required to make thousands of telegraph poles for the War Office. As some of these poles were used on the battlefields they had to withstand considerable strain, especially if the surrounding poles were destroyed by a burst of shrapnel. Therefore the poles were subjected to vigorous testing before they left Rippers. All sizes of tent poles, and prefabricated wooden huts were also made and despatched to the Near East at the same time.

When air stations were built at Goldhanger and on the coast around Essex, Suffolk and Norfolk, Rippers supplied the wooden huts which were used in the men's quarters. Similar huts were also used at Pembroke, South Wales and Anglesey, North Wales. In Anglesey Rippers undertook the construction of a large drainage system as well. The task produced several problems due to the hard rock formation and thick strata of soft rock; however the men completed the job satisfactorily.

In 1914 Rippers built the men's quarters for the Royal Naval Air Service at Cranwell, Lincolnshire and supplied the temporary buildings and equipment for the air station at Cardington, near Bedford, where the Short Brothers airship sheds were situated. Harry Ripper, a young man of eighteen, was in charge of the Anglesey and Cranwell jobs, with Donald and Ashley both only sixteen years assisting at Cranwell and Pembroke respectively. In addition Rippers produced over mantels, mouldings, conservatories and other joinery work through the Commonwealth Office for South Africa, Bolivia and Europe, and camp dining forms for the military authorities.

During the Second World War the manufacture of special joinery resumed to support the war effort and Rippers worked closely with Evans Bellhouse. Among the items produced were army huts, pontoons, bomber parts, navigation tables, ammunition boxes and army bedside shelf units. Rippers also produced packing cases, some of which were large enough to carry motor cycles overseas.

The Royal Air Force needed to build airfields in East Anglia and required land to be cleared of trees. At the same time Rippers were using a great deal of timber and required the wood, but lacked transport to remove the heavy logs off the sites. As it was impossible to buy new or second hand vehicles, a timber tractor and trailer was designed by Bertram Hogarth and built in Ripper's engineering workshops. The tractor was made from a single decker Leyland bus obtained from a breakers yard in Chelmsford. The chassis was cut and shortened and the body removed, the winch and jib crane were fitted, and also a steadying spade. The trailer was made using two lorry rear axles, again acquired from the breakers yard. The cab behind the driver's seat was marked "Bill Ditton's Sleeping Compartment"! (Bill sometimes undertook long journeys with overnight stops).

The timber tractor and trailer built in Ripper's engineering workshops. The photograph was taken in Station Yard, "S/D" department with the loading dock and "B" mill in the background. On the left is Jack Holden and on the right is Bill Ditton

In 1939 when the young men at Rippers enlisted they were replaced once again by older men and by women. It was said that after six weeks training the women were as good as the men. To prove this, the women made a set of hexagonal table mats in plywood at the end of their training; if they were satisfactory the women passed the test and received the mats as a 'passing out' present.

The large sawmill being rebuilt and repaired following extensive bomb damage in February 1941

Interior of the bomb damaged sawmill
Note the blackout shield on one headlight of the lorry, which was driven by a Mr. Ruffle. This Bedford Goods truck, ATW 817, was owned by Rawlinson Brothers of Alderford Mill, Sible Hedingham to whom it was registered on 31st January 1934

Once again the factory was running at full stretch and hundreds of bomb doors were made for the Royal Air Force, which were used on their Stirling, Wellington, Halifax, Lancaster and Mosquito aircraft. They also produced propellers, bunk beds and lockers.

As Rippers was a large factory it was inevitably a target for German bombers and on 29th October 1940 six high explosive bombs fell in marsh land either side of the River Colne and railway line near the Railway Station and the Works. In February 1941 the pilot of a lone Dornier bomber spotted the Works, changed its course and dropped four bombs in succession. Extensive damage was caused to buildings and machinery, six workmen's houses were lost and another forty were damaged. Luckily, as it was a Sunday afternoon, only maintenance men were at work in the factory, no one was killed and only minor injuries were sustained. The military authorities took possession of the Works for nearly a week because, it was thought that an unexploded bomb was buried near the power house, but excavations proved that was not the case. Immediate steps were taken to clear up the appalling mess and within a week production started again, contract dates were not allowed to go by default. Unfortunately the saw doctor's shop was demolished by one of the bombs, and the large sawmill was badly damaged and had to be practically rebuilt. However quite a few of the machines survived serious damage and within a month the company was sawing timber again. Despite these setbacks within a year Rippers had increased its production, all contracts were completed and fresh work was undertaken. Therefore by 1942 and throughout the remainder of the war every department was fully employed. The Works continued to be targeted by the Germans and production was halted in air raids by bombers, doodle bugs and long distance rockets. On 13th December 1944 a flying bomb damaged the Works, Rookwoods House, the Senior School and the Gas Office in Station Road.

In 1943 and 1944 war work increased too, especially with the production of pontoons for Bailey bridges, and storm boats. Ripper's factory also featured in a film which showed the manufacturing process of the storm boats from selecting the wood, sawing, planing, machining, assembling, painting, testing, loading for despatch, to shipment on the boats. The film also showed actual footage of the Rippers made storm boats being used abroad in the War areas.

During the war years Rippers had its own air raid shelters, fire brigade, fire engine, fire station and a separate fire watcher's hut, with the fire watch duties at night carried out by Fred Corder. Other employees served in the Observer Corps at the Castle Hedingham Post including, Jack Coates, Stanley Finch, Jack Guilding, Bertram Hogarth, Ted Marjoram, William Meadowcroft and Tom Vale.

The headquarters of the London Scottish Regiment at Horseferry Road, Westminster was badly damaged by bombing, including the First World War memorial which was almost completely destroyed. Rippers restored the memorial using between 1300 and 1400 separate pieces of oak. The joiners completed the task so well that none of the restored parts were visible on the memorial. The joiners who carried out the repair work, were very proud to have played a small part in honouring the gallant men, who sadly lost their lives and whose names appeared on the memorial.

Rippers personnel during the two World Wars

A large number of men employed by Rippers served in the forces during the First World War. Unfortunately eight men lost their lives including Hubert Ripper. In a private ceremony on 10th September 1921 a memorial was unveiled in memory of the eight men. The oak memorial, on the outside wall of the workshop near the entrance to the Works, had been designed and made at the Works. It featured a carved cross with a wreath entwined and in the centre panel were engraved the names of the men surmounted by the words "In Memoriam". At the base was inscribed "Their name liveth for evermore 1914-1918". The unveiling was carried out by James Redgewell, the oldest employee, in the presence of the employees and parents of the fallen. They are also commemorated on the Castle and Sible Hedingham war memorials.

The following details of the fallen are courtesy of the Commonwealth War Graves Commission:

Bertie Ambrose, of the Norfolk Regiment, was a son of William Henry and Sarah Jane Ambrose of St. James Street, Castle Hedingham.

Private Frank Drury, 1575, 1st/5th Bn., Essex Regiment who died 1st October 1915 aged 20. He was son of Charles and Kate Drury of Pye Corner, Castle Hedingham and was buried in 7th Field Ambulance Cemetery.

Private Rupert Frederick Hawkins, 56981, 10th Bn., Lancashire Fusiliers died on 26thAugust 1918 aged 19. He was son of Frederick William and Lydia Hawkins of Rose Cottage, Castle Hedingham and was buried in Bagneux British Cemetery, Gezaincourt.

Private Edward Mead, G/14708, 2nd Battalion, Royal Sussex Regiment died on 9th September 1916. He was commemorated on the Thiepval Memorial.

Sidney Partridge, 5865, 13th Bn., Royal Sussex Regiment who died on 30 January 1917 aged 24. He was son of Dennis and Ellen Partridge of Church Street, Sible Hedingham and husband of Mrs. E. Partridge, of 1, Riding Street, Werneth, Oldham, Lancashire. He was buried in the Viamertinghe Military Cemetery.

Edward C. Thornton served in the Royal Flying Corps and originated from Castle Hedingham.

Alfred James Vale, 6696 of the Essex Regiment and later the 1st/9th Bn., London Regiment (Queen Victoria's Rifles) who died 9th October 1916 aged 22. He was a son of Joseph and Fanny Vale, of Alexandra Road, Sible Hedingham and was commemorated on the Thiepval Memorial. (His brother, Thomas Mumford Vale served in the Essex Regiment and later in the Northumberland Fusiliers and was also employed at the Works).

Ripper Family Members involved in the Wars:
Hubert Ashman Tucker Ripper was the eldest son of Harry Tucker and Edith Sarah Ripper of Castle Hedingham. Early in September 1914 Hubert answered the call of King and Country and joined the 18th Battalion, Royal Fusiliers, Public Schools Corp. He was drafted to France in November where he saw action. In February 1916 his parents received a letter from a Chaplain at one of the Casualty Clearing Stations in France advising them that Corporal Hubert Ripper was seriously ill with cerebrospinal meningitis and had lost consciousness. This was followed a few days later with another letter to say that Hubert died on the 23rd February 1916 aged 21 years. He was buried in the Lillers Communal Cemetery, Pas de Calais.

Ashley Edward Ripper volunteered for military service in early 1917. He trained for the infantry, joining the 1/13th London Regiment and was in active service in France by the end of the year. In 1918 he was completely buried when a shell burst near him. He was dug out and fortunate to escape with his life, suffered from shell-shock and sent home.

Harry Joseph Edward Ripper served in the Royal Flying Corps and in June 1917 became a despatch rider in German East Africa. Towards the end of 1918 he was hospitalised in Durban. He arrived home at Hedingham Railway Station just before Christmas 1918, when the employees of Rippers workshops lined the boundary fence between the factory and the railway and gave a great cheer to welcome him home. During the Second World War Harry was associated with Civil Defence in the Hedingham District, and was Deputy Chief Warden as well as Group Warden for "B" area. He was also the 'food organiser' for the Castle and Sible Hedingham parishes.

Hubert Ashman Tucker Ripper

Ashley Edward Ripper

Harry Joseph Edward Ripper
First World War

Harry Joseph Edward Ripper
Second World War

Donald Charlton Claybourn Ripper served in the East Surrey Regiment and transferred to the 15th Essex Regiment in April 1918. He served in France, where he was injured by shrapnel and taken to a Hospital in Calais before being relocated to a Hospital in Eastbourne.

Norman Charlton Ripper served in the Royal Artillery during the Second World War and reached the rank of Lieutenant.

Left to right: B.Q.M.S. Morgan, Norman Ripper and Sgt. Hudson

Harry James Hubert Ripper (Jim) with his wife Joan

Harry James Hubert Ripper (known as Jim) was a Flight Lieutenant in the Royal Air Force, Bomber Command. He flew a Halifax on 30 operations and was discharged in April 1946. His future wife Joan was in the Women's Royal Air Force and worked in the Met. Office.

During the Second World War the following memoranda were circulated to employees:

Roof Spotters
"It has become necessary for the company to again become responsible for the sounding of the air raid warning siren. To do this the roof spotters have had to move to the fire watchers hut. This does not mean any lessening of the protective measures against sudden raids, as the Observer Corps will continue to function as before.
Signed: S. K. Finch"

A.R.P. and Fire at Rippers Limited
"Works Buzzer Signals:
From 5th July, 1943, the following signals only will be given apart from starting, leaving off and break times:

Series of Short Blasts:	Observer Corps alarm; everyone to go to shelters.
One Long Blast:	All clear, return to work.
One Blast of 15 seconds:	Fire Brigade Call. No action to be taken by anyone other than Fire Brigade and department affected.

<u>Fire</u>

1. While men at work:	Tackle the fire with water buckets and extinguishers but send a messenger immediately to the Power House for the Fire Brigade. If necessary wait there until the Fire Brigade musters to direct them to the fire.
2. During an Observer Corps Alarm:	During an alarm, the Fire Brigade stand-to by the Fire Station at the bottom gates. Send to Fire Station and not to the Power House.
3. Outside Working Hours:	Before taking any action report the fire to the Fire Watchers hut".

Comfort Fund

The following notice was issued by Stanley Finch, Works Director in 1943.
"Comfort Fund' 10/- to be given to every employee of the company serving in the forces.

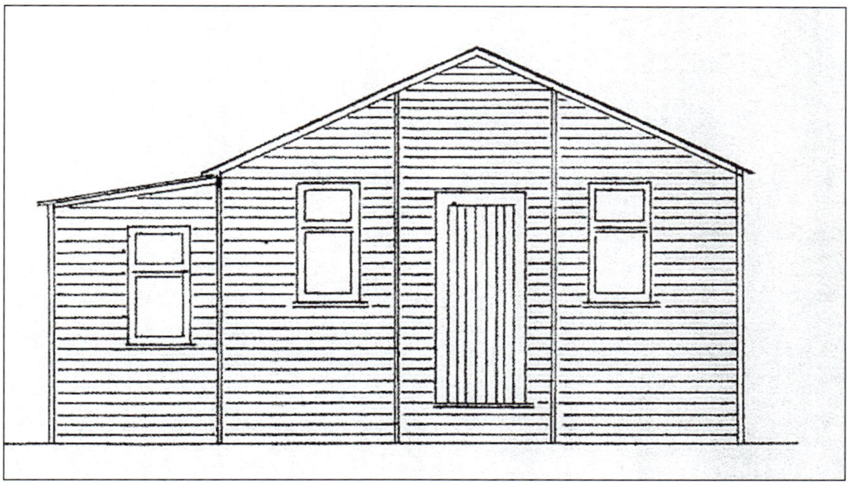

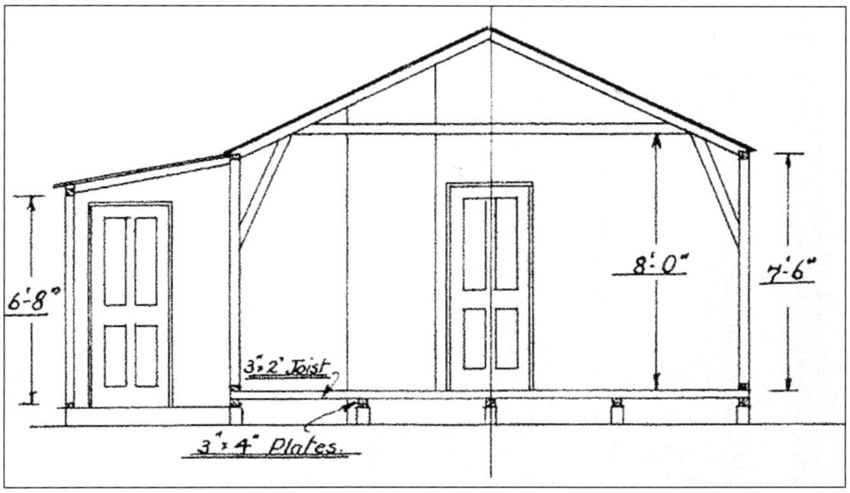

Architect's drawings of end elevations of Firewatcher's Hut

The firewatcher's hut being renovated by apprentices after the Second World War under the supervision of Spencer Hayward

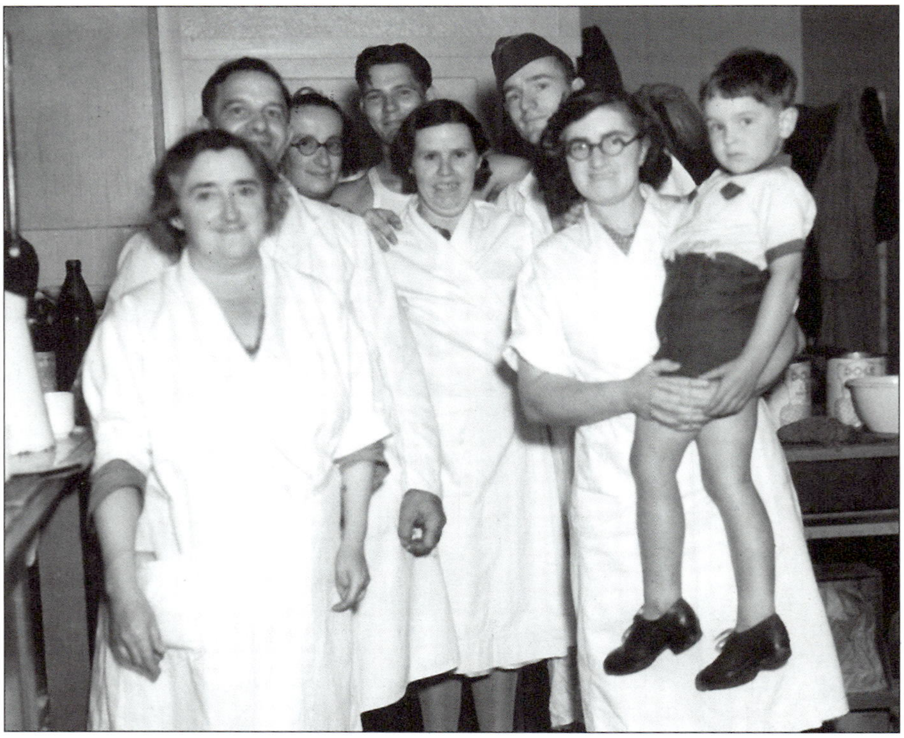

Wartime Canteen Staff
Front row left to right: May Corder, Nellie Brett (later Everitt) and Hilda Ruffle

Chapter 8

Fires and Firemen

The fire appliance, used by the Castle and Sible Hedingham Joint Volunteer Fire Brigade, was a horse drawn "Merryweather modern manual" purchased in 1886 and housed in Castle Hedingham. It was dependent upon the availability of two horses but if no horses were available the fireman ran it to the scene of fires by hand. The Castle and Sible Hedingham Joint Fire Brigade Committee comprised of five representatives from Castle Hedingham and five from Sible Hedingham Parish Councils. The Joint Fire Brigade existed until 1929 and the three volunteer captains were Robert Balls, William Radley and Nunn Schooling successively.

In the early 1900s Rippers had its own manual fire engine, which had "The Steam Joinery Works" painted on the sides. It remained at the works until 1973 when it was restored. During the Second World War the works fire engine trailer pump, a more modern appliance, was housed in a purpose built brick garage to the left of Crosspath near the Brook House entrance. The works had its own Fire Brigade for the duration of the war for which Len Day was latterly the chief fireman.

A Nissan Hut, which served as brigade headquarters and a fire appliance belonging to the National Fire Service, was situated on the opposite side of Swan Street (on the site now occupied by the Library). In 1948 the Essex County Fire Brigade was established and in 1962 a new Fire Station was built in Sugar Loaves Lane (now Rectory Road), which remains in service.

Working with wood and machinery meant that there was always the risk of fire at the factory. It was inevitable that occasionally a spark from a machine could set sawdust or wood shavings alight. Most of these fires were dealt with swiftly and damage was minimal. However larger fires did occur which were much more serious and dangerous, particularly the fires of 1914, 1925 and 1962.

Damage caused by a fire which occurred on Sunday 4th October 1914
Tucker Ripper is standing on the right hand side of the photograph talking to the fireman

1914 – A fire started at 4am on Sunday 4th October 1914 and it was feared that the whole works would be razed to the ground. The fire originated in the engine shed and quickly spread to the joinery workshops which surrounded it. Robert Webb, who lived close by, raised the alarm. The Fire Brigade did not waste time waiting for horses and arrived at 4.20am with the appliance, which had been pulled to the scene manually by firemen: Robert Smith, Horace W. Alpe, Harry Wright, Tills Kendall and James Earey, who were assisted by Will Smith, Harry Smith and Harry Baines. Under William Radley, the Fire Brigade Captain and the many willing helpers, the fire was under control by 9am but not before the premises had suffered considerable damage. One volunteer was Percy Corder who, with others, worked many hours without a break. It was fortunate that there was a good supply of water at the site and thanks to the men who worked the pump an excellent pressure of water maintained. Also present at the scene were Police Officers: Inspector Bretton, Sergeant Edwards and Police Constable Reid. After the Fire Brigade left Scout Master Frank Westrop and a number of Boy Scouts guarded the site, ready to put out any minor outbreaks of fire that occurred. Ripper's employees returned to work on Monday although auxiliary power had to be provided by an engine which belonged to F. G. Bishop, (George Bishop).

Fire damage - 1914

1925 – A fire occurred in the main Power House at the centre of the works. A large quantity of sawdust and wood shavings in one of the hoppers which were situated above the Power House caught fire. One of the large engines in the Power House back-fired when it was lit and it is thought that this may have blown back through one of the 'producers', forcing the cowl on the hopper which then projected through the ceiling above and ignited the surrounding material. George Ruffle, the generator attendant raised the alarm as the whole upper part of the building was engulfed in flames. The Rippers Fire Brigade with its manual engine was rapidly on the scene accompanied by the Castle and Sible Hedingham Joint Fire Brigade under their Captain Nunn Schooling. The Halstead Fire Brigade, under Captain William Arthur Nicholson, and Sudbury Corporation Fire Brigade under Captain Percy Brown, were also in attendance. By 4am the fire was prevented from spreading due to the bravery of the firemen who fought the fire from precarious positions on the adjoining workshop roofs, but the Power House suffered severe damage. The massive iron girders which supported the storage roof were in danger of melting in the terrific heat. Above the staging on the roof there were large tanks of water and luckily when the wood which supported them burnt away they collapsed and emptied their contents onto the flames. To ensure the factory could resume operations as soon as possible a breakdown gang was organised into three shifts which worked through the night clearing the debris. Naturally there was some disruption and production in the factory suffered for a few days until the employees could resume full time work. The damage caused by the fire was estimated at around £2,000 and was covered by insurance.

Castle and Sible Hedingham Joint Fire Brigade photographed during the early 1900s outside The Three Crowns Inn, St. James's Street, Castle Hedingham, with driver and captain, William Radley.

Members of the Police Force present at the time of the fire were: Sergeant Brown (Castle Hedingham), Sergeant Smith (Halstead), Constable Feakes (Sible Hedingham), Constable Martin (Ridgewell) and Constable Ling (Belchamp St. Paul).

1962 – One of the biggest fires in the district occurred on 28th November 1962 in the early hours of the morning. Eight fire engines rushed to the scene where a fire had started in the television cabinet department, known locally as 'The Old Malting', which was situated on the approach road to Hedingham Railway Station. The building was completely gutted. As the twenty foot flames roared through the building explosions from containers of polishing material could be heard over six miles away. It was a foggy night and a dramatic glow could be seen through the mist.

The alarm was given at 3am by Bill Ambrose, a member of the local Fire Brigade. Within minutes Sible Hedingham Fire Brigade was in attendance joined by two fire engines from Halstead. These were followed by engines from Braintree, Clare, Coggeshall, Wethersfield and Sudbury. With the River Colne close by there was a plentiful supply of water but it was not possible to save anything in that section of the works. Chief Fire Officer, E. J. Ellis directed operations and the blaze was under control in about two hours although it took another three hours to extinguish the flames when relief Brigades from Clacton and Brightlingsea took over.

The day after a fire swept through 'The Old Malting' on the 28th November 1962

Fire damage at 'The Old Malting', showing a Second World War air raid shelter in the left foreground, with the Hedingham Gas office and Gasometer behind. In the centre background is the embankment of the Colne Valley Railway

The fire, which caused £80,000 of damage, destroyed the building and left just a few bits of interior wall standing, twisted metal and useless machinery. Stanley Finch, a director reported that every effort would be made to resume production as soon as possible, and that most of the 90 employees in the television department would be found alternative work; unfortunately about 30 women had to be laid off. A massive 'clear up' operation was put into place, a new building was erected and by June 1963 they were back in production.

Rippers considered various options to protect the company against serious fire damage, and an automatic sprinkler system was considered to be the best option. It was designed to send jets of water down onto a blaze before the fire could take hold, and therefore prevent a disastrous fire. It also had the benefit of reducing insurance premiums, and gave a sense of security by being operational in case of fire. Not long after the system had been put in place, in the early 1930s, it proved to be well worth the expense. About half an hour after workmen had left the machinery room for their lunch break, chippings, which were lying on the wooden floor suddenly burst into flames. This was witnessed by a director who summoned the Fire Brigade immediately, however before they had time to arrive, the sprinkler heads opened and water fell onto the fire which was extinguished very quickly. The damage was minimal and disaster averted.

1962 – Tribute to Part-Time Firemen at Sible Hedingham (Extracts from the Halstead Gazette).

"Tributes to the efficiency and enthusiasm of part-time firemen were paid by Lady Beatrice Plummer, J.P. of Berwick Hall, Toppesfield, when she opened the new fire station at Sible Hedingham in October 1962.

The brigade had come a long way since 1914 when a hand pump was stationed at the Bell Inn at St. James Street, Castle Hedingham. It was drawn by two horses that had to be caught first before setting out to a fire. When a fire occurred at Rippers in 1914 the firemen did not waste time waiting for the horses, with the appliance being run to the scene by hand. In 1918 a lorry was provided to tow the pump and the men were paid one shilling an hour plus beer.

In 1948 the Essex County Fire Brigade was established and equipped with some of the most modern equipment to be found anywhere. In 1962 a new permanent fire station was built in Sible Hedingham of which the brigade and the people of the village could be proud. In addition to the main appliance room, there was storage and recreational accommodation, cloakroom and other facilities.

Between 1957 and 1962 the Hedingham brigade answered 250 calls, and 49 calls out of the district to assist other stations. (In 1961-62 no less than 50 farm fires had been attended by the brigade in the area). The station was manned by retained men, and great credit was due to the employers, especially Rippers for their co-operation, and full praise was given to the men themselves for their efficiency and their keen unstinting service."

The majority of the firemen worked for Rippers; once the alarm was sounded the firemen would stop work and dash to the fire station to answer the call. Rippers released the men for duty but did not stop their money. The firemen also had fire bells fitted in their houses. Once Bowater took over, the number of firemen retained gradually dwindled.

The following is a list of Rippers employees who were also part time firemen with the Sible Hedingham Fire Brigade. Those marked * were also members of Rippers own Fire Brigade during the Second World War.

Bert Abraham – a joiner.

***George Alliston** – a joiner.

Bill Ambrose - a joiner.
***Hubert Ambrose**
John Blanden - a joiner.
Doug Blazeby - a fitter with responsibility for fork lift trucks and other vehicles.
***Ernie Boreham**
***Joe Boynes**
***Bob Brett** - worked in the Power House.
John Catterwell - a joiner.
***Charles Clarke** - a joiner.
***Bert Cox**
***Len Day** - a pipe fitter and welder in the maintenance department from 1942 until 1970 and the chief fireman of Rippers Fire Brigade during the latter half of the Second World War.
Robert Deal - a fork lift truck driver.
Reuben Debenham - responsible for the assembly of window frames.
Roy Drury - a fork lift truck driver and also regularly drove the fire engine.
Harold John Earey
Ian John Harrington - a charge hand.
Trevor Hazell - a machinist.
Brian Hoadley - a machinist 1963 to 1985.
***Arthur Kibble**
***Les Martin** - worked in the Power House until 1965.
***Dick Nichols** - a joiner.
Dave Orbell - a joiner and later a charge hand.
Derek William Sidney Pratt - employed from 1949 to 1999 initially as an electrician, then in the tool room and latterly a wood machinist. His first wage was £75 a year. He was a long serving fireman and was Chief Fire Officer for some years.
Keith Stribling - a machinist.
Fred Wells - a machinist and later a foreman.
Tom Wells, jun., - a joiner and later a foreman of "D" department.

Rippers Fire Brigade during the Second World War
The men are photographed in front of Ripper's fire appliance building. Left to right back row: Hubert Ambrose, Ernie Boreham, George Alliston, Joe Boynes, Bert Cox and Leslie Martin
Front row: Arthur Kibble, Dick Nicholls, Len Day (Chief Fireman), Charlie Clarke and Bob Brett

Sible Hedingham Fire Brigade 1952
Left to right back row: Thomas Wells, Bill Ambrose, Ted Overall, ? Hopkins, Bert Ambrose, Fred Lewis and Fred Wells Front row: Arthur Kibble, Charlie Clarke, Bert Abraham, Len Day, George Alliston, Doug Blazeby and Roy Drury

Sible Hedingham Fire Brigade
Derek Pratt standing in front. Left to right: Greg Cocks, Keith Haddow, Robert Deal, Dave Orbell, Ian Harrington and Derek Wheeler

Stephen Ripper presenting a cup to fireman Billy Ambrose in 1968

Chapter 9

Transportation by Road, Rail and Ship

Horses and carts

Whilst operating at Castle Hedingham during the 1880s and 1890s, Ripper Brothers relied solely upon horses and carts to transport timber and goods manufactured by them.

Railway

When Rippers moved from Castle to Sible Hedingham in 1899 their new premises were conveniently located close to Sible and Castle Hedingham Station on the Colne Valley and Halstead Railway. A siding was constructed from the railway into the works, which was used to bring in timber and to take away completed goods. Rippers advertised free delivery on all orders of £5 and over to customer's nearest station or a site if it was within the railways delivery radius of one hundred and fifty miles of London.

Rippers used the railway extensively until its closure to goods traffic on 31st December 1964. Sometime earlier Rippers had asked British Rail for an assurance that the railway would not close. British Rail confirmed that it would not and on the strength of this a gantry was installed on their siding to lift tree trunks up to 15 tons from railway wagons into the sawmills. When the railway closed a few months later, the company was left with an expensive gantry. Following the closure of the railway Rippers purchased the railway station, goods shed and all the land owned by British Rail between Station Road and the River Colne. In 1973, Norman Ripper, allowed the Colne Valley Railway Preservation Society to remove the former station building, which was reconstructed brick by brick on their site at Yeldham Road, Castle Hedingham. This clearance enabled Rippers to erect new factory buildings on land formerly owned by British Rail.

Sible and Castle Hedingham Station viewed from the works with Ripper's sidings in the foreground. A passenger train is on the main line to the right of the signal box and the large building in the centre background is the goods shed.

The sidings, adjacent to Ripper's Joinery works, during the early 1900s with coal being unloaded. The truck in the bottom right is a Colne Valley Railway No. 54 carriage truck, specially built for the conveyance of road carriages.

A diesel passenger train at Sible and Castle Hedingham Station bound for Haverhill. Ripper's joinery works is in the background with the gantry and crane on the left and the works chimney and cyclones on the right. Note the goods trucks on Ripper's sidings beyond the signal box.

Sible and Castle Hedingham Railway Station is in the centre background with the main lines on the right and Ripper's sidings on the left, circa 1962. Two painters are standing on the loading dock outside the 'hut' department and the man on the right is believed to be Ernest ('Gus') Boreham.

An imported hardwood log being moved by a jib crane from near the sidings into the saw-mill.

A wooden packing case used by Rippers to transport goods now in the collection of the Colne Valley Railway Preservation Society and photographed with their kind permission.

Road transport
When road transportation increased, particularly after the First World War, Rippers purchased lorries to transport goods. Among early lorries were the following:

A Foden steam lorry possibly acquired from the War Department.

AB 75 Thornycroft wagon, engine no. 88, built by John I. Thornycroft & Company Limited of Chiswick and Basingstoke, was registered new on 21st December 1901 to D. W. Goodwin & Co of Kidderminster, Worcestershire. In 1918 it was sold to Rippers who became its last recorded owner and it is therefore assumed that it was later scrapped by them.

Thornycroft goods lorry TW 4618 registered new to Rippers Limited on 13th July 1926

TW 4618 The Thornycroft goods lorry's unladen weight was 3 tons 6cwt, 50 h.p. It had four forward gears and was described as a "Commercial J Type" with four open spoke wheels. J types were built from 1923 to 1926 and the cost in June 1926 was £924 and included an open lorry body.

ANO 95 Bedford goods lorry, registered on 30th June 1933. Its unladen weight was 2 tons 18 cwt.

MHK 589 Crossley goods lorry, registered on 18th July 1947 of 6 tons unladen weight, in Station Yard with Fred Cornell left and Bill Ditton right.

Quite apart from using their own lorries, Rippers also engaged local contractors to transport goods. These contractors included Robert Roger Gatward of Nunnery Street, Castle Hedingham and Rawlinson Brothers of Sible Hedingham. During the 1930s they both owned Bedford goods lorries, which were used extensively by Rippers for haulage work.

From the 1940s to the 1970s the principal haulage contractors engaged by Rippers to carry out distribution work were Cousins Transport. This business was started in 1932 by two brothers, Leslie George Albert Cousins and Herbert John William Cousins, when they mainly carried agricultural goods. Herbert Cousins was tragically killed on 23rd April 1944 whilst serving in the Home Guard leaving Leslie Cousins as sole proprietor. In 1960 the business was incorporated into a limited company as Cousins Transport Limited. Its fleet of over twenty vehicles transported doors, window frames, stair cases, kitchen units, television cabinets and other joinery manufactured by Rippers to all parts of England. Among other large customers of Cousins Transport Limited were Brobat Limited of Colchester and Whitlock Bros. Limited of Great Yeldham. Cousins Transport Limited operated from a yard off Swan Street, Sible Hedingham, which was formerly Arthur Frank Gibson's builder's yard. The yard was initially rented and later purchased from his son Hubert George Start Gibson. It comprised offices, workshops and storage buildings and was conveniently located within half a mile of Rippers joinery works.

The trailer on the right was made in the wheelwrights shop and the wheels and axles were cast at the foundry of Charles Portway & Son Limited, Halstead. On the left is a stack of sawn softwood and on the right hardwood logs ready for moving into the sawmill to be sawn into planks.

A Bedford lorry, 8196 PU, in front of the works, circa 1969

Internal transport

In the early 1900s Rippers installed a narrow gauge tramway around the works to facilitate the transportation of timber around the ever growing premises. These small trolleys were initially pushed by manpower.

An internal trolley on narrow gauge rails normally used for moving timber around the factory
On this occasion Ted Ripper's children and friends are enjoying a ride in the trolley. Ashley Ripper, on the left, Evelyn sitting behind him and twin sisters, Ethel and Nellie seated front right. The three sisters are wearing similar dresses.

After the First World War lorries were also used for transporting timber around the factory. However from the beginning of the Second World War there was a severe shortage of petrol and therefore a cobb horse was purchased to pull trolleys around the works. This horse was stabled near Brook House for the duration of the war.

After the war Bertram Hogarth designed and supervised the construction of a variety of purpose made internal transport trolleys for various uses, some of which are as follows:
Twelve trolleys to move window frames from the assembly shop to the hangar. There were six trolleys in each train with safety couplings.
Twelve machine shop trolleys.
Six low loading panel carrying cars with split rollers for easy loading; one car carried fourteen panels (previously one man had moved one panel balanced on a roller skate!).
Four finger cars for drying curtain coated boards, which were purpose made to suit European sizes.
Four tow trolleys with detachable sides for movement of coated panels.
In addition Lister three-wheeler trucks were used to move timber and products around the works.

Timber storage yard, with a Rapier crane. The stored timber was sawn imported softwood

Keith Pilgrim (left) and Roy Drury (right) loading standard window frames from the T2 hangar store onto a Douglas truck to take to the 'Hut' department to have sashes and fasteners fitted.

Roy Smith (left) and Derek Bunton (right) wheeling a trolley load of stair strings to the new stair case assembly shop, opposite 'C' department, circa 1966-67. The open door at the end of the brick shop in the background, led into the works manager's office.

Workmen's transport

The majority of workmen who lived in Sible and Castle Hedingham either walked or cycled to work. Many living in surrounding villages also cycled to work. However some workmen who lived outside the Hedinghams travelled to and from work by train on the former Colne Valley and Halstead Railway and, also by buses provided by the once numerous local bus operators.

During the mid 1920s, Harry Stanhope Theobald (1878-1963), an employee of Rippers, who lived at Long Melford and travelled to and from work by bus, thought, it would be a good idea if he purchased a bus to drive his fellow workers. He continued his employment with Rippers and parked the bus each day at the works. In due course he decided to become a full time bus operator and upon leaving Rippers commenced a bus service between Sudbury and Long Melford; he ultimately developed a network of services.

Cars for Rippers representatives

The company provided its representatives with company cars to visit clients. These cars were purchased by Bertram Hogarth from Leslie Drury of Tills V. Smith & Co. Limited of The Garage, Bayley Street, Castle Hedingham.

Transportation at Manchester

Ripper's associate company, George Evans & Sons Limited, timber importers and merchants of Manchester initially used horses and carts. Following the First World War lorries were gradually introduced and both methods of transport were used simultaneously for some years.

Four horses and carts alongside five motor vehicles outside Newton Heath Saw Mills

George Evans and Sons Limited used a Clayton and Shuttleworth steam lorry, which frequently towed a four wheel trailer, both loaded with timber. (Photograph dated 15th May 1928)

Evans Bellhouse Limited later owned a fleet of lorries, including Commer lorries to transport packing cases and other joinery manufactured by them

Ships and trips abroad

When the three Ripper brothers started their business they used native English timber for most of their woodwork. However, after the First World War, many forests and woods in the United Kingdom had been stripped of trees to make wooden items to help the war effort, therefore joinery manufacturers began to look further afield for timber.

Travelling was not as easy as it is today and most trips would have been rather gruelling as they involved rail and ship and probably some form of native transport too! It appears that Tucker Ripper was the adventurer and travelled abroad on behalf of both Evans Bellhouse and Rippers. It is doubtful that his brothers would have been well enough to make some of the arduous journeys which he undertook.

Tucker was primarily responsible for the introduction of British Columbian Red Cedar, a soft wood, into the United Kingdom. He travelled to the USA and visited the Pacific Coast and Canada to obtain first-hand information. Tucker knew that the Americans called Red Cedar, 'the everlasting wood' and used it in 'roof shingles, weatherboarding, fence posts, telephone poles, garden fixtures and whenever resistance to the weather and decay was a vital factor'. However he did not know how it would react in centrally heated buildings. Following three years of experimental use Tucker was so impressed with the timber that he recommended it to British architects as it did not warp or twist and could be used for highly decorative work such as 'panelling, ceilings and finishing'.

A few more years passed with visits to sawmills and lumber operators in America and Canada before Tucker became a serious importer of Red Cedar, mainly through Thurston & Flavelle Limited, Vancouver, Canada, whose sole business was to produce Red Cedar lumber for home and export.

The timber was used daily in the factory alongside other woods which included conifer and many decorative hardwoods from around the World, for example African padauk, black bean and Indian laurel.

The following is a brief resume of some trips undertaken by Tucker Ripper between 1924 and 1939:

1924, February **Austria** – to check on timber situated at Wiedhofen for Evans Bellhouse. This trip involved travel from Vienna by horses and sleigh.

1926, March to May **USA and Canada** – firstly as a rest cure and secondly to investigate the timber situation on the Pacific Coast and to establish business contacts. This trip was via the West Indies, across Panama, along the Pacific Coast to San Francisco, then onward to British Columbia and across Canada. Tucker returned home from New York.

1927, October to December **Canada and USA** – to follow up previous contacts with a view to commencing business and to visit Thurston & Flavelle Limited, Red Cedar lumber exporters.

1929, April to June **Canada and USA** – a further trip to the Pacific Coast was undertaken to consolidate work achieved on the previous visits. Edith accompanied him on this trip.

1929, August **Germany** – Tucker investigated a patent for a Lamella roof.

1930, **Germany** – He carried out further investigations in Berlin to patent a Lamella roof.

1931, **Germany** – His business is unknown, but it was possibly for further discussions about the Lamella roof?

1932 **Germany** – Bremen, Hamburg and Osnabruck to look at specialised machinery. This included a visit to a foundry to test a wood cutting machine and to negotiate a license to use the machine in England, which was granted.

1933, April **Finland** – Tucker reported upon the condition of a consignment of timber, which had been salvaged from a stricken vessel, off the Finnish coast. Evans Bellhouse intended to bid for the wood through Lloyds Agency, who offered it for sale to the highest bidder.

1934, March **Yugoslavia** – Tucker travelled with his brother Charlton and nephew Stanley Finch to select and purchase high quality oak trees for Rippers.

1934, late summer **Germany** – Hamburg and Augsburg. Tucker travelled with his son Harry to investigate a very ingenious German window.

1935, May **Lithuania** – Tucker travelled with his brother in law John Porkess to Memel to inspect timber.

1935, October to December **Canada and USA** – Tucker continued business investigations and visited Vancouver Island to see a logging camp in operation. It was on this trip that he visited his old school friend Edward Corder (1868-1940) who was then living at Gibson's Landing, to which Tucker travelled by speed boat up Howe Sound. A number of Edward Corder's close relations were employed by Rippers.

1937, April to June **Canada and USA** – having acquired a tract of virgin forest up the Fraser River in British Columbia with English and Canadian associates, Tucker travelled to the Pacific Coast to visit the project.

1937, October to December **Canada and USA** – Tucker investigated the British Columbian forestry problems and discussed the financial implications of the project, with bankers and investors.

1939, Easter time **Switzerland** – Tucker and his nephew Kenneth investigated a prefabricated wooden building, which was causing much interest in the woodworking industry.

Edith and Tucker Ripper on board ship

Edith did not usually accompany Tucker on his trips, but in 1929 she was persuaded to join him. They left Liverpool on the 6th April aboard the S.S. Scythia bound for Canada and the United States of America. Edith proved to be a good sailor when they ran into a bad storm. When Tucker and Edith landed at Halifax the countryside was covered in snow and everywhere was ice-bound. They took the night train to Montreal and slept in a carriage that appeared to have square wheels! Although it was primarily a business trip for Tucker, time was spent visiting old friends and family while on the trip. They travelled to Winnipeg and were surprised to bump into Frank Woodcock's sister in law in the Christian Science Church. (Frank was a Ripper's employee). They visited Vancouver and whilst in Port Moody met Mr. and Mrs. Stock, she was Percy Bareham's sister. (Percy was also a Ripper's employee). Tucker and Edith also spent time in California, the Grand Canyon, Chicago, Buffalo, Pittsburg, Philadelphia and New York, which they left during a heat wave on the German ship, Stuttgart and arrived back in England on 29th June.

During the Second World War business trips abroad were curtailed and both Rippers and Evans Bellhouse struggled to operate smoothly. Following the war years there was difficulty in obtaining timber. This was caused by the introduction of timber licences and price control which were not lifted until 1st March 1951, when Harold Wilson was Secretary to the Board of Trade. (Licences were also adopted in other countries and were introduced to protect the forests and woods from 'over felling' as they had been depleted during the war. New tree plantations were underway and by the 1960s and 1970s wood was readily available again).

As flying became an easier mode of travel it was no longer difficult to travel abroad on company business or to visit distant timber forests. Opportunities also arose for apprentices to travel to Europe as part of their training to visit other companies and learn new techniques.

The Flandre
A French ocean going liner, the Flandre was built in 1913 for Compagnie Generale Transatlantique. Tucker Ripper sailed on the Flandre on 1st March 1926, departing from Plymouth, when he visited the West Indies, United States of America and Canada. It was Tucker's first experience of a long sea voyage and one that he thoroughly enjoyed. The Flandre struck a mine in 1940 and sank.

S.S. Scythia
The S.S. Scythia was a luxury liner launched in 1920 by Cunard. She initially sailed between Great Britain and the United States of America. S.S. Scythia was requisitioned at the end of 1939 when she was used as a troop ship and took part in the British Army landings in North Africa. The liner was taken to the ship-breaker's yard in 1957 having spent her last few years' service as a passenger ship. Tucker and Edith Ripper sailed on her in 1929.

(Other ships Tucker Ripper sailed on were: Aquitania, Britannic, Columbus, Duchess of Bedford, Duchess of York, Empress of Australia, Homeric, Jamaica Producer, Manchuria, Montclare, Mauretania and Stuttgart).

Chapter 10

Process and Products

In a 1920s Rippers brochure it was stated with pride that the woodwork produced was the creation of the individual craftsman and that wood, 'blossomed into beauty of line and shape beneath these men's hands'.

As the company grew, and Rippers started to make standard joinery as well as specialist joinery, the products inevitably changed, especially during the war years. Working for the building trade, doors and windows in all sorts of shapes and sizes provided Rippers with constant revenue and became the mainstay of their operations.

Process

Logs would arrive at the works either on large trailers or by train into the Ripper railway sidings, where they would be unloaded by a gantry crane. Some logs were taken into the sawmill while others were stacked away for years to dry and season. The stock of raw materials (wood) was extensive and at one time comprised over 30,000 cubic feet of hardwood and over 8 acres of softwood storage.

Alec Tait stripping bark, known as "barking", from an English oak log - 1965

The sawmill was equipped with a travelling crane capable of carrying 5 ton logs, which were fed onto a battery of saws. Before English logs, especially oak were sawn they underwent "barking". This involved a man stripping the bark from the logs looking for nails, wire, metal or even bullets, which were sometimes found in the post war years.

A heavy duty band saw could cut a 5 foot diameter log into planks at speed. Logs which had been sawn into planks were known as "in stick" and some were stored in timber sheds and others outside so that the air could circulate.

Softwood was stored in sawn sizes and routine inspections were carried out to determine the moisture content of the wood which would be used later for joinery products, this was particularly important where centrally heated buildings were concerned. Drying kilns and condition chambers, designed at Rippers, ensured that all the wood used was in the finest possible condition.

Logs waiting to be sawn in the background and sawn logs in planks in the foreground. Note the gantry crane on the right of the photograph which was used for lifting and moving the logs; the crane driver in the 1960s was Stan Boreham

A horizontal band-saw and a mahogany log on a moving carriage being prepared for converting into planks - 1929

In the Setting Out Department drawings were prepared for customer's orders. Full size sections and details were made ready which included timber cutting lists of all the items ordered. These were passed to the timber department and to the machine mills.

The Setting Out Department – 1929
Left to right, front row: Allan Webb, Arthur Cleghorn and Bert Evans who is setting out for a signal box at Liverpool Street Station, London

The Setting Out Department – 1965
Left to right, foreground: Gordon Faiers and Billy Wilkin

The Cutting Out Department was used primarily to convert timber to a size suitable for machining to required profiles for assembly.

Cutting Out Department
Len Cansell can be seen operating the gantry crane

A moulding machine being operated by John Waldron on the left and Alan Sibley in "B Mill"

From the sawmill, the planks went on trolleys to subsidiary mills, where other specialist machines could reduce the raw material to its finished thickness and shape. For example, a square piece of timber could be fed into a "moulding" machine and emerge with intricate mouldings and curves.

The Machine Shop prepared material for assembly, and in "B" Mill there were large cyclones, (extractor pipes) which carried the shavings and sawdust to the gas producing plant where it was used as fuel.

In the Assembly and Joiner's Shops the various units were assembled by skilled craftsmen. Although the factory was equipped with modern machinery it was the joiner's expertise and capable hands that produced the high class woodwork.

Top floor of "C" Department - 1935
George Alliston with a cross cut saw; joiners in the background are assembling machined parts

When the units left the shops they were primed or polished, and then the finished products were ready for packing and despatch. From covered sidings and loading docks, the railway, trucks and lorries took the goods to all parts of the country. Products which, were destined for overseas were taken to various ports to await shipment.

List of some of the products made at Rippers:

1880s: General carpentry including wooden troughs used in bread making.

1885 – 1920s: Coffins.

From 1902: Prefabricated wooden buildings for the Congo and South Africa.

1915: War work, including wooden huts and duckboards.

1916: Rippers advertised "Specialities"; good class contract joinery for the trade which was called Architects and Decorators' joinery; Ecclesiastical joinery including, altars, reredos, screens, seating and stalls. Timber framed temporary buildings. Composition enriched mouldings and mantels. Horticultural Buildings and Conservatories, (this work they acquired when Crompton and Fawkes Limited of Chelmsford, closed down).

1917 and 1918: Aeroplane parts and laminated propellers.

From 1920: Ripper's indispensable step chair and space saving, gold medal award revolving cupboard; both were considered ingenious inventions as the country was economising on the space inside newly built houses.

1922: An article featured in The Timber Trade Journal Annual Issue stated that in addition to joinery, Rippers turned out: shop fronts, counters, show cases, wall fittings, window enclosures, staircases, lift enclosures, cash offices and desks. They also produced windows, frames, doors, sashes, coffee tables, pulpits and church pews.

Rippers were responsible for the introduction of British greywood, which was English elm treated by a special process to change the natural light brown to a grey tint. The wood was suitable for parquet flooring, furniture, panelling, doors, windows and anything that needed a decorative feature. In addition to wood, Rippers handled glass, metal, marble, granite, tiles and other building materials.

It was in 1923 that Rippers started to make 'standard' joinery, and the mills for bulk joinery and special joinery were separated. Standard joinery included both doors and window frames which were all made to specific sizes. These could be stored easily and transported to building sites or 'one off' jobs when required, without the customer having to wait for them to be specially made. This was especially useful from 1924 to 1927, when Rippers built a large number of houses in Sible Hedingham for their employees.

Assembly shop for softwood windows and bays with Ernie Pannell, Fred and John Sturgeon - 1929

1923 and early 1930s: Standard joinery included:

Angle mullions.
Bay windows.
Combined frames.
Door frames.
Garage doors.
Vestibule frames.

Standard joinery

A Trade Price List of Rippers stock joinery for April 1927 quoted: *"Terms of business – Net monthly account against approved references or less 2½% cash with order. In the case of new customers delay will be avoided if order is accompanied with a remittance or a Banker's reference. Carriage – Prices include free delivery to customer's station or to a site if within Railway Company's delivery radius, in quantities of 8 and over. Under 8, prices are F.O.R. Time for delivery – Windows and doors within 48 hours of receipt of order to approved accounts. Bays (bay windows) and primed orders take longer, according to size"*.

The carriage later changed to: *"free delivery to customer's station or site if within Railway Company's delivery radius, on all orders to the value of £5 and upwards within a radius of 150 miles"*.

Example of prices:	Kitchen dresser	67/6d.
	Oak garden gate	21/- to prime or stain 1/- extra.
	Doors	from 11/9d to 31/6d.

1930s: Rippers were involved with a number of large London contracts, supplying offices and blocks of flats with their joinery.

1938: Militia huts.

1939: War work including: Pontoons, storm boats, ammunition boxes, bomber parts including bomb doors, navigators tables, folding chairs and packing cases for vehicles.

From 1939: Standard joinery included:

Bay windows	Casement doors
Combined frames	Door frames
Door linings	Draining boards
Storey frames	Vestibule frames
Windows	Window boards

Rippers provided boxes for fisherman at Lowestoft for the transportation of fresh fish, and flower boxes which were sent to the Channel Isles. They also made packing cases for the Irish linen trade in Belfast.

Circa 1945: Rippers were reputed to have made wooden parts for Dutch windmills to replace those destroyed by the Germans when withdrawing from Holland during 1944-45.

1946: Standard joinery included:

Bay windows	cant, circular end, segmental or square.
Casement doors and frames	
Combined frames	for doors opening in or out.
Door frames	for external and internal doors.
Door linings	
Draining boards	
Storey frames	
Vestibule frames	
Windows	bulls-eye, landing, larder, W.C., with bars, with bars to fan only, with lay bars, without bars.
Window boards	

From 1948: Back doors for dust carts (Ministry work).
Packing cases for Electrolux.
Refrigerator parts in beech.
Tables for barracks.
Tables and locker doors for miners.

Late 1940s to the late 1960s: Standard joinery included:

Casement windows	Standard pivot-hung windows
Bay windows	Double glazed windows
Door frames	Stairs

General specification stated that all components were made from selected softwood with hardwood thresholds to door frames.

Following the Second World War Rippers supplied joinery for the 'Cornish Unit' prefabricated houses built by Selleck Nicholls & Co. The Cornish Unit house was constructed using precast concrete made with 'spoil' from the china clay industry. Selleck Nicholls was the building division of the English China Clay Company. Ripper's joinery was used in these houses until the 1960s when the houses were built by local authorities across the country.

From circa 1953: Clock cases Radiator casings

Between 1955 and 1965 Rippers were manufacturing radio cabinets and about four thousand television cabinets a month.

During the 1960s: 'Up and over' garage doors Kitchen units

"S" Mill, Stair Assembly Shop
Bob Mills on the left and Jack Leathers on the right

"C" Department assembling up and over garage doors, designed and made on premises
Cyril Reeve (left) and Peter Cook (right)

Bob Turner making the finishing touches to a television cabinet in 1965

In 1965 Rippers received orders for their new Regency range of kitchen units for four hundred houses. This new range of kitchen fittings proved very popular as maintenance was cut to a minimum by the use of laminate facings on doors and cupboard fronts, all in fadeless colours that would never need painting. Work tops could be purchased separately to use as links between units such as breakfast bars. Sink units were available too and came in a choice of enamel or stainless steel, single or double with tap fittings, all easy to clean and modern in design. Also hob units were included in the range and Rippers were able to supply the necessary cooking equipment for this increasingly popular style of fitting. It was stated that: *"Ripper's Regency range of kitchen units gave an atmosphere of luxury to your kitchen"*.

Kitchen Unit Assembly on ground floor of Brick Shop in 1965
Left to right: Ray Piper, Bob Moore (in background) Ted Corder (in centre), Mick Brown and John Wright (in foreground)

1967: Easiform and Storiform dwellings were built and constructed with prefabricated timber infill panels to front and rear elevations.

Windows included:
Casement, picture, landscape, larder with fly screens, double glazed windows and bay windows. External and internal frames were produced with standard doors.

With the introduction of metrication into the building trade Rippers were one of the first companies to introduce a range of metric windows in 1970.

Although kitchen units always featured in Ripper's order book, it was the building boom of the last two decades that saw specialist kitchen departments evolve at the beginning of the 1970s.

By 1972, Europlan was introduced as the new metric range of kitchen fittings, once again in laminated plastic. There were four worktop and six door and drawer finishes which included olive green, natural teak, midnight blue and bright orange colours. These cabinets were available in fully assembled or component form for the "D.I.Y." home market. Flat packed units, reduced transport and warehouse costs for Europe. Brochures promoting the Europlan kitchen range were written in both English and French, the two official languages of the Common Market.

1972: A new range of products included "Viking" PVC door linings, skirting boards and architraves. These were marketed by Rippers under an agreement with the Swedish manufacturers.

1972: Rippers and Tomo Group of Uxbridge pooled resources and technical knowledge to produce Tomo high performance windows, which were designed to combat gruelling weather conditions, noise and heat loss, and were used in hospitals, schools, offices and public buildings.

Europlan Module 2 range of unit furniture was also based on the metric module of 500mm.

The Regency Range with employee Mary Hart in the showroom kitchen

1972: In their Annual Report and Accounts, Rippers stated that they produced:
EJMA (English Joinery Manufacturers' Association), imperial standard windows, EJMA metric dimensionally co-ordinated windows, curtain wall units, external doors and frames, Regency kitchen units, Europlan metric kitchen units, staircases, internal door frames, Viking PVC internal linings, architraves, skirting boards and the 'TOMO' double glazed window.

Although the exact years of production are unknown Rippers also made:

Ironing boards	Bedside cabinet
Coffee tables	Small nest of tables

In 1973 Rippers quoted: *"Rippers are organised for the seventies"*.

In addition to the above Rippers made carpet strip manufactured from hardwood and serving hatches.

The above paragraphs are an outline of the principal products made by Rippers during a period of nearly one hundred years. In addition they made numerous 'one off' items for customers in the UK and abroad.

Chapter 11

The use of Products in Buildings

Rippers made joinery for all types of buildings including abbeys, chapels, churches and synagogues, factories, hospitals, hotels, schools, public buildings, private dwellings, blocks of flats and large stores in London; for example Harvey Nichols, Libertys and Selfridges.

In some cases Rippers carried out the whole, or major part of the joiners' work and, on other jobs made a single specialist piece of joinery. The following are brief details of a few contracts undertaken by Rippers on buildings principally in Essex during a period of eighty years and constitute evidence of Rippers' wide experience in all kinds of woodwork.

In 1895 the Empire Theatre in Southend was destroyed by fire. It was rebuilt in 1896 by the proprietor, Fred Marlow and renamed the New Empire Theatre. Walter J. Wood was the architect and Heffer and Gillett were the builders. The joinery work together with the block flooring and four first class refreshments bars were supplied by W. C. Ripper's joinery works.

It was also stated that a great part of the joinery at the new Capital Bank and business premises adjoining the Empire Theatre were also being supplied by 'this rising firm'.

Ilford Town Hall, in High Road, Ilford was opened in December 1901 having been built for £24,900. It contained a large variety of woodwork made by Rippers including the Council Chamber from Indian Laurel, the Members Room in oak panelling, the Ladies Room in pine panelling and the Engineers Room with columns and panelling made from oak. Rippers also supplied a walnut mace stand, which was carved by Bryan Saunders, an ecclesiastical master wood-carver of Coggeshall.

Ilford Town Hall – Council Chamber in Indian Laurel

In about 1922 Rippers supplied their scientifically designed hygienic flush doors to many hospitals including the Cottage Hospital Halstead, the Nurses' Home at Romford, County Hospital at Colchester and numerous other buildings listed in appendix two. In 1922 Rippers was awarded a bronze medal by the Sanitary Congress at Bournemouth for these hygienic doors, which were made in oak, walnut and mahogany.

The oak choir stalls and the priest's stall, in the chancel at St. Peter's Church, Sible Hedingham, were designed by architect, Wykeham Chancellor F.R.I.B.A. They were dedicated by the Bishop of Colchester on the 6th March 1929 who stated 'that the massive oak used was of high quality and the exquisite workmanship was a source of admiration'. The choir and priest's stalls are no longer in their original position having been moved in 1993 towards the altar rails, to accommodate concerts, plays and a piano. Rippers also constructed the pulpit and much of the other woodwork in the church.

Choir stalls at St. Peter's Church, Sible Hedingham

In 1929 they provided the joinery for a signal box at Liverpool Street Railway Station in London.

In 1936 Rippers made the main staircase of Columbian Pine and Austrian Oak for Bonds of Chelmsford at High Street, Chelmsford. In the same year they supplied woodwork for the four courtrooms and the picture room in the Shire Hall at Chelmsford. On the 5th February 1937 Tucker Ripper attended a luncheon at the Shire Hall to celebrate its reconstruction.

In 1937 Norman Ripper erected a wooden house in Sible Hedingham. It was designed by Gordon O'Neil, L.R.I.B.A., and was constructed of red cedar on a brick foundation. The roof was also made of red cedar shingles laid in a similar way to a tiled roof. It was light and stopped heat loss. The house, which was known as Crows Cross, was damaged in 1940 when a land mine exploded in 'the top field' close to the house. It was repaired by Ripper's joiners and the charges included 2/- for nails!

Crows Cross, Sible Hedingham – 1938

In 1939 Rippers supplied a new pulpit and pews in Columbian pine and six choir pews, stained, varnished and finished with a skin of button polish for the New Congregational Church, Parsonage Street, Halstead for £41 17s 6d, including delivery.

After the Second World War one of the first large housing estates to be supplied with Ripper's joinery was the Moulsham Lodge Estate at Chelmsford and during the 1950s and 1960s Rippers supplied significant joinery for building Harlow new town. In 1963 they supplied the windows and joinery for Sible Hedingham Village Hall, including laminated timber trusses and hardwood floor.

The pulpit at All Saints' Church, Maldon – erected 1951

The pulpit in All Saints' Church, Maldon was made by Rippers and erected in 1951 as a memorial to Edward Thomas Baker, churchwarden for 27 years. The panels were carved by Bryan Saunders and mark Edward Baker's many public interests in Essex and in Maldon where he was Mayor six times. The carving work on the pews was also by Bryan Saunders and it is possible that they were also made by Rippers.

In October 1960 Norman Ripper presented a beautifully carved oak pamphlet and gift table to Sible Hedingham Church. The Rev. Dr. William Porkess, D.D., of the Cathedral Church of St. John the Divine, New York, (a brother of John Wilkin Porkess) preached at the commemoration and dedication service. Another brother, the Rev. Frank Porkess, was for thirty years at St. Margaret's Episcopal Church, Glasgow.

The dedication of the oak pamphlet and gift table at Sible Hedingham Church in 1960
Left to right: Rev. Glynne Howard-Davies, B.A., C.F., (rector), John Cecil Goodchild (churchwarden), Norman Ripper, Frederick Connell (churchwarden) and Rev. Dr. William Porkess, D.D.

Some work was subcontracted out by Rippers to other craftsmen. This included Bert Corder, a cabinet maker and joiner who undertook specialised joinery work, which the company was unable to produce. Work was also subcontracted to George Argent, a joiner, builder and undertaker of Great Yeldham. He made one-off special sash windows, staircases and other products. Rippers were geared up to make large quantities of the same product but Bert Corder and George Argent made individual items more economically than Rippers could. George Argent had been apprenticed to Bert Corder before trading on his own account and when George retired he sold his business and premises to Jim and Stephen Ripper.

The majority of carving work was passed to Bryan Saunders who undertook the following work on behalf of Rippers:

Wendover Court	Hatfield Catholic Church
St. Barnabas Church, Purley	County Hall, Chelmsford
Little Wakering	Church Hall Farm, Broxted
A coat of arms at Braintree Police Station	Arnos Arms, Southgate
Becontree Church	A frieze for Codham Hall

During the late 1950s, the Lady Chapel in the south aisle of St. Peter's Church, Sible Hedingham was restored and an oak altar and oak panelling installed. The carving has two hawks incorporated in the design relating to Sir John Hawkwood. Bryan Saunders worked on this carving with Harry Hewlett, a joiner from Rippers and a Litany desk was also provided.

In connection with another church, Rippers sent Bryan Saunders oak for fifty-eight pew ends "to be carved and incised with a Maltese Cross on each" for which Bryan only charged 3s 6d for each cross. Unfortunately not all jobs ran smoothly. On one occasion Bryan complained to Rippers about a fourteen foot oak seat, which had been wrongly jointed and his client would not accept it. There seems to have been a quid pro quo system as in many cases wood was ordered for carving whereas in others Rippers did the joinery work and then delivered the item to Bryan for carving. Not all work undertaken by Bryan for Rippers was ecclesiastical, he also provided carving for the International Tea Co., and for the Shell-Mex building in London. The latter included Monkey Tails, which were the scrolled ends of handrails. In many cases the orders from Rippers were for carving long lengths of wood of various types. For one job he was asked to carve 230 feet of oak moulding and twenty lengths of mahogany moulding, which he completed for just over £90! Other work included brackets, notice boards, picture frames, paterae, panels, rails and enormous quantities of carved lettering. Rippers also sent Bryan orders for large wooden malt scoops for use in a local brewery. At busy times Bryan hired extra men and boys to assist him.

Standard joinery
Rippers supplied 1700 central pivoted teak windows to the Fleet building in London for the Post Office. Completed in 1960, the 11 storey building was a vast telecommunications centre

In 1970 the company secured a £54,000 contract with J. E. Lesser (Buildings) Limited of Hounslow, Middlesex for the supply of joinery and wall panelling for 140 houses at Basildon.

In the early 1970s Rippers supplied all the wooden windows and external joinery for the St. Mary's Vale Estate at Stratford St. Mary on the Essex-Suffolk border. The developer was H. C. Housing Limited a division of the Hey & Croft Group, winners of the 1968 and 1970 'House of the Year' awards. At the same time other H.C. sites in Essex were at Fingringhoe, Witham, Hatfield Peverel, Bicknacre, Eastwood and Shoeburyness as well as sites in Suffolk and Norfolk.

In about 1972 Rippers supplied standard joinery for the Manor Rise Estate, Brightlingsea, the Mount Estate at Feering and for another development in East Bergholt, which were all designed and built by W. & C. French (Developments) Limited. Rippers also supplied external joinery and doors for Lanson Contractors Limited, part of the W. & C. French Group, probably the largest construction and civil engineering organisation in East Anglia.

Sites supplied with Rippers standard joinery
Top left: Chequers Estate, Crowborough, Sussex. Top right: An estate at Lancing, Sussex
Bottom left: Manor Estate, Brightlingsea, Essex. Bottom right: Estate at East Bergholt, Suffolk

A list of many other buildings for which Rippers supplied the joinery is contained in appendix two.

Chapter 12

Exhibitions and Festivals

During the latter part of 1919 and throughout 1920 Rippers made a few specialist items suitable for use in small flats and houses. These pieces were shown at various Homes and Building Exhibitions held at Olympia, London and in other large towns in England and Scotland. Two of these items, a dresser with a table attachment to seat six people and a very ingenious cupboard with a revolving interior were each awarded a gold medal at the third Bristol Home, Life and Economy Exhibition held in 1919.

It was when these two award-winning items were shown again at Olympia, that a lady took a leaflet advertising the furniture to show her husband who was connected to a building firm which was negotiating contracts for several municipal housing schemes. When he discovered that Rippers could supply housing joinery in bulk they were awarded the contract. This led to one of the biggest post war orders Rippers had received up to 1922.

Rippers also produced a flush door known as 'Rippers Hygienic Door' which was exhibited in 1922 at Bournemouth where it proved to be very popular and the company was awarded a Bronze medal by the Sanitary Congress.

At the Builders Exhibition held in 1932 at Olympia, Tucker Ripper spoke to many exhibitors of wood products about the need for a country wide organisation to bring wood, in all its forms to public notice. At the time products made from a variety of materials competed with wood. An informal meeting took place to consider importing timber and the trading and manufacturing interests. In 1934 Tucker was a founder member of the Timber Development Association, today known as TRADA, (The Timber Research and Development Association). He was a member of TDA education committee and for many years members of the Ripper family were very active in this organisation.

The company exhibited at the Bath and West of England agricultural shows and received many favourable comments on their 'excellent examples of joinery'. In 1936 Bonds of Chelmsford held an Ideal Homes Exhibition which featured a staircase in Columbian pine and oak which was made at the works.

Rippers exhibited a cellulosed sideboard fitment for use in a dining recess at the 'Britain Can Make It Exhibition', which was held at the Victoria and Albert Museum in South Kensington, in 1946.

In the summer of 1951 a national exhibition was held throughout the United Kingdom, which was organised by the Government to give the British people a feeling of recovery in the aftermath of the Second World War. Known as the Festival of Britain, one of the venues was on the south bank of the Thames. Harry Hewlett, an estimator with Rippers, with George Argent, a local builder, carried out much of the building and construction work for the Rippers stand where Mahogany and Brazilian pine doors were among some of the products exhibited.

George Argent sometimes built displays for Rippers when they exhibited at the Building Exhibitions at Earls Court, London, and on one occasion built two flights of stairs.

Rippers Limited became regular exhibitors at the Building Trades Exhibitions at Olympia until the early 1970s. Stephen Ripper, as sales director, arranged these exhibitions and used a company in London to set up the stand, and arrange for brochures and tickets to be printed. Invitations were sent out in advance to Rippers customers inviting them to attend the exhibitions where new products were displayed.

A display being assembled in "S" Mill circa 1958
Left to right: Fred Lewis, Peter Cracknell, Allan Dowsett and Maurice Wiseman

Peter Kirk M.P. with Norman Ripper looking at a kitchen display at the works in 1965

At a by-election in 1965 Peter Kirk was elected as Member of Parliament for the Saffron Walden constituency in succession to the Rt. Hon. R. A. Butler, who then entered the House of Lords as Lord Butler of Saffron Walden. In July 1965, shortly after his election, Peter Kirk visited Rippers joinery works where he was conducted around the factory by Norman Ripper who was then managing director. They made a tour of the various workshops in which standard windows, special joinery and television cabinets were made. He inspected a new range of kitchen units for which orders had been received for 400 houses. The Hedinghams were then in the Saffron Walden constituency and the visit enabled the new M.P. to familiarise himself with the villages and meet electors.

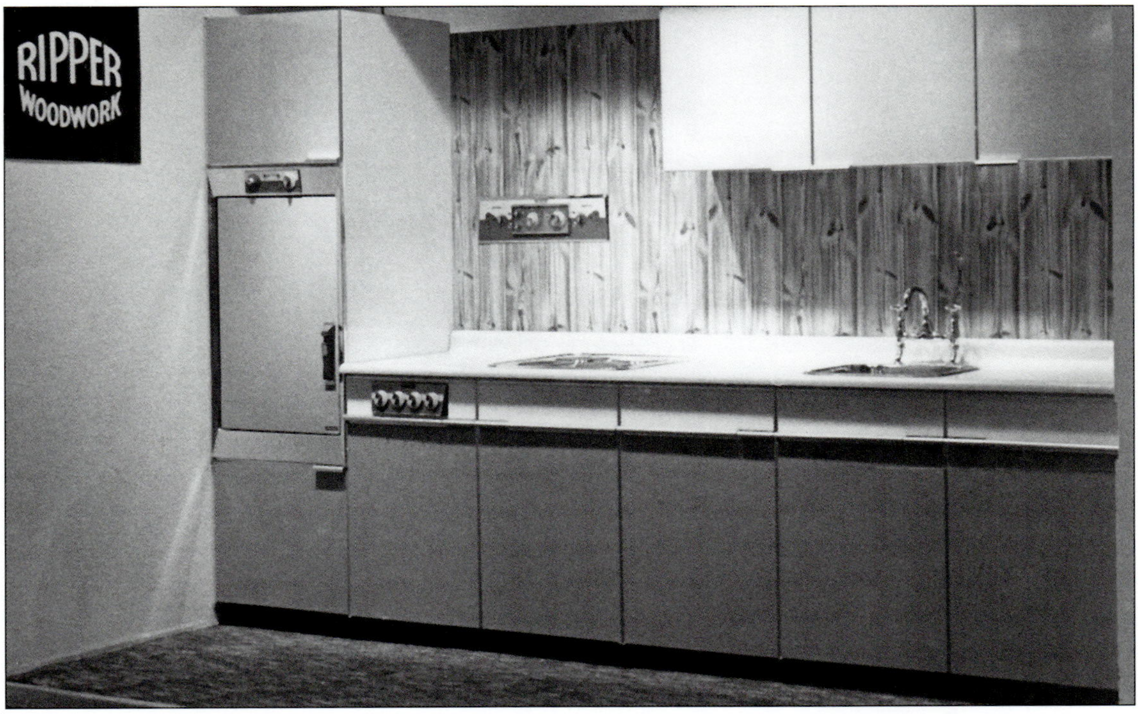

A kitchen display on show at an exhibition circa 1970

"Rippers and the Hedinghams" History Exhibition 2013

On the 13th and 14th September 2013 an exhibition was held at the Village Hall, Sible Hedingham called "Rippers and the Hedinghams" which was hailed a triumph. The organisers produced about sixty boards which detailed not only the Ripper family and the history of the works, but a comprehensive insight into the products made at the factory, and buildings where Ripper's joinery was installed. They embraced Rippers contributions to the Boer War and First and Second World Wars. They looked at the fires which had destroyed parts of the factory over the years and at the firemen who served in both the Ripper and Hedingham Fire Brigades. Industrial housing was featured with examples of the houses which Rippers built for its employees, from wooden huts to semi-detached houses. There were plans showing the factory layout and maps; some of the craftsmen's tools were displayed as were wooden bowls turned on the lathes, alongside old union books and photograph albums; but most importantly there were many photographs of employees taken from the early days to the 1970s. Boards headed 'Recollections' were a great success with both the subscribers and the other employees. The three associate companies were not forgotten with boards depicting the history of George Evans & Sons Limited later Evans Bellhouse Limited, William Kay (Bolton) Limited and The Sible Hedingham Red Brick Company Limited. The atmosphere in the village hall was buzzing for two days as old friends met up and reminisced.

The organisers of the Rippers exhibition held in September 2013
Left to right: Adrian Corder-Birch, Nick Ellis, Fran Ripper, Pam Corder-Birch, Anne Shellim (formerly Ripper) and Angela Weatherley

Fran Ripper (centre) with members of her family
Left to right: Cathy Malone, Martin Malone, Fran, John Malone and Anne Shellim

Chapter 13

H.R.H. Princess Marie Louise visits Rippers

On the 24th July 1933 Her Royal Highness the Princess Marie Louise (1872-1956) visited Castle Hedingham and inspected the timber yards and works at Rippers. The Princess was President of the Forum Club, who's "Buy British" Sub-Committee had recently organised a very successful exhibition of Empire timbers. Her visit to tour the works had materialised through connections at the exhibition.

The Princess who was accompanied by Sir Stephen Tallents, Secretary of the Empire Marketing Board, and Mrs. Claude Wilson, Chairman of the Forum Club, who acted as her lady in waiting travelled down to Castle Hedingham by car. The party stopped on route at Great Leighs and visited J.S. Wright and Sons, producers of 'willow clefts' which were used in the making of cricket bats, before they were entertained to lunch at the 'Old White Hart' in Great Yeldham by members of the Ripper family.

The party were shown over the works by Tucker, Harry, Charlton and Ashley Ripper and Stanley Finch. The Princess witnessed the different processes involved in the manufacture of woodwork, from the rough log to the finished article. Inside the sawmill she saw one of the largest English Oak trunks Rippers had ever handled, being sawn into pieces. The Princess watched all the operations with great interest and ended her tour of inspection in the offices where she was presented with a small coffee table made by Tom Waterman.

Princess Marie Louise watching a morticer being used in "B" Mill

Tucker Ripper presenting Princess Marie Louise with a coffee table after her tour of the factory

Later in the afternoon the Royal party enjoyed tea in the garden at Cherry Lawn with all the members of the Ripper Family. Harry and Winifred Ripper's young son, Stephen, presented the Princess with a bouquet of sweet peas before the Royal party returned to London.

Stephen Ripper presenting Princess Marie Louise with a bouquet of sweet peas, when she visited 'Cherry Lawn' for tea on the 24th July 1933
Left to right: Edith Ripper, Stephen Ripper, Princess Marie Louise and Tucker Ripper

Part of the garden at Cherry Lawn which was situated on the opposite side of the road to the house

Chapter 14

Patents

When designing and making a new product that was unique, it was wise to take out a patent so that your competitors could not copy your ideas. Tucker Ripper applied for patents in the United Kingdom, Canada and the United States of America, with most applications taking place between 1920 and the mid 1930s.

The following are some of the patents, which were taken out by Tucker Ripper:

1920 November 8th – GB153625 – Revolving cupboard fitment.

A drawing showing the Revolving Cupboard

The Chelmsford Chronicle of 31st December 1920 reported: *"Particulars are just to hand of some rather novel improvements in kitchen dressers for which Tucker Ripper of Castle Hedingham has obtained a patent: Number 152115.*

The outward shape of the dresser is of the usual type, but pivoted to the front part is a collapsible table supported by a pair of hinged legs, which can be folded to lie behind the table and inside the body of the dresser when not required. Cupboards are provided in the sides of the lower part of the dresser while above there are two or more sets of sliding shelves. On each side of the front top two sides, a cupboard is provided containing a number of rotatable shelves. These innovations are decided improvements as you have a table, sideboard and dresser all in one, the components of which, when not required fold up and occupy a minimum of space".

1922 December 15th – GB190191 – Improvements to wooden coffins.

A Canadian firm exported a flush door called 'the Gilmour' in about 1922 which caused considerable interest, and the manufacturers found they could not make enough doors to meet the demand. A British Government department approached Rippers and asked them if they could design a similar, efficient flush door at a reasonable price. Rippers obliged and the 'Rippers' Hygienic Door' went into production.

1923 March 8th – GB194336 – Improvements in or relating to doors.

1923 November 6th – US1473320 (United States of America). Patent taken out for the Ripper's flush door.

British patent numbers 194336/21 and 326983/29 for the "Hygienic" flush doors, described the 'patent' edging as the exclusive feature. It both secured the ply so that fraying was impossible and gave a generous margin for adjustment. The core of the door was built from stock kiln dried wood and was finished to ensure a perfectly uniform surface.

For hospital use the door could be supplied in any size (wood type mentioned below). The doors were suitable for commercial or public buildings, such as offices or banks and could be supplied in either hardwood or softwood. They could be fitted with sound-deadening insulation and for hospitals they could be made with observation panels and special insulation for X-ray rooms. Used with the flush type 'miracle partition' they offered a complete solution to a modern office layout.

An advertisement for Ripper's Hygienic Flush Doors

The following Hospitals were using Rippers' Hygienic doors by 1923:

New Infirmary, Christchurch
Eton College Sanatorium
Cottage Hospital, Halstead
Royal Herbert Hospital, Woolwich
Billericay Union New Infirmary
Queen Mary Maternity Hospital, Hampstead
Jewish Hospital, Stepney
Women's Hospital, Derby

Dr. Elsie Inglis Memorial Hospital, Edinburgh
Nurses' Home, Romford
Redhill Hospital, Edgware
Stamford Infirmary, Lincolnshire
Bethnal Green Hospital, Casualty Reception Rooms
County Hospital, Colchester
Brompton Hospital, London

1924 July 15th – CA241570 (Canada) – Door.

1929 November 14th – GB321527 – Improvements in or relating to doors.

1930 March 27th – GB326983 – Improvements in or relating to the 'Rippers' Hygienic Flush Doors.

In the 1930s other buildings which used Hygienic Flush doors under patent 194336/21 and 326983/29 included:

Kent and Sussex Hospital
Mount Royal Flats
Watford Joint Isolation Hospital
Flats at Hendon, Finchley and Ealing
West London Hospital
Prudential Assurance Offices
Daily Sketch Offices
Shell Mex House
Bristol Baths
L.M.S. Railway

1931 February 17th – CA308644 – Door and CA308645 Door and wall panelling.

An office constructed of miracle sectional partitions

A patent was granted for 'the miracle sectional partition' which was an efficient and speedy way to subdivide large floor areas. All units were reversible and interchangeable and made to suit any height or width. They could be used to create offices and sound deadening insulation could be provided if required. The partitions were easy to erect and beams, projections or irregular ceilings presented no problems. The partitions could also be reused many times when a change to office layout was required. Ripper's technical department was available to provide plans, fixing instructions and to erect the partitions if necessary.

1930 March 13th – GB326295/29 - Improvements in or relating to the construction and erection of partitions in buildings.

1933 March 3rd – CA308994 Building partition.

Ventilock Window, patent number: 390320/32. Rippers stated in their catalogue: *The Ventilock Window is a sliding sash, without any of the defects usually associated with this type of window. When closed it is absolutely weather and rattle proof and it is impossible to open it from the outside without breaking the glass. When open either sash can be operated by one finger and, in addition to the ordinary openings, the lower sash can be hoppered forward for night ventilation and can be locked in position.*

Lamella

In 1921 Friedrich Zollinger of Germany patented a form of roofing called 'Lamella' (Laminated Veneer Lumber). Rippers were offered the opportunity to sell the 'English rights' and in 1929 Tucker Ripper, with employee William Calver and the patentee's agents travelled to Berlin to visit buildings which used 'Lamella'.

Whilst Tucker was in Berlin, Rippers joiners were busy erecting a new workshop ("C" Department) and a store at the factory. Tucker evidently approved of Lamella because he sent a telegram dated April 1929 to Hedingham from Berlin which said: "Defer store roof until hearing from me later". Both the above buildings were built with a Lamella roof.

Rippers eventually operated the Lamella patent in England collaborating with licensees of 'Lamella' in the United States of America and Canada.

Definition of a Lamella Roof

Lamella roofs were self contained arched wooden roofs which were supported by the walls of the building and therefore required no beams, trusses or other supporting parts. They were made in spans up to about 100 feet with either Gothic arch or segmental roof profile. The 'lamellas' were made to templates with ordinary machine tools such as a band-saw, circular saw and drilling machine. The roof was easily assembled and could be readily dismantled and used again elsewhere.

Lamella roof in "C" Department prior to being demolished

In about 1973 Rippers signed an agreement for the sole manufacturing rights of the Alco Ripper timber and aluminium window in the United Kingdom. (The Alco Company was situated in Germany).

Chapter 15

The London Offices, Logos and Letterheads

The London Offices

In the 1911 census, 44 Silver Crescent, Gunnersbury, London W. was the home of William Bell, a commercial traveller in joinery. By 1917 to circa 1919 this address was described as being that of Rippers Limited, joinery manufacturers with the telephone number Chiswick 614. It would appear that William Bell was a commercial traveller for Rippers and used his home address for company purposes.

In about 1920 a permanent London office was established to help with maintaining contacts in the area and to provide a service to customers. The addresses of the London office changed over the years and are as follows:

1920 – 1936
Rippers Limited, 165 Grays Inn Road, London WC1. Tel: Terminus 5623 & 5624

1936 – 1939
Rippers Limited, British Industries House, Marble Arch W1. Tel: Mayfair 6624 & 6625

1941 – 1945
Rippers Limited, Shop Fitters, 11 Grosvenor Mansions, W2. Tel. Paddington 1076 and Rippers Limited, 11 Grosvenor Court Mansions, Marble Arch, W2. Telephone: Paddington 1076-7. (These two slight variations in addresses were clearly one and the same).

1947 – 1969
Rippers Limited, 9 Southampton Place WC1. Tel: Chancery 8306-7

Rippers maintained a department to deal with contract work. The Setting Out Department at Hedingham, which comprised of more than thirty men, acted in collaboration with the London Office liaison staff and therefore maintained the closest possible contact with the Clerk of Works and the General Foreman on each contract.

Transfer Office

1930s - 1973
Rippers Limited and Evans Bellhouse Limited
Transfer Office, 10 Copthall Avenue, EC2. This was the address of Messrs. Wrigley, Cregan, Todd & Co., chartered accountants who were Ripper's auditors.

Registered Office

The London offices must not be confused with the company's registered office, which always remained as Castle Hedingham. Although the actual postal address was Station Road, Sible Hedingham, this address was not used for official purposes. Castle Hedingham was always used as the registered office because this was where the business had started.

Logos

The company logo 'Ripper Woodwork', which was in use until the late 1960s, was used on all advertising, company brochures, annual reports, invoices and letterheads. It was recognised by local authorities, architects and builders throughout the country as the logo of a company producing specialised and standard wood products of the highest quality. The logo was white lettering on a blue background and also appeared on 'Ripper' vehicles and packaging, quite apart from documentation.

In the late 1960s more colour, was introduced into brochures and although the design of the 'Ripper Woodwork' logo remained it appeared in various colours.

In the early 1970s the logo was completely changed and consisted of a circular saw blade followed by either 'Rippers Limited' or 'Ripper Products'.

Rippers Logo until the late 1960s

Name plate attached to some products

Rippers Logo from the early 1970s

Letterheads

An early letterhead was in the name of 'W. C. Ripper, Steam Joinery and Wood Block Flooring Works, Castle Hedingham', which was used from the late 1890s until 1905. This was followed by 'Ripper Brothers' until 1915 when the private limited company was incorporated. The 'Rippers Limited' heading from 1915 until the end of the First World War made it clear that it was a Government Controlled establishment and that the company were contractors to H.M. Government Departments. The address was given as 'Station Joinery Works, Castle Hedingham'. During the 1920s the letterheads promoted the English Timber Mills and Drying Kilns and that Rippers Limited were joinery and cabinet manufacturers. The close proximity of the works to Sible and Castle Hedingham Railway Station was advertised on numerous letterheads. The reference to Colne Valley Railway prior to 1923 was changed to London North Eastern Railway that year. Later letterheads included details of successive London offices and the logos of the 'National Scheme for Disabled Men' and the 'Timber Development Association' of which the company were members. Although the works moved from Castle Hedingham to Sible Hedingham in 1899, Castle Hedingham Post Office continued to be used for incoming and outgoing post and the Castle Hedingham address was retained on all stationery and was only changed by successor companies during the late twentieth century.

Examples of some letterheads and invoices used by Rippers:

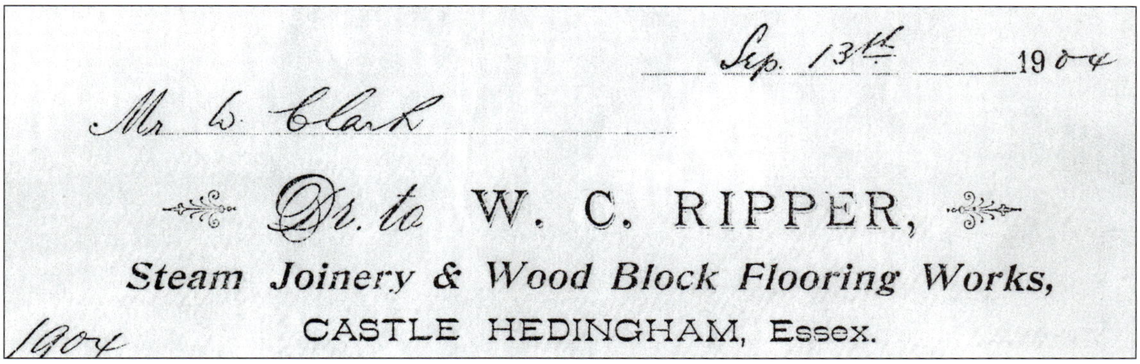
Sep. 13th 1904

Mr W. Clark

Dr. to W. C. RIPPER,

Steam Joinery & Wood Block Flooring Works,

CASTLE HEDINGHAM, Essex.

1904

1904 when William Charlton Ripper was sole proprietor

23rd May, 1917

GOVERNMENT CONTROLLED ESTABLISHMENT.

CONTRACTORS TO H.M. GOVERNMENT DEPARTMENTS.

Rippers Ltd

TELEGRAMS: RIPPERS, CASTLE HEDINGHAM.

TELEPHONE No.: 9 CASTLE HEDINGHAM.

RIPPERS, LTD.,

JOINERY MANUFACTURERS.

SPECIALITIES:

GOOD CLASS CONTRACT JOINERY FOR THE TRADE.
ARCHITECTS' AND DECORATORS' JOINERY.
ECCLESIASTICAL JOINERY: ALTARS, REREDOS, SCREENS, SEATINGS AND STALLS, &c.
TIMBER FRAMED TEMPORARY BUILDINGS.

*COMPOSITION ENRICHED MOULDINGS AND MANTELS, &c.
*HORTICULTURAL BUILDINGS AND CONSERVATORIES.
**In succession to CROMPTON & FAWKES, Ltd. (late of Chelmsford).*
**See Special Catalogues :: Special Designs Prepared.*
HOME AND EXPORT TRADE.

Station Joinery Works, Castle Hedingham, Essex,

23rd May 1917

1917 following the incorporation of Rippers Limited in 1915

NATIONAL SCHEME FOR DISABLED MEN

Telegrams "RIPPERS" CASTLE-HEDINGHAM

Station: SIBLE AND CASTLE-HEDINGHAM. (Colne Valley Rly.)

Rippers Ltd.

JOINERY & CABINET MANUFACTURERS.

ENGLISH TIMBER MILLS AND DRYING KILNS,

Telephone Nº 9 CASTLE-HEDINGHAM.

Our Reference

Your Reference

Castle Hedingham, ESSEX.

After the First World War until 1923 – note reference to Colne Valley Railway

Station:
SIBLE AND CASTLE HEDINGHAM,
(L.N.E.Rly.)

Ripper's Ltd.

JOINERY & CABINET MANUFACTURERS.

Telegrams
"RIPPERS"
CASTLE-HEDINGHAM.

Telephone
Nº 39
HEDINGHAM

ENGLISH TIMBER MILLS
AND DRYING KILNS,

Our Reference
Your Reference

Castle Hedingham, ESSEX.

From 1923 when the railway was recorded as London North Eastern Railway

RIPPERS LTD
CASTLE HEDINGHAM
ESSEX

LONDON OFFICE:
BRITISH INDUSTRIES HOUSE
MARBLE ARCH: W. I.
PHONE: MAYFAIR 6624

TELEGRAMS: RIPPERS
CASTLE HEDINGHAM
TELEPHONE NO. 39
HEDINGHAM (2 LINES)

1936 to 1939 when the London Office was at British Industries House

RIPPERS LTD
CASTLE HEDINGHAM
HALSTEAD, ESSEX

LONDON OFFICE.
9, SOUTHAMPTON PLACE
(SUITE 16)
· LONDON, W.C.1 ·
PHONE: CHANCERY 8306/7

TELEGRAMS: RIPPERS
CASTLE HEDINGHAM
TELEPHONE NO. 191
HEDINGHAM (4 LINES)

1947 to 1960s when London Office was at 9 Southampton Place

RIPPER
WOODWORK

rippers ltd
castle hedingham
halstead essex

telegrams
Rippers, Castle Hedingham
telephone
Hedingham 391 (4 lines)
London Office
9 Southampton Place, Suite 16
London W.C.1
telephone
Chancery 8306/7

17th August, 1966.

A letter head dated 1966, which was used during the 1960s

Chapter 16

Industrial Housing

St. James's Street, Castle Hedingham

St. James's Street, Castle Hedingham

In about 1892, the Ripper brothers built three red brick houses in St. James's Street, Castle Hedingham. Curiously only two had cellars and one did not. In the rear garden is a brick shed which was built at the same time as the houses. One house was occupied by the brother's parents, Edward and Louisa Ripper until their deaths in 1906 and 1913 respectively. It was also the home of their youngest son, Charlton, until his marriage in 1906. The brick shed was used by the brothers for storage, when they were operating from their premises at Back Lane, Castle Hedingham, prior to moving to Sible Hedingham. These houses are now 18, 20 and 22 St. James's Street.

Station Road, Sible Hedingham

In 1899 the brothers built four red brick houses with slate roofs in Station Road, Sible Hedingham on the south west side of the entrance road to Castle and Sible Hedingham Railway Station. They were built to accommodate key workmen and to provide some security for the new premises at the rear. In 1901 three of these houses were occupied by the following:
William Drury and his son Arthur Drury, who were both described as 'joiners in wood'.
Anthony Howard, 'carpenter and joiner'.
William Robert Blowers, 'machinist at woodworks – sawyer' and his brother in law, William Calver, a 'joiner and carpenter' William Calver later moved into a new house at Alexandra Road and continued his employment with Rippers for many years.

Two of these cottages later became part of Rippers offices and sadly all four cottages were demolished, in 1978 during the Bowater era.

The first cottages at Station Road, Sible Hedingham

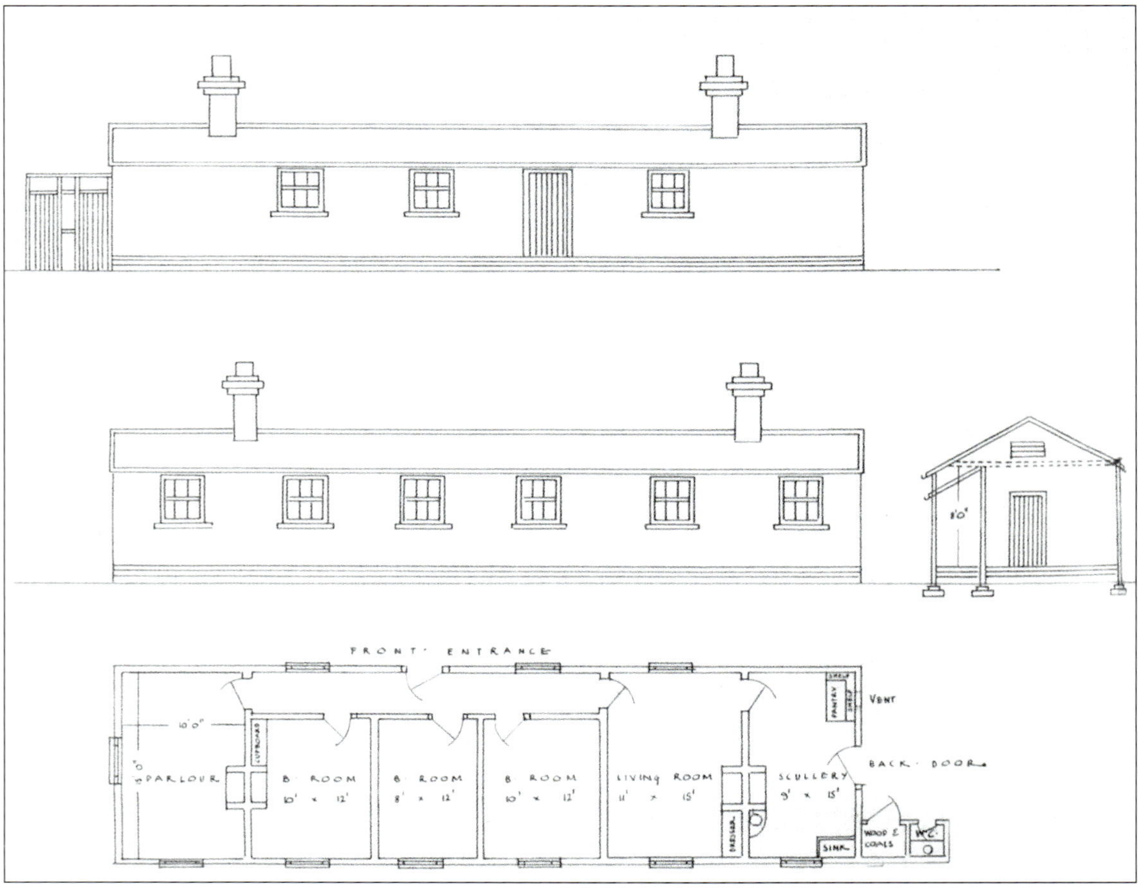

Architect's drawing of one of the Huts (Wooden Bungalows), Sible Hedingham dated 1920

The Huts, Sible Hedingham

After the First World War there was a shortage of housing. To help the situation, Rippers presented plans to the former Halstead Rural District Council in June 1920 for the erection of ten wooden bungalows at Brook Farm for which permission was granted. By September 1920 two wooden bungalows, which were erected experimentally, were already occupied. Plans were approved by the Medical Officer of Health and a subsidy granted to Rippers, who built eight more followed by another four. In fact a total of fourteen wooden bungalows were built during 1920 and 1921. They were built on plots of land, which varied in size from 42' by 130' to 31' by 176' and were erected from surplus army hut sections mostly in English timber of various species. Each bungalow contained maximum accommodation of six rooms with a hall running full length. The bungalows, which were known as "The Huts" and latterly as "Brook Bungalows", were demolished during the late 1970s to make way for extensions to the factory. The employees, who occupied "The Huts", during nearly sixty years of their existence, described them as being extremely comfortable.

Nunnery Street, Castle Hedingham

On 11th October 1920 Rippers Limited purchased five houses in Nunnery Street, Castle Hedingham in which to house employees. They were purchased for one thousand pounds from the Rev. Martin Church Taylor (then chaplain of the House of Keys on the Isle of Man), as Executor of his father in law, James Dyson, who had died in 1909. In 1898 James Dyson, a baker and corn dealer of Church Ponds, Castle Hedingham, purchased 44 perches of land being part of Pound Field, formerly Dragons Croft, at the junction of Nunnery Street and Kirby Hall Road, then called Dragon Lane. James Dyson was an elder of the Congregational Church at Castle Hedingham, where the Ripper family then worshipped, and Pound Field was very close to Cherry Lawn where they lived. The five houses were built by James Dyson in local red brick in typical Edwardian style, and were then known as 'Lobster Cottages'. They are now 26, 28, 30, 32 and 34 Nunnery Street. These five houses were occupied by key workers of Rippers until they were sold in 1972 when they were lived in by employees including Lionel Brown, John Leathers, Cuthbert Mitson and Stephen Wooding.

The five cottages at Nunnery Street, showing Anne Brown (later Bambrick's) mini parked outside.

Wooden Bungalow on the left opposite Hedingham Railway Station

Hope Cottage, a wooden bungalow opposite Hedingham Railway Station

In June 1921 approval was given to Rippers for a single wooden hut. Although the site is not clear it was possibly for a wooden bungalow opposite Hedingham Railway Station. It was not built but in 1930 Messrs. Palmer and Corder, builders of Sible Hedingham submitted plans for a timber famed bungalow opposite Hedingham Railway Station for George Ruddock. It comprised of a bedroom, living room and scullery, with a brick chimney, wood and concrete floors and

4" x "2, studwork covered with corrugated iron. The bungalow was supplied with water by agreement with the nearby Hedingham Gas Works. This bungalow, which became known as "Hope Cottage", was demolished many years ago. Following removal of the railway and station buildings the site was later used by Rippers for additional factory buildings.

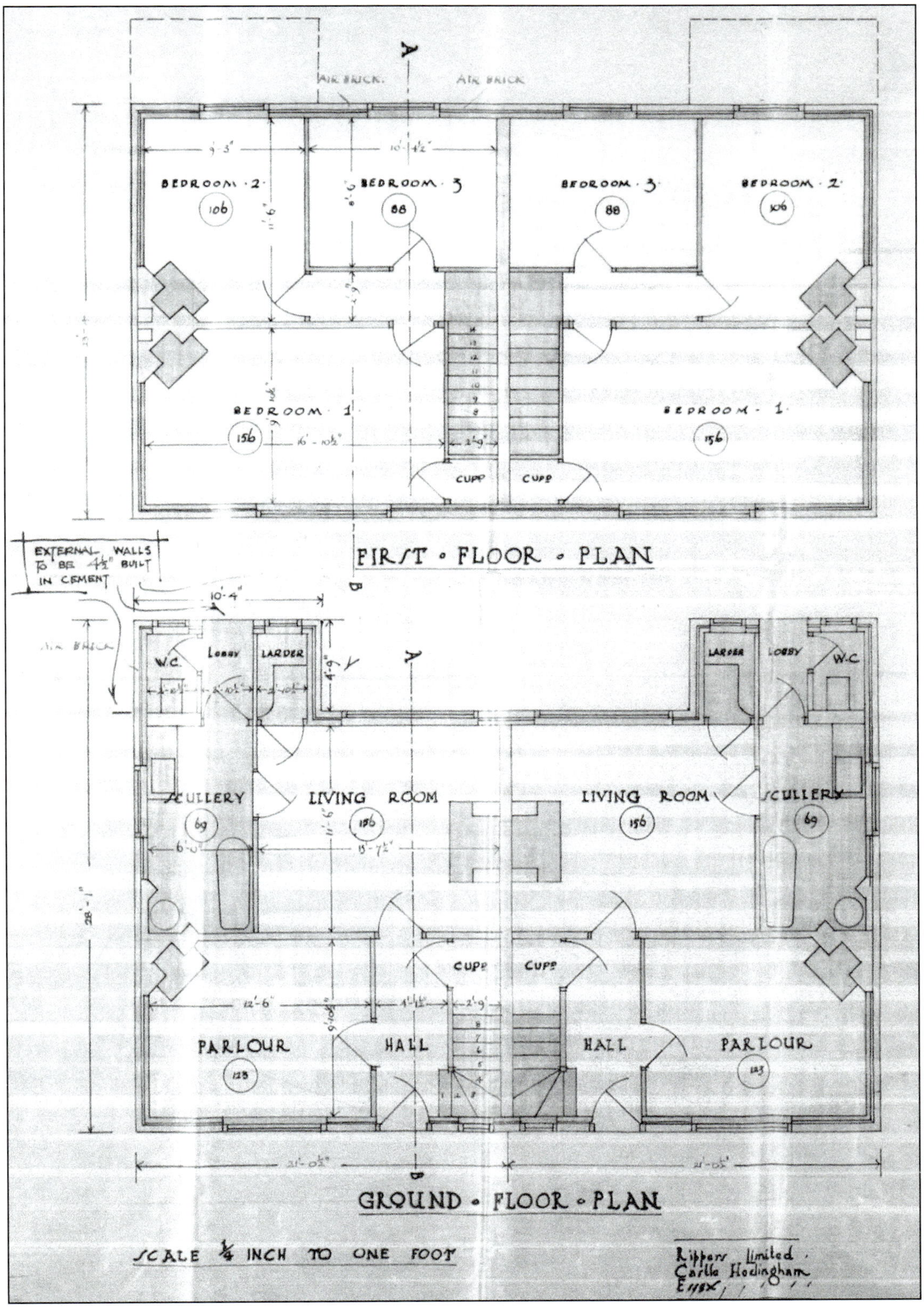

Architect's drawings of floor plans of houses in Swan Street and Brook Terrace, Sible Hedingham

The pairs of houses on the left are Ripper's housing in Swan Street built circa 1924-1926

Ripper's housing on both sides of Brook Terrace built circa 1924-1926

Swan Street and Brook Terrace, Sible Hedingham

In addition to "The Huts", further industrial housing was erected during the inter-war period. This comprised two considerable estates totaling 94 houses, built in 47 semi-detached pairs of rendered brick under tiled roofs. The first estate in Brook Terrace and Swan Street was built c1924-1926. It consisted of 154-188 Swan Street (evens) and 1-23 and 2-24 Brook Terrace. These houses were built on land which was originally part of Brook Farm, of which 23 acres was purchased by Rippers on 10th June 1918. Approval for these houses was granted on 23rd May 1924 by Cyril Tobitt as surveyor to the former Halstead Rural District Council. Articles of agreement were entered into on 29th May 1924 between Rippers Limited as owner and George Thomas Elsdon, the builder. The plots were 50 feet by 150 feet for each pair of houses and a 15 feet building line was to be observed. Although the plans and articles of agreement included a pair of houses in Crosspath they were not constructed until the second estate (below) was built as evidenced by the slight variations in the design such as the canopies over the front doors. As part of the first estate an additional 3 pairs of houses were planned on the north side of numbers 3 to 7 "The Huts" but not built.

Yeldham Road, Sible Hedingham built 1926-1927

Yeldham Road, Station Road and Crosspath, Sible Hedingham

The second estate known as "Christmas Field" situated in Yeldham Road and Station Road was built 1926-1927 to a slightly different design, including an additional small pitched and hipped canopy over the front doors, many of which still exist. These houses are 1-24 Yeldham Road (consecutive) and 1-31 and 35-53 Station Road (odds). The site was laid out for building and contracts were entered into on 15th and 16th November 1926 when building commenced. These houses were completed and occupied before the end of 1927.

Houses in Yeldham Road before it was, realigned. Note the Rippers Woodwork sign on the left.

Houses in Station Road, Sible Hedingham, built 1926-27. Note the canopies over the front doors.

Crosspath

At the same time (1926-27) a pair of houses namely 1-2 Crosspath were built to an identical design as the houses in Yeldham Road and Station Road. On 12th October 1923 an application had been made by John Wilkin Porkess on behalf of Rippers Limited for a timber bungalow on this site which was described as on the opposite side of Crosspath to the Engine House. This application was approved by the former Halstead Rural District Council on 9th November 1923 but the bungalow, which was to be of timber on brick foundations, was never built and it later became the site of 1-2 Crosspath. In view of the close proximity of this pair of houses to the factory they were always occupied by senior members of the maintenance staff.

At a meeting of Halstead Rural District Council the clerk Sydney Long, reported that the Rippers houses had been valued at £400 each. The subsidy payable by the Government for each house was £76 18s 0d, which reduced them to £323 of which the Council agreed to loan 90% (£290). Whilst the building work proceeded, the Council advanced 50% of the cost of the work as it was carried out.

Both estates were very uniform in design, equal-status houses, being architecturally plain typical inter-war semi-detached houses. A further twelve houses were planned for this estate in Christmas Field but never built. If they had been built ten would have faced what is now Hedingham School and erected along the south side of the public footpath between Yeldham Road and Station Road. If these houses had been built the footpath would have been replaced by a new 36 foot wide private road. The remaining two houses would have been built on a vacant plot, next to 53 Station Road. The area in the centre of Christmas Field was designated as a Recreation Ground but later became the site of prefabs and now of replacement bungalows.

Grays Hall Farm

"Christmas Field" was part of Grays Hall Farm, comprising about sixty acres, which was purchased by Tucker Ripper, John Porkess, Harry Ripper and Charlton Ripper on 29th September 1926. On 22nd January 1927 they conveyed it to Rippers Limited. It included Grays Hall, which from 1946 became the home of Jim and Joan Ripper and their children, Christopher and Judith. The farm included eleven acres of land, including Nine Acre Field and part of Christmas Field, which Rippers sold to Essex County Council in May 1938 where Hedingham School was built between 1938 and 1939. On 19th April 1952 Rippers sold a further fourteen acres of land to the former Halstead Rural District Council where the Oxford Meadow and the Brook Meadow housing estates were built. This included Lawn Meadow now owned by Braintree District Council and leased to Sible Hedingham Football Club. The field northwest of the Baptist Church, which was used by Rippers for storing logs and extended to about 7½ acres was sold in December 1963 with outline planning permission for 75 dwellings and is now the Graysmead Estate. The remaining land originally owned by Rippers and later by Bowater Ripper Limited was conveyed to RBT (London) Limited on 14th November 1985. Part of this land eventually became Abbey Meadow, Castle Meadow and Friars Close housing estate. Another part was Grays Hall Meadow, which RBT (London) Limited conveyed to Braintree District Council on 19th June 1986. The meadow had been partly used to extend Sible Hedingham Churchyard and the remainder was conveyed to Sible Hedingham Parish Council on 11th May 1990. A small area was allocated for a Garden of Remembrance which was opened in 1992. The majority of Grays Hall Meadow is now a public open space, which remains in the ownership of Sible Hedingham Parish Council.

The Maltings Cottages, Station Road, Sible Hedingham

When Rippers purchased the Maltings in Station Road in 1926, a pair of cottages was included that were formerly part of the malting complex and occupied by malting workers. The cottages were of brick and plaster with tiled roofs. It is assumed that they were later occupied by Rippers employees. These cottages were in existence until 1950 when the last occupier, Thomas Playle moved to Christmas Field and they were later demolished.

The Maltings Cottages when in the ownership of Thomas Bradridge & Co. with Benjamin Smith standing in front of the tumbril.

Church Lane, Castle Hedingham and cottages at Ridgewell

Quite separate from the company houses, Charlton Ripper owned a number of houses personally. These included 8 cottages in Church Lane, Castle Hedingham and some cottages near the Kings Head Public House at Ridgewell. Some of the former were occupied by employees of the company.

Proposed Brook Hill Estate

In 1929 a third estate was planned by Rippers to be known as the Brook Hill Estate, but was not built. The plans comprised forty plots or houses, of which five 50 ft plots would face Swan Street and the remainder behind. The original 1929 layout included a vehicular access opposite Brook Farm House. The Fire Station was later built on the site of the proposed access, prior to being relocated to Rectory Road. The County Library now stands on the site of the former Fire Station. In 1952 Rippers sold the remaining land to the former Halstead Rural District Council and it became the Brook Meadow Housing Estate comprising 58 houses. The upper half was built by Bert Corder and the lower half by Arthur Thomas Coppock, a builder of Gosfield. The vehicular access off Rectory Road is significantly safer than it would have been off Swan Street.

Sale of Rippers industrial housing

The 'Rippers' housing schemes were completed before the majority of Local Authority housing schemes, with the exception of 20 council houses built in Alexandra Road, Sible Hedingham by the former Halstead Rural District Council in 1920. The occupants of all the Rippers industrial housing in Sible Hedingham initially obtained water from an artesian well at the joinery works until mains water was connected. During 1971, Rippers sold some 90 houses, having taken care to protect the interests of all the tenants. The surplus was invested in the business to provide finance for technical improvements to the factory. The dwellings of this major employer were the only example of industrial housing in Essex associated with the joinery industry.

Chapter 17

Employees

During the twentieth century Rippers expanded and the number of employees increased. There were substantial brickworks in the Hedinghams, which gradually declined and closed between 1905 and 1953. Many of the unemployed brickmakers were fortunate enough to find employment with Rippers, which prevented any large scale unemployment. Brickmaking was principally an outdoor and seasonal occupation, Rippers, on the other hand, provided indoor and full time employment. They eventually became one of the first employers to provide paid holidays and were also able to offer housing. These benefits were very attractive to former brickmakers. Rippers became one of the largest employers in the area for which figures are included in chapter eighteen. The following is an alphabetical list of many employees, their positions and other relevant information where known. It gives an indication of the large variety of positions available to employees quite apart from carpenters and joiners. This list has been compiled from many sources but is not complete because, unfortunately, no records survive of all employees. It is mainly Ripper's employees but some are included who worked for successor companies until 2009. Details of employees are also included in other chapters such as firemen, long service awards, retirements and union membership.

Tom Abbott worked in the Power House.

Bernard Abraham was a joiner.

Leonard Allen was a woodcutting machinist.

Samuel Edward Allen of Halstead worked on a saw bench, circa mid 1930s.

Eddy Alliston worked in the electrical shop.

Roy Alliston was an electrician and engine manager.

Fred Alston from Haverhill was a carpenter prior to the First World War.

Alfred Thomas Ambrose was a machinist and previously a brickmaker.

Ernest Ambrose was a sawyer. In 1905 he sustained two broken ribs when a piece of wood, which he had sawn off, dropped on the opposite side of the circular saw and flying back, struck him with great force.

Pat Ambrose (later King) was a typist from 1949 to 1958.

Stanley Ambrose was a representative.

William Alfred Ambrose commenced a five year apprenticeship as a joiner at the age of sixteen years on 16th August 1935 and left on 29th January 1940.

Sybil Amey worked in the office.

George Anderson was an apprentice joiner and continued as a joiner for over 40 years. He became a charge-hand, then a foreman and in 1961 was appointed labour manager. Upon his retirement in 1970, after fifty two years, Jim Ripper presented him with a gold watch. George was clerk of Castle Hedingham Parish Council for many years.

Peter Anderson was a personnel manager.

Arthur John Andrews known as Jack Andrews was well known in the Hedinghams and Halstead initially as a lorry driver and later as a pig farmer. After driving for R. R. Gatward, haulier of Nunnery Street, Castle Hedingham, who regularly hauled for Rippers, Jack was employed by them until service as a Gunner in the Royal Artillery during the Second World War. He remembered many kind people who worked at Rippers donating to a Comforts Fund for those who served in H.M. armed forces and had left the company to do so. He was one of the recipients of ten shillings from the Comforts Fund. After the war, Jack and one of his brothers, Bernard, made a living selling wood. They collected old splines and offcuts from Rippers in their old covered wagon for 7s 6d a load, which they hawked around surrounding farms and villages for £2 10s 0d a load, with a target of three loads a day.

George W. Andrews was employed for 33 years from 1976 to 2009 as an S-loader driver, loading and unloading timber.

William James Andrews was a fitter. During the Second World War he was a Craftsman in R.E.M.E. serving in North Africa.
Arthur Anson was a welder.
Ernest Ashton was foreman of the machine shop, known as "B" Mill and became works manager in charge of production. He started work in London as a woodworking machinist and when he later joined Rippers he assisted Bertram Hogarth with developing machinery and jigs.
Douglas Frederick Baggaley was a mechanic who had served with R.E.M.E. in the Second World War.
Brian Bain assembled stair cases in the stair shop in "S" Mill workshop.
Alfred Frederick Charles Ballard left Catford, London during the blitz and moved to Mill Lane, Little Yeldham. He was employed by Rippers until his death in 1943.
Geoffrey Frank Ballard was employed at the works for the majority of his working life and occupied a Rippers house in Station Road.
William Bangs, a labourer, was frequently seen walking home to Little Yeldhan carrying a sack full of fire-wood on his bicycle.
Charles Arthur Barber known as **Arthur**, moved from Leiston, Suffolk and started work at 14 years old, serving his apprenticeship as a carpenter. During the last war he helped make Nissan huts and landing craft. Later, when work was slack he transferred to Whitlock Bros. Limited of Great Yeldham. His father, also **Charles Barber**, was a labourer at Rippers.
Delyss Barber commenced work in 1941 at the age of 16 years as a cost and wages clerk and comptometer operator under the supervision of Ashley Ripper. She continued working for the company until March 1952.
Percy Ralph Bareham was a joiner.
Herbert Barnes worked on a moulding machine in "S" Mill.
Roy Barnes was an apprentice joiner from 1963 to 1967 and now has his own building business.
Susan Barnes worked on the assembly line putting window frames together.
Sandra Barty employed from 1976 to 1977 and 1990 to 2004.
William (Bill) Beadle was a saw doctor, responsible for sharpening saws in the Saw Doctor's Shop.
Don Beadle was a woodcutting machinist from 1938 to 1985 including work on a moulding machine in "S" Mill. He was presented with a gold watch after thirty nine years. His wife **Dorothy Beadle (nee Wegg)** worked in the office in "B" Mill.
Edward 'Teddy' Beadle was an apprentice joiner before WWII and later a machinist in "S" Mill.
Heather Beadle (later Robinson) worked in kitchen assembly for two summers in 1972 and 1973 whilst a student.
Wally Beadle served his apprenticeship as a joiner before the Second World War and later assembled stair cases in the stair shop in "S" Mill workshop.
William John Francis Bell and his wife **Pauline Margery Bell (nee Harrington)** were both employed by Rippers. Pauline worked in the TV Department.
Charlie Berry was employed by the company for 33 years, including service in "F" Department.
John Beswarick was mill foreman.
Stephen Billings was an apprentice joiner and in 1970 was the first trainee that Rippers sponsored on an 800 mile cruise on the 300 ton sail training schooner Sir Winston Churchill.
Cyril Bishop worked on double ending machine in "B" Mill.
Tony Bishop served his apprenticeship at Rippers and later worked as a carpenter and joiner for Alf Pannell, a builder of Swan Street, Sible Hedingham.
S. E. Blake was foreman of the timber yard and later worked in the office.
Robert (Bob) Blamire was a long standing employee who achieved the age of 104 years.
A. W. Blythe was a member of the production staff.
Cecil Boorer followed in his father's footsteps to be employed by Rippers. The company employed two, three and, even in some cases four generations of the same families. Cecil helped construct the pulpit for All Saint's Church at Maldon.
Lewis Boorer was one of the earliest and longest serving employees and is included on the 1949 photograph of Tucker Ripper with employees who had completed fifty years loyal service.

Ernest H. Boreham was a painter.
H. Boreham was employed for 16 years.
Stan Boreham was a crane driver.
Stuart J. Boreham was a joiner during the early 1970s and was employed for 13 years. His wife Hazel (formerly Shipperley) worked in the office.
Bert Borrett worked in the office.
Margaret Mary Bowles who lived at Tidings Hill, Halstead was a clerk at Rippers in 1939.
Charles Brady initially worked on the boiler in "D" Department, but when it was taken out of commission transferred to the main boiler.
Jane Brett (nee Nichols) worked on the assembly line putting window frames together.
Leslie Verdun Brett was a brickmaker and later employed by Rippers prior to joining the Essex Regiment in April 1940. He died in the Middle East in August 1941.
Oscar Robert (Charlie) Brett was a woodworking machinist and completed 51 years service.
Robert Brett, sen., and Robert Brett, jun., were foreman and fitter respectively in the Power House.
Charles William Bretton moved to Hedingham in 1914 when his father was appointed as Police Inspector at Castle Hedingham. In the First World War, when he was wounded in France, Charles served in the Kings Royal Rifles and later transferred to the Royal Engineers. He worked in the Estimating Department for about 30 years from 1918 to 1948 and was a member of the Observer Corps during the Second World War. From 1948 until his death in 1960 he owned a confectionery and tobacconists shop in Swan Street. He was a founder member of the Hedingham and District Branch of the British Legion in 1924, secretary for 13 years and later a Vice President.
Herbert Britton of Halstead was a machinist who in February 1916 sustained a severely lacerated finger at a machine saw.
Alan Brown drove a Lister three-wheeler truck within the works.
Albert Brown was a timber buyer and his secretary was Shirley Seaman.
Albert George Brown was employed as a woodworker from May 1927 when he was 15 years old until about 1970. By 1953 he worked in "L" Department.
Fred Brown was a labourer in "D" Department commencing employment following service in the Second World War and continuing for over 20 years.
Marion Brown (nee Bacon) was a secretary in "B" Mill office for a few years.
Michael Brown started in August 1959 as a labourer and at 16 years of age commenced a five year apprenticeship as a carpenter joiner, when he gained experience by working in all departments. He later worked in the kitchen cabinet and stair departments. After working for Crittalls for two years he returned to Rippers. Following other employment he joined JSR Joinery when it started.
William (Bill) Edward Brown was a joiner and later promoted to foreman.
Lennie Broyd was a charge-hand circa 1960s.
Dennis Brunner was a labourer in "B" Mill.
Maurice (Morrie) Bugg worked in the shavings loft.
Susan Butcher worked on the assembly line putting window frames together.
A. Edgar Byford of Long Melford worked at Rippers before he enlisted in the First World War. He served in the Canadian Infantry and was killed in action at Pas de Calais, France on 17th June 1915 age 36 years.
Malcolm Byford was an apprentice in 1958.
William E. Calver was a joiner who became foreman of the Joinery Department and later personnel manager.
Harry Cansell met with a nasty accident in February 1914 when a teak sash fell on a finger and crushed it. He was treated by Dr. James Bromley and in 1949 completed 50 years loyal service.
Cecil Ernest Chatten commenced his five year apprenticeship as a joiner at 15 years of age on 23rd August 1929, which ended on 23rd August 1934. His father Ernest Henry Chatten was a party to the indenture. Cecil later worked in "C" Department.
Ernest (Ernie) Henry Chatten was a joiner and completed 50 years service.
Colin Chatters was employed from 1975 to 2004.
Iris Crisford worked in the office.

Hubert E. C. Clarke was a foreman.
Mr. Clegg was a foreman.
John (Jack) William Coates was apprenticed to W. C. Ripper in 1899 and employed by Rippers for fifty years. He became foreman of the general timber department and latterly worked with Jim Ripper in the English timber department. Jack served in the Essex Regiment during the First World War and retired with the rank of Acting Sergeant Major and in the Second World War served in the Observer Corps at the Castle Hedingham post. He was a founder member of the Hedingham and District Branch of the British Legion.
Peter Cock joined following service in the Second World War and became a wood machinist on a morticer machine.
Bert Cocks was a foreman.
Robert Edward (Bob) Cocks was an apprentice and later became a charge hand in the machine shop. Following retirement he ran the Social Club in the former Ripper's Canteen. His wife, **Sheila Cocks**, worked in the television department for a short time.
A. Codling whose responsibilities included conducting visitors around Ripper's showroom at Castle Hedingham during the early 1970s.
Wilfred Alan Collar of Little Yeldham was employed as a lorry driver for many years.
William Walter Collar, D.F.M., was a costing clerk before volunteering for the Royal Air Force Voluntary Reserve in 1941. Following the completion of numerous operations he was awarded the Distinguished Flying Medal for gallantry and devotion to duty in February 1945.
Stan Connell was a personnel manager.
Paul Cook was a joiner during the early 1970s.
Peter Cook assembled up and over garage doors in "C Department.
Bertie William Corder served his apprenticeship as a carpenter and joiner with Rippers during the early 1900s when it was still a comparatively small concern. He left in 1924 to commence business, initially in partnership with Charles Horace Palmer as Palmer and Corder and later on his own account as B. W. Corder, master builder, contractor, decorator, carpenter, joiner, cabinet maker and undertaker. In 1927-28 he built timber storage sheds for Rippers. They often subcontracted specialised work out to him, which they were unable to undertake.
Edith Ethel May Corder was employed making wooden parts, including propeller blades, during the First World War and worked in the canteen during the Second World War. Her service was confined to helping with the war effort in both World Wars as she did not work during peace time.
Edward John Corder was employed at Rippers by 1907 until 1911 when he became a brick and tile maker at The Manor Brick Works, Thundersley. By 1913 he had returned to Rippers where he remained until his death in 1938.
Edward Stanley Corder joined in 1933, became a carpenter and joiner and worked in the systems joinery department. At the outbreak of the Second World War his skills were urgently required by de Havillands of Hatfield, Hertfordshire and Luton where he worked on the wooden frames of Mosquito aeroplanes until 1943. By this time women had been trained to carry out much of this work and he joined up. From 1943 to 1946 he was an armourer in the REME serving in Burma, India and the Afghan border. In 1946 he returned to Rippers where he was a joiner and later made TV cabinets until becoming a charge hand in the kitchen units department. He retired in 1983 having completed 50 years service including his war work with de Havillands and service in the REME.
Fred Corder commenced employment with Rippers at the beginning of the Second World War and remained until his retirement in 1950. During the war he undertook night time fire watch duties, being used to night work as he had previously fired the kiln at Southey Green Brick, Tile and Pottery Works during nights.
Rayner Valentine Corder known as **Ray** was employed by Rippers for the majority of his working life with the exception of service in the Suffolk Regiment during the First World War.
Walter Edward Corder left the brickmaking industry during the Second World War and joined Rippers where he remained until retirement in 1961.
William Dan Corder served his apprenticeship between 1902 and 1906 with Harry Gooch, a joiner and builder of Sible Hedingham and thereafter continued to be employed by Gooch until

1909 when the business was sold. William then joined Rippers as a carpenter and joiner where he remained, with the exception of First World War service, until he retired in April 1959 at 72 years of age having completed 50 years including war service.

William Ross Cowan, M.S.M., was formerly a marine engineer and had served in the Merchant Navy. During the First World War he joined the Royal Engineers, became a Staff Sergeant and was awarded the Meritorious Service Medal. In 1919 he moved to Sible Hedingham where he set up a haulage business in partnership with his brother. He subsequently became proprietor of his own business as a vulcanizer (of rubber tyres) operating from the rear of Alderford House. He later worked in the Power House as a maintenance engineer.

Ben Cox was a fitter.

Peter Cracknell made staircases.

Fred W. Craven was an electrician and a member of the electrical maintenance and installation team who became electrical supervisor.

Christine and Carole Cutmore worked on the assembly line putting window frames together.

Joan Darkins (nee Margetts) worked in the office.

Pip Darkins worked in the windows sales office for one year.

Alfie Deal was employed by the company for 27 years and worked in "D" Department. Following retirement from full time employment at the age of 71 he returned part time to work in the maintenance department.

Reuben A. Debenham whose responsibilities included the assembly of window frames had two brothers employed at the works for a time namely **Alfred Debenham** and **Ivor R. Debenham**.

Mr. Dell worked at Rippers circa 1950s and later became head of the building department at the North East Essex Technical College and School of Art. Upon his retirement in 1974 he donated a shield, known as 'The Dell Shield' for the best student in machine woodworking. This was won by Dawn Pilgrim in 1976 (see below).

Sid Denny worked in the Turbine Room.

Bill Ditton was a lorry driver during the 1930s and 1940s.

Alan Dowsett worked on stair case assembly in the stair shop in "S" mill workshop.

Dennis Cyril Dowsett known as **Den**, was employed from leaving school until joining up. At the outbreak of war in 1939 he was serving in B Company 2/5th Battalion, Essex Regiment, Territorial Army and later transferred to the Royal Engineers. He became a prisoner of war of the Japanese and died on 2nd December 1943 in Burma aged 23 years.

Francis Ralph Dowsett known as **Frank** served his apprenticeship and became a carpenter and joiner. Following service in the Second World War he returned to Rippers and in December 1977 he received a gold watch having completed 29 years service. He died in 1980 about one year before he was due to retire.

Beryl Drury worked in the offices, circa 1930.

Ernest Drury started at the age of 14 in the machine shop and 49 years later finished as foreman of the kitchen and television cabinet department.

Frank Drury worked at Rippers before he enlisted in the 5th Essex Regiment during the First World War and was killed in action in the Dardenelles. Another **Frank Drury** was later switchboard attendant for the distribution of power attached to the Power House.

Harold Charles Drury of Pye Corner, Castle Hedingham who was born in 1905 left school when he was 12 years old and joined Rippers as an errand boy. One of his duties was the collection and delivery of mail between the works and Castle Hedingham Post Office. He was apprenticed as a joiner two years later when he moved to the saw-mill under the supervision of Archibald Ross. In November 1922 he had the forefinger of his left hand amputated as a result of an accident. He particularly enjoyed trips out with Tucker and Charlton Ripper when he accompanied them around the area buying timber; Harold held one end of the tape measure! After his apprenticeship was complete he earned £3 a week. He worked at Rippers for 54 years.

Harry Drury was a wood machinist for 50 years and received a gold watch from Jim Ripper in 1970.

Jack Drury was a foreman.

James Ernest Drury of Halstead was an assistant labourer to a sawyer in the mid 1930s.

John Drury was sadly the first fatality to occur at Rippers in 1937. The following report is courtesy of the Essex Newsman 1937. *"Dr. J. F. MacDonald, coroner, held an inquest at Halstead on John Drury, 58, labourer, of Alderford Street, Sible Hedingham, who was fatally injured at Ripper's Joinery works at Castle Hedingham. John Leathers, machinist at Rippers stated that he was working in the sawmill, where there were a pile of logs. He heard a rumbling, and seeing Drury coming round the corner from a passage between two large stacks of logs, called out, "look up Jim". Drury tried to run, but tripped against a piece of wood, and fell in a sitting position. A log fell down straight onto Drury. The log weighed about a ton and a half. The coroner: "If he had not fallen, would he have escaped"? – "I think he would possibly have got through". Archibald Ross, sawmill foreman asked by Miss McWilliam, (H.M. Inspector) if he had any idea why this log fell out the stack, replied, "I think the log which was being lifted by the crane moved another log, and this moved the one that caused the trouble." The jury returned a verdict of Death by Misadventure while following his employment and added that no blame was attached to anyone".*
Another **John Drury** was the sawmill foreman during the late 1940s, by which time he had been employed by Rippers for 30 years.
Reg Drury worked in the office.
Robert Drury was at work with a surfacing machine in 1907 when his left hand came into contact with the knife and was so injured that it had to be amputated. The machine was properly guarded. Drs. Bromley and Twamley were called in and the patient was taken to Halstead Cottage Hospital.
Roy Drury was a fork lift truck driver and later a charge hand in the stores. His brother **Peter Drury** was employed shortly before his National Service. Their younger brother **David Drury** later worked for Premdor from 1998 to 2007 when his duties were successively wrapping flat packed doors, working on the bench, a fork lift truck driver and latterly assistant store-man.
William Drury (1874-1939) was a large man and had the nickname of 'Buller' Drury. He was originally a railway porter on the Colne Valley and Halstead Railway. He later worked for Rippers where he sorted out timber after it had been delivered by rail and he became a foreman. In 1893 he, married Alice Edith Corder. ('Buller' was a cousin of John Drury who was killed in 1937).
Dorothy (Dot) Earey (formerly Louth) was a French polisher.
Dorothy Beatrice Earey (later Unwin) was a member of staff.
Herbert John Earey of Potter Street, Sible Hedingham was killed instantly on 30th April 1948 when engaged in unloading trees from a trailer. Donald McLeod of Swanton Morley, Norfolk, who was the lorry driver delivering the trees was also killed but he was not employed by Rippers. Unloading had commenced when two of the trees, an oak and a poplar fell from the trailer and crushed the men. Dr. Philip Putnam of Sible Hedingham was immediately called to the scene but sadly both men were dead by the time he arrived. At the inquest, when Rippers was represented by solicitor Ronald Long, the Coroner returned a verdict of "Accidental Death".
Jeff Elkins worked in the Turbine Room.
Allister Evans who had served in the First World War was employed at Rippers in 1929 when he sadly got into difficulties whilst swimming in Gosfield Lake and was drowned.
Bert Evans was a foreman.
David Bryan Evans was born in 1906 and initially worked on the bench; a job obtained for him by his grandfather and he appears on the 1926 photograph of employees. David loved working with wood and carved many beautiful items. He later worked in the office as an estimator and following the hit and run air raids by the Luftwaffe in 1941, decided to transfer from Rippers to Evans Bellhouse where he worked until his tragic death in a car accident in 1958.
Eddie Evans was an estimator for standard joinery.
Bert Everitt was an employee who lived at Christmas Field. He was a long standing clerk of Sible Hedingham Parish Council and Everitt Way, off Station Road, was named after him.
Ian and Daphne Everitt – Ian completed 31 years service and his wife Daphne assembled staircases.
Ron Everitt worked in the Turbine Room.
Victor Everitt assembled stair cases in the stair shop in "S" Mill workshop.
Alfred Eves caught his right hand in a planing machine in January 1929, severing part of his fingers.

Gordon Frederick Faiers worked in the Setting Out Department.
Malcolm Firman started as an office boy from 1948 to 1950 when he was paid 9¼d an hour. He was later employed by Bert Corder.
Thomas Augustus Firman was a native of Cambridge who moved to Sible Hedingham and was a joiner for 20 years, living in a 'Rippers' house in Brook Terrace. He was a Sergeant in the Home Guard and sadly one of six killed in a tragic accident at Gestingthorpe on 23rd April 1944 when he was 45 years of age.
George Leonard Foster served in the Royal Fusiliers in the First World War and afterwards became a postman until being employed by Rippers until his early death in 1942. He was one of the first members of the Hedingham Platoon of the Home Guard and became a Sergeant.
Percy Alfred George Foster was a carpenter and joiner and later employed by his uncle Bert Corder and then by George Argent, a builder and funeral director of Great Yeldham. In about 1939 Percy Foster, George Hilsden and other employees of Rippers were engaged in erecting search light batteries around Sible Hedingham.
Peter Foster worked in the Stair Department.
Alf Francis was employed by Rippers variously as a blacksmith and as an electricians mate.
Florence Freear made wooden parts for aeroplanes, including Wellingtons, during the Second World War and later worked in the canteen.
Jane Frost (later Ripper) was secretary to managing director Michael Ripper at Hedingham and later at Bowater's office in West Stockwell Street, Colchester.
John Fuller worked in the office and was responsible for the clocking in and out machine. He was also the rent collector for the Ripper's houses.
Arthur Gardiner worked in the estimating office and was chief estimator for special joinery.
Leonard Gardiner was employed by Rippers all his working life and his wife **Hazel Gardiner (nee Steward)** also worked there during the 1970s.
Ernest Edward Gepp was initially a brickmaker, but later a machinist for about 50 years.
Ruby Florence Gepp worked in the office.
William Bernard Gepp was a woodworker who initially lived at New England and later in one of Ripper's Bungalows (The Huts).
Brian Gooderham was a tree feller during the late 1950s.
Thomas James Goodfellow joined Rippers when he was 46 and lived in Christmas Field. He was a member of the Congregational Church at Castle Hedingham and sang in the choir.
Annie Ruth Goodge worked in the office as Bertram Hogarth's secretary for many years and retired aged 60 in 1966. She died in 1997.
Leonard Arthur John "Jack" Guilding was employed from 1926 to 1970 in the timber yard latterly as a leading hand. Upon his retirement Michael Ripper presented him with an Omega watch.
Gloria Halls drilled parts for television cabinets.
Linda Halls worked from 1978 to 1984 on the assembly line on 'A' frames (window frames) which came off 'the press' and had to be put together.
Susan Halls worked in the kitchen department.
Thomas Hammond was employed at Rippers during the 1920s and early 1930s. He lived at Falcon Square, Castle Hedingham and was a member of the British Legion and the local bowls club.
Hugh Hanscombe lived at Chappel and from 1924 until the 1960s he used to cycle to work.
Robin Harding was employed from 1961 to 1966.
Alma Hardy joined as an apprentice joiner in 1920 and in 1927 moved to the Setting Out Department of which he was in charge from 1947 until 1956. He was then promoted to the production planning office with special responsibilities for delivery to sites.
Nancy Hardy worked in the office.
Ernest Harper was a stationery engine driver and engineer for 22 years.
Lionel Harper was a fitter.
Reg Harrington worked in the Setting Out Department.
Janet Harrison was engaged in administration.

John Hart, known as Jack Hart, started work in 1938 at the age of 15 years. Following service in the Navy during the Second World War he returned to Rippers in 1945 and remained with the company until 1965. He worked on timber wagons and collected tree trunks, which were brought back to Hedingham. He sometimes helped with cutting down trees and removing the branches prior to transportation and collected logs and timber from docks. His wife, **Gladys Hart**, worked in the French polishing department and her sister, **Kay Brown (later Turner)** helped make wooden aeroplane parts during the Second World War. Jack and Gladys's daughter, **Jackie Hart**, was also employed by Rippers and successor companies.
Mary Hart worked in the estimating office for several years before joining Stephen Ripper as his personal assistant specialising in sales and advertising.
William Harvey was a joiner from 1939 to about 1969.
Spencer Hayward worked in the Setting Out Department and part of his work was drawing plans not only for Rippers but also for The Sible Hedingham Red Brick Company Limited.
Stan Heard worked in the office.
John Heather was a member of the sales department with responsibility for standard products.
Derek and **Roy Hewitt**, two brothers living at Church Street, Sible Hedingham were long standing employees of Rippers. Derek worked in "B" Mill and Roy in 'Tom Wells' shop. The brothers were well known for making and showing films of the history of Sible Hedingham and in particular the annual carnivals. They were also leading members of the local model aero club.
Harry Hewlett was a joiner and later an estimator. He worked at Rippers for approximately 40 years from 1928-9 to about 1969. He also made drawings of joinery to be manufactured by the company, particularly for the interior of churches.
Paula Hilsden worked in the stock office 1959 to 1960.
David Hilton was a representative.
Keith Hopkins was an apprentice joiner from 1964 to 1968 and joined the production planning department in 1969. By 1973 he had been promoted to production manager for purpose built joinery and staircases.
George Arnold Howard lived in Station Road. He was a member of Sible Hedingham Parish Council and chairman from 1934 to 1946.
Mary Howard later Sullivan worked in the wages and cost office.
Graham Hume joined Rippers in 1965 when he was 15 years old. An apprenticeship of four years included day release at Braintree College to take a City and Guild examination. Graham trained under Tom Wells making standard joinery and completed 43 years.
Hector Silas Hunwick moved from Kelvedon to 'Halcyon', Sible Hedingham in about 1899. For a number of years he was shop foreman in the joinery department before he died in 1939. Hector took a great interest in the Village Club at Castle Hedingham.
Aubrey Ince was a member of the electrical maintenance and installation team.
William (Bill) Ince was a foreman.
Hedley James Iron was a member of the clerical staff until joining the Beds and Herts Regiment during the Second World War. He transferred to the RAF and was latterly a sergeant in the First Glider Pilot Regiment. He was killed in May 1943 in the Italian campaign.
Eleanor Irvine worked at Rippers during the Second World War.
Jack Jarman was in charge of the drawing office.
Harry E. Jay was a representative.
William James "Billy" Jay was employed for 52 years, including 41 as a sales representative, with the exception of the war years when he took over the buying of home-grown timber.
Ian Johnson worked in the office on costings, and sales of standard joinery.
Maureen Kelly worked in the Accounts Department for 24 years from 1958.
Doug Kendall was an apprentice.
Arthur W. King was a wood machinist and on 19th October 1918 he was admitted as a member of The Amalgamated Society of Millsawyers & Woodcutting Machinists.
David King was a joiner.
Frederick Charles King was initially a brickyard labourer for the Rayner family at Maiden Ley Brick Works, followed by 18 years at Rippers and was finally employed by Essex County Council.

Marlies Kuhnert became one of the first qualified lady wood machinists in the country.
Hilda Larbelster assembled kitchen cabinets.
Peter Large was a lorry driver from 1998 to 2009.
Douglas A. R. Laver known as **Roy** worked in the electrical shop.
William (Bill) Laver worked in the shavings loft.
June Lawrence worked in the office.
Jack Leathers assembled stair cases in the stair shop in "S" Mill workshop.
Stanley Letch was a charge hand.
Walter Edward Letch was a brickmaker and later employed by Rippers.
Fred Lewis assembled stair cases in the stair shop in "S" Mill workshop.
Leslie Ling, son of Charles Ling trained as a carpenter/joiner and joined Rippers. Later he became an area representative for the company in Hertfordshire and lived near Watford. Leslie's wife **Jessie**, formerly **Jarrow**, worked in the office for a short time about 1930.
Alan Lowe employed from 1962 to 2009. He served a five year apprenticeship as a joiner and later became joinery supervisor for windows and door frames.
Andrew Lynch was employed from 1979 to 1991 and 2002 to 2009.
Jim McAleese, D.F.M., was born in Ireland in 1915. He joined the Royal Air Force in 1934 and in 1940 received the Distinguished Flying Medal from King George VI. When Jim was demobbed Cyril Martin offered him the opportunity to train as a representative for Rippers and 'his area' was Kent and Sussex. When Cyril retired Jim was promoted to Head of Sales and travelled to the London Office at Holborn daily. When the Holborn office closed in 1970 Jim transferred to Hedingham. He retired from Bowater Ripper in 1980 and died in January 1982.
C. MacBean was a foreman.
Duncan (Jock) McCulloch was a blacksmith.
Patrick McGlown was a member of the maintenance team for 4 years.
Bernard (Jock) McGraw was a machinist from 1971 to 2009.
Edward George (Ted) Marjoram was a sawyer in "S" Department and served in the Observer Corps during the Second World War at the Castle Hedingham post.
Peter Marlton was a polisher.
John Marsh whose responsibilities included, conducting visitors around Ripper's showroom at Castle Hedingham during the 1970s.
Aubrey Martin was a polisher.
Cyril Rigby Martin was a commercial traveller commencing on 1st January 1946 and entered into a seven year agreement with Rippers on 1st April 1946. He later became manager of their London office, where his much valued secretary was Miss Gale. He moved to Castle Hedingham to work and lodged with Mrs. Sarah Ambrose. Cyril married her daughter, Winifred Eva Ambrose who had worked in the office at Rippers in 1923. Cyril was a loyal and dedicated employee who retired when he was 72 years old.
Leslie Martin was a steam and boiler fitter in the Power House.
Ernest H. Mead served in the East Kents (Buffs) during the First World War and became a prisoner in Germany. In December 1917 the sum of £2 14s 6d was collected in the works on his behalf.
Col. Frederick John Mead, C.B.E., started as a sawyer's mate on a power driven saw bench. He emigrated to Canada and joined the Royal Canadian Mounted Police at Regina, Saskatchewan in 1910. He served in the Great War when he made his only return visit to Sible Hedingham. He prospered and rose through the ranks until in 1944 he was appointed Deputy Commissioner, the second highest rank in the RCMP. In 1946 he was appointed a Commander of the British Empire by King George VI. During his visits to Canada Tucker Ripper met up with Frederick on three occasions. He died on 9th September 1961 at his home in Vancouver and was buried with full Military Honours.
Stanley Mead was an apprentice joiner until serving in the Royal Engineers from January 1940 to 1946 when he returned to Rippers until 1948. He was son of Sgt. George William Mead, M.M., who also worked at Rippers and nephew of Col. F. J. Mead (above).
William (Bill) Meadowcroft was initially employed by The Sible Hedingham Red Brick

Company Limited as manager and later transferred to its associate company, Rippers Limited, where he was in charge of the stores. He served in the Observer Corps during the Second World War.
Oliver J. Metcalf worked in the office.
John Metcalf was chief engineer from 1972 to 1976.
Cuthbert Mitson was a long standing employee who lived in a 'Rippers' house at Nunnery Street, Castle Hedingham. He served in the Home Guard during the Second World War and was later a member of Castle Hedingham Parish Council.
Fred Mitson was a foreman.
Noreen Metson was a stock control clerk from 1972 until 1979.
John Moles was a joiner who later worked in the office and became a director of JSR Joinery Limited.
John Ambrose Moore was apprenticed in about 1930 and became a carpenter and joiner. Following service during the Second World War he worked in the building industry before returning to Rippers during the late 1950s where he remained until about 1970.
Harry Morrell was employed for six years, which included his apprenticeship. His siblings, **Rene, Pat, Alan and Valerie** were also employed by Rippers at various times.
James (Jim) Morrell was employed as a labourer when he came out of the army in 1946 and retired because of ill health in 1975. He mainly worked in "B" Mill.
Patricia Marion Morrell (later Dakin) worked in many departments and was the first woman to work on the stair press to assemble staircases. This was unique and other manufacturers, including the Chinese, visited and inspected it. When equality for women started in about 1972 she was one of the first women to be offered an apprenticeship as a machinist but declined as she was getting married and wanted to start a family.
Sandra Mortimer (formerly Hume) was employed from 1970 to 1972 initially in the main Mill and later in the Maltings. Her tasks included working on window presses and filling in holes in wood where knots had existed.
Alf Mulley was an early employee in the 1890s and became foreman in the Machine Shop in about 1913.
Aubrey Newton was a joiner and in 1973 at the age of 78 he came out of retirement to restore the hand-pumped water tender to working order. This fire appliance dated 1720 had been stored at the works and was used to fight fires there during the early 1900s but it is very unlikely that it was used after 1929. (See chapter 8)
Richard Nice was a labourer in "B" mill.
Gordon A. J. (known as Jim) Nichols originally had an inside job but later transferred to the sales team. He became a representative for the Kent area and lived just outside Tunbridge. In 1941 he married **Kathleen Joyce Meadowcroft**, daughter of Bill Meadowcroft and both were employed by Rippers.
Harry Norman was a receptionist and telephonist.
Peter O' Halloran was a machinist.
Robert B. Oakey was a machinist and supervised over 50 other employees.
S. Oakey worked in the office for four years.
Edmund (Ted) Oliver from Wallington, Surrey successfully applied for the position of turbine driver at Rippers in December 1938. He moved into a Ripper's house at Yeldham Road for which the initial rent was 11/- per week including rates. His wages were £4 per week plus overtime. He left in 1958.
Julie Owen (nee Williams) was an assembler in the Maltings.
Steve Owen was employed from 1971 to 2009 latterly as a joinery supervisor.
Joyce Palmer worked in the office.
Lucy Pannell, known as **Nurse Pannell**, was a long serving nurse at the factory surgery.
Arthur Charles Parr was a machinist and towards the end of November 1915 had the fingers of one hand crushed in the rollers of a machine. Although painful injuries were sustained no bones were broken and under the care of Dr James Bromley, the injured hand recovered.
Frederick William Parr was a machinist until his early death in 1914 at 26 years.

Herbert Partridge worked for his father who was a builder in Castle Hedingham until he was 'poached' by Rippers!
Brian Phillips was a representative.
Aubrey Pilgrim was a polisher.
(Edith) Dawn Pilgrim initially worked part time from 1957 and returned full time in 1971. She attended North East Essex Technical College one day a week for three years and became one of the first qualified lady wood machinists in the country.
Keith and Laura Pilgrim a husband and wife collectively employed for over eighty years.
Leslie Pilgrim started in the Setting Out Department in 1943 at the age of 14. One of his first jobs was putting up the wartime blackout shutters in the evening and removing them in the morning. He later worked in "D" Department as a carpenter and in about 1963 was promoted to charge hand in the 'Maltings' Department.
Lionel Pilgrim was employed from 1975 to 1990.
Pat Pilgrim was the yard manager.
Ray Piper was a charge hand.
Fred Pizzy worked in the accounts office until service in the Second World War.
Ron Plaistow drove an articulated lorry.
Clifford Potter was a joiner and was presented with a gold watch for 43 years service.
Norma Radford worked in the TV Department.
Gladys (Bunty) Ranger was the nurse in charge of the factory surgery.
Bobby Rash assembled staircases.
Glen Rawlinson started in 1971 as a labourer undertaking general yard maintenance work and later became an apprentice, passing his City and Guilds as a wood machinist in 1976. He remained as a wood machinist for about 15 years and then reverted to maintenance work. He continued working for successor companies until closure by Premdor in 2009 completing 38 years service.
Olive Jean Raymond was a secretary at Rippers nearly all her working life.
Marcel John Rayner completed his apprenticeship as a joiner in 1951 and remained with the company for many years until joining Courtaulds Limited.
Capt. William Wright Raynham, D.C.M., was a soldier who took part in the South African and Egyptian campaigns and later became a brickmaker. He rejoined the army during the First World War and was given a commission. After the war he was employed by Rippers and in 1926 became Provincial Grand Master of the Colchester and Maldon District of the Manchester Unity of Oddfellows.
William Raynham, jun, was an apprentice electrician for five years and worked in the Power House.
Dick Read joined in 1926, became charge-hand in "D" Department and completed 48 years service.
Fred Read was a representative.
Jim Redgewell originally drove an engine on agricultural work and commenced work for Ripper Brothers in the 1890s as a 'rough' carpenter. He later volunteered to look after their steam engine and developed a great empathy towards all types of engines and ultimately worked on the wood and coal producer engines. He remained at the works for the rest of his working life and died in October 1941 aged 83 years.
Cyril Reeve assembled up and over garage doors in "C" Department.
Derek C. Reeve left school in 1965 and joined Rippers as a labourer under Lennie Broyd, who was his charge-hand, and John Smith who lived at Earls Colne. He was an apprentice bench joiner for four years and subsequently trained for a further six years at Braintree College. Derek remained with the company until 1972.
Horace William Alfred Reeve was a fitter's mate for 29 years from 1942 until 1971. He was born in the Thingoe District of Suffolk in 1902 and was in service at Gosfield Hall prior to joining Rippers. Horace and his wife Evelyn were proprietors of the Off Licence at Gestingthorpe from 1944. He joined the Amalgamated Engineering Union in 1948 and in 1971 was presented with a gold watch upon his retirement at nearly 70 years of age. He died on Christmas Day 1983 at his home in Gestingthorpe.

Jacqueline Reynolds became one of the first qualified lady wood machinists in the country.
John Reynolds was a member of the office staff.
Alan Rice was a foreman in charge of a workshop.
Ennice Lavina Richards was employed as a clerk. In 1939 at the age of 15 years she was accidently killed by a car when cycling to Braintree from Sible Hedingham.
Freddie Ridgewell who formerly served in the Royal Navy became an electrician and supervised apprentice electricians at the works.
Harry Riley worked in the Accounts Department with responsibility for wages from 1965 to 1969.
Charles Henry Rippingale of Brook Terrace left school in 1931 to work in the maintenance section where he remained until his retirement in 1978 with the exception of service in the RAF during the Second World War. He served as a special constable for over 25 years and died in 1980.
Archibald Ross worked as foreman of the English Timber Department and was sawmill manager for 21 years. Previously he had been engaged in this line of work all over the country. During his early years he served with the Lanarkshire Police Force reaching the rank of sub-inspector. Following his retirement he moved to Holland on Sea.
Robert "Bob" Ross joined in 1923 and progressed to estimator, sales representative and special joinery sales manager.
George Ruddock was a native of Bradford and moved to the village in 1921 when he worked at the old Gas Works for ten years before joining Rippers in 1931. He lived in the wooden bungalow opposite Sible and Castle Hedingham Railway Station.
Arthur Richard Ruffle was apprenticed to Bert Corder, a builder and contractor and worked for him before the Second World War. Arthur served in the Tank Corps during the war and afterwards continued working for Bert Corder. In 1954 he started work for Rippers where he initially worked in the Hardwood Shop making oak doors and then moved to the Setting Out Mill. He completed 25 years service and received a gold watch.
Cecil George Ruffle was employed during the late 1940s as a tractor driver unloading logs delivered by lorry.
Frederick Ruffle was employed at Rippers when he left in July 1916 to join the C.N.A.S at Brook Green, Hammersmith, London.
George Ruffle was a stoker in the Power House.
Stan Ruffle worked in the office.
William (Bill) Ruffle assembled stair cases in the stair shop in "S" Mill workshop.
Ron Sevill was a machinist.
Arthur Nunn Schooling known as **Nunn Schooling** was a carpenter and joiner by trade but as a young man served in the Essex Constabulary for 9 years. Upon leaving the Police he returned to his old trade with Rippers remaining for 43 years. He was captain of the works fire brigade and latterly foreman packer not retiring until he was about 72 years of age.
Herbert A. H. Schooling worked in the Setting Out Department. In 1961 a carved oak table was dedicated at St. Peter's Church, Sible Hedingham in his memory. He was the second of four generations of his family who were employed at the works. (Nunn Schooling, Herbert, Ben Cox, Colin and Kathie Hoye).
Harry Scott a long serving employee who in 1913 accompanied Hubert Ripper and carried out some beautiful work on Belladrum House, near Beauly, north of Inverness. He was later a charge hand and then a foreman in the building situated near Crosspath.
Joan Scott worked in the stores and was the daughter of Harry Scott (above).
Kath Scrivener worked in the office.
P. Seabrook was a setter-out for 30 years.
Shirley Seaman was secretary to Norman Ripper and Albert Brown timber buyer, from August 1953 to January 1961
Alan C. Sibley worked on a moulding machine in "B" Mill.
Arthur Simmonds was a carpenter but also cleaned the boards on the turbine cooling tower. He had been a prisoner of war.
Len Simpson was a foreman.

J. Smee (nee Wells) was employed in the Abstracting Setting Out Department.
Cyril Smith worked in the office.
Derek Smith was a highly skilled French polisher who worked at Rippers for 27½ years and was a son of Stan Smith (see below). Derek started work with Turner's French polishing firm, which was run by Bob and Albert Turner, whose business was situated close to Rippers during the 1940s. At the time Turners were involved with the finishing process of cabinets for the Government, which were used by the 'Forces' during the Second World War. Albert retired and Bob went to work for Rippers in their television department when Derek also transferred to Rippers. He worked on Bush and Echo televisions and radiograms, made specialised pieces for exhibitions and experimental pieces before production, as well as working in many other areas; he was also involved in hand polishing several very large solid mahogany worktops for an Irish Linen Company. Working upstairs in another department was **Gladys Cook** and they were married in 1957.
Evelyn Smith worked on the assembly line putting window frames together.
Fred Smith was a wood machinist from 1923 to 1973. Fred's daughter **Carol Smith** was a shorthand typist at Rippers.
George Gusterson Smith, M.B.E., was born in Castle Hedingham and bought up in the woodwork tradition, his father and grandfather being first rate joiners and carpenters. He joined Rippers in about 1890 and worked at Cherry Lawn reinstating the woodwork, including a fine oak staircase. This house was to become Tucker Ripper's home in 1893. He later left Hedingham and by the First World War ran a very successful business in Holloway Road, London giving Rippers valuable assistance in making war material of great complexity. Towards the end of the First World War he joined the Aeronautical Inspection Department of the Air Ministry and specialised in the inspection, selection and use of wood for aeroplanes and ultimately became principal inspector on wood to the Ministry of Aircraft Production. In 1944 he received a Member of the British Empire medal for his services.
Humphrey Sidney Smith of Bottle Hall, Sible Hedingham was initially employed by Bert Corder and later by Rippers.
John Smith was a foreman.
Louis Gordon Smith was an apprentice in the Setting Out Department and eventually became a progress chaser. His wife **Elsie Smith** worked in "C" Department – the window framing department.
Peter Smith was a joiner from 1941 until 1990 completing 49 years service.
Another **Peter Smith** worked for Rippers and all successor companies becoming manager for Premdor Crosby until closure in 2009.
Stanley Smith, nicknamed **'Spindle' Smith** was a machinist for 50 years, with one break when he was called up for service during the First World War.
Victor Harold Smith who was chairman of Sible Hedingham Parish Council from 1947 to 1952.
Walter F. (Wally) Smith was a lorry driver.
M. Southgate employed from 1959 to 1966.
Barry Sparke was a member of the electrical maintenance and installation team and was the last apprentice to be taken on by Bertram Hogarth. His wife **Veronica** assembled kitchen units.
Dennis Sparke (father of Barry) represented the Amalgamated Society of Woodworkers.
Cecil Springett was a joiner who made wooden parts for aeroplanes during the Second World War and radio and television cabinets during peacetime.
Walter Springett was a machinist in 1917 when he caught his hand in a trenching machine and cut the top off his first finger.
Harry Steward was a brickmaker and later employed by Rippers.
Joe Stoker was a long standing employee and became a charge hand.
Arthur Sutton was a mechanic.
Alexander Tait was a labourer and part of his job was to measure timber logs and remove the bark, known as 'barking'. His wife **Doreen Tait** assembled window frames.
George Tarbin was a boilerman.
J. Tarbin was a joiner for 45 years.

Harry Stanhope Theobald who lived at Long Melford purchased his own bus to transport fellow workers. He continued his employment and parked his bus each day at the works. He eventually left Rippers and became a full time bus operator.
Ann Thomas worked in the Maltings Workshop.
Harry Thompson was a wood machinist.
Alan Turner was a joiner for 43 years.
Alfred Turner was a French polisher.
Bill Turner joined in 1948 and completed 26 years as company car driver.
Bob Turner was a French polisher.
Leslie Turner worked in the Setting Out Department.
John H. Twiggins was a fitter.
Thomas Mumford Vale lived in Alexandra Road. He was a member of Sible Hedingham Parish Council and chairman from 1952 to 1954 and 1964 to 1966. He was apprenticed to the building trade with Frank Gibson and later worked for Rippers for many years until retiring in 1958.
John Waldron worked on a moulding machine in "B" Mill and represented the Transport and General Workers Union.
Norman Walls was a foreman at the works during the early 1900s and brother of Tom Walls.
Tom Walls was a carpenter in his native Northampton before moving to Hedingham and being employed as a joiner. When still a teenager he worked under the supervision of Mr. Cuthbert on the next bench to Jack Coates. Tom later became a policeman in London, a jockey in Australia, farmer, concert party pierrot, actor, film star and sportsman. His colleagues at Rippers, including Charles Drury, described him as having a good voice and frequently sang at local concerts. He was always sky-larking, full of fun and the despair of his foreman. Following a successful stage career, Tom died in November 1949.
Tom Waterman was a joiner who made the coffee table presented to H.R.H. Princess Marie Louise.
Brenda Weavers worked in the machine shop for 25 years.
George Webb was a saw doctor and later promoted to take charge of the Saw Doctor's Shop.
Robert Lewis Webb worked in the office from the First World War until 1935 and was also secretary of the Loyal Webster Lodge of Oddfellows.
Dorothy Weight was an assembler in the Maltings.
Bert Wells was a foreman
Tom Wells, sen., was a machinist in "K" Department.
Frank Westrop was employed for 50 years, becoming foreman of the workshop at the Maltings. He was a member of Castle Hedingham Parish Council, Church Warden and for over 65 years a member of the Church choir. His main hobby was photography and some of the photographs in this book were taken by him.
Charles Wildash worked in the Accounts Office.
Cecil Wilding was a carpenter.
Phyllis Wilding worked in the office.
William Wilkin was a setter out for stair cases and also involved with making panelling for churches.
Alfred Williams was removing some timber in 1917, when a considerable weight fell upon him and seriously hurt his toes and injured his hip.
Brenda Williams became one of the first qualified wood machinists in the country.
C. E. (Ted) W. Williams worked in the estimating office, and was an estimator for special joinery.
E. Williams sen., worked in the office.
Fred Williams joined the company in 1954 as a paint sprayer in the kitchen unit department. He retired on his 65th birthday in 1973 when foreman, Ernie Drury, made a presentation.
Frederick George Williams who was a native of Castle Hedingham worked for Rippers practically all his life apart from service during the First World War. He lived in Brook Terrace and died in 1964.
Hubert S. G. Williams worked in the Setting Out Department.
David Williamson passed his City and Guilds in 1976.

Arthur Wiseman was employed for 25 years as a machinist.
Frederick Charles Wiseman was initially employed for about 20 years by Hovis Limited of Hulls Mill as a lorry driver delivering flour until the mill closed in 1957 when he became a driver for Rippers.
Harry Wiseman was employed before and after the First World War when he served in the army.
Maurice William Wiseman commenced his five year apprenticeship as a joiner on 25th September 1936 at the age of 16 years working a 44 hour week. He was provided with his own set of tools which cost £6 5s 5d less 20% discount of £1 5s 1d leaving a balance of £5 0s 4d which was deducted from his salary at the rate of 3/- per week. His apprenticeship ended on 25th September 1941 and following service in the Second World War, when he became a sergeant in the Essex Regiment, he returned to Rippers. He was principally engaged making staircases and in December 1976 was presented with a gold watch upon completing 40 years service including war service.
Frank Woodcock, J.P., was born in 1883 and his first job was a carpenter with Mr Wicks at Wethersfield. When he moved to Greenstead Green he worked for Charles Wash of Earls Colne. During the First World War he served in the Royal Flying Corps and his first job after demobilisation was with Crittall's at Witham. When Rippers erected the wooden bungalows (which then shared a field with cattle) Frank was offered one and he joined the company. On 29th August 1920, their daughter Jean was the first baby to be born in the bungalows and Tucker Ripper was a frequent visitor to see how the baby progressed. When her younger sister Eileen was born the Woodcocks became one of the first families to move into a new Ripper's house in Brook Terrace. Frank worked as a joiner, later in the Setting Out Department and when he retired in 1953 was the Labour Officer. He was secretary of the local branch of the ASW (see chapter 20); was the first chairman of Governors of Hedingham Secondary School and served as a Justice of the Peace for 24 years.
Jean Woodcock (later Cooper) left school aged 16 and started work in Rippers office. She first learnt to operate the telephone switchboard before commencing evening classes for shorthand, typing and book keeping so that she could work in Harry Ripper's office with Joyce Meadowcroft. At the outbreak of war with the younger men enlisting, Jean took the place of Fred Pizzy who worked in the accounts office with Charlie Wildash and Ashley Ripper. As Jean was in a reserved occupation, she was refused enlistment so she became involved with the First Aid Post evening duty in the village. After the war Rippers gradually returned to normal work and Jean continued working in the accounts office until she left to have her first child in 1950.
Steve Wooding worked in the T.V. Cabinet Department at the Maltings and lived in a house owned by Rippers at Nunnery Street, Castle Hedingham. Wooding Lodge, the Scout and Guide Headquarters, at Sheepcote Road, Castle Hedingham was later named after him.
Archie Wright commenced his apprenticeship in 1921 and later specialised in hardwood joinery. He was a charge-hand during and after the Second World War and in 1955 joined the staff as a foreman of one of the special joinery shops. He took charge of the stores in 1963, moved to the Despatch Department in 1965 and retired in 1970 after 49 years service.
Alec John Yerbury was originally apprenticed to William Sudbury of Halstead, before he joined Rippers, where he worked in the stores and remained for over 40 years until he retired in 1947.

The following were also employed by Rippers:
George Alliston, William G. Alliston, Horace Ambrose, R. Amey, Rene Armriding, Annie Bacon, Ivy Barber, Cecil Bareham, Eileen Barnes, Henry G. Barton, Ray Barty, Edward Beadle, Willie Beadle, D. Beckett, Austen Beckwith, Emmy Best, Michael Bocking, Barbara Boreham (later Holmes), Cecil Boreham, Derek Boreham, Doreen Boreham, Jack Boreham, Margaret Boreham, William E. Boreham, Dot Bowen, David Bowers, Barbara Bowles, K. G. Bretton, Dick Britton, Faith Britton, Mrs. M. Brooks, Cyril Brown, Gordon F. Brown, Derek Bunton, George Button, Joseph G. Carder, Angela Chatters, D. Chatters, Charlie Clark, Doreen Clark (later Patmore), Michael Clark, Victor L. Clark, John Clarke, Arthur Cleghorn, Fred Cobbold, Edward Cock, Les Collar, Dennis Crisford, George Cross (nicknamed Solomon), Janet Day, Jenny Deal, Harold Debenham, Thomas W. Dowsett, Charlie Drury, Bernard G. Duce, Harold J. Earey, Sidney C.

Earey, Timothy Edwards, A. H. Evans, Herbert Everett, Jean Everett, Maureen Everett, Reginald F. Fairclough, William Finch, Flo Francis, David Gambell, S. Gardiner, Frank Happe, Roy E. J. Harper, Fred Harris, Roy Hasler, Bill Hazelwood, Frank Headland, Malcolm Hoadley, Jack Holden, Dick Hunwick, Alan Ilett, Ruth Joslyn, Kath Kemp, Jack Kibble, J. Lake, T. Lawler, Albert Leivers, George Lewis, Dennis Lock, Bill Lynch, Ronald H. Mallott, Bill Mansfield, Keith Metson, Bert Miller, Bob Moore, C. Mortimer, H. Moules, D. Mowles, George Needham, Hubert G. Needham, Fred Noble, Brenda Norman, Cecil North, Alastair Nye, Nicky Nye (nee Steward), Nigel Palmer, Ernie Pannell, Jack Pannell, Percy Pannell, Frederick Stanley Parr, George James Parr, Reginald J. Paynter, Captain Peachy, Gordon Peacock, Harry Pickering, Arthur H. Pilgrim, Jeff Pilgrim, Stanley D. Pilgrim, Maurice Raymond, Jack Reeve, Jim Ridgewell, Stephen F. Ruffle, Rosemary Shipperley, Eddie Skeggs, Maureen Skeggs, Dot Smith, Doug Smith, Frank Smith, Roy Smith, Alf Steward, Mollie Steward, Peter Steward, Albert Richard Stockdale, Fred Sturgeon, John Sturgeon, Fred Suckling, C. E. Symonds, Eric Symonds, Bill Theobald, Peter Turner, Mr. Twitchett, R. Underwood, Alan Webb, Colin Westrop, H. Westrop, H. White, Roy Wilding, William Wilding, William Charles Willett, Peter Winch, John Wright and Jimmy Writtle.

'A' Department	J. Allen	**'G' Department**	Arthur Cleghorn
'B' Department	R. Rayner	**'K' Department**	E. Smee
'C' Department	George Hilsden, S. Staines	**'L' Department**	A. Daines
'D' Department	R. Ambrose, R. Gould	**'R' Department**	William (Bill) Ellis
'E' Department	A. Fenner	**'S' Department**	E. Farrant
'F' Department	D. Cook, W. Raymond		

Hedingham office staff: William Bell, A. Brown, R. Drury, E. Evans, Mrs. Nicholls, W. Ross, A. Steward, Mrs. Westrope, H. A. White
London office staff: T. H. Ricks (sales), B. Willis
Hedingham works staff: F. Connell, S. Liddiard, B. Nunn, Mrs. F. Ruffle, Miss. Spurgeon.

Finally, the following anecdote of an unnamed Rippers employee during the Second World War is courtesy of the late Stanley Randall who was for many years a senior and well respected reporter with the Halstead Gazette.

"There had been a night long air raid with little activity in the area until one or two dog-fights were heard high above the clouds as the returning enemy bombers were attacked by our fighter aircraft. Then the warning went out that an enemy parachutist had been seen to come down between Sible Hedingham and Wethersfield and very close to the USAAF air base (at Wethersfield). A full search was mounted but without result and with the coming of dawn many of the civilian searchers were called off. With day light a very young, dazed and terribly frightened German airman decided to leave the cover of the woods beside the Wethersfield Road and give himself up. Slightly wounded, scratched by the undergrowth in which he had hidden during the night and covered with mud he came out onto the main road. Within a short time a cyclist came pedalling along the road and raising his hands high in token of surrender, the airman tried to tell the cyclist that he wished to be taken prisoner. This, however, was a situation in which the man had never dreamed to find himself and he clearly did not know what to do. Finally, he said he was sorry but could not stop, as he had got to be at work at Rippers in about fifteen minutes, jumped on his cycle and went off leaving the enemy airman completely nonplussed. The young German then struggled up the chase to nearby Wrights Farm where he gave himself up to two elderly sisters, the Misses Alice and Kate Wallace, who gave him a piece of their chocolate ration while they waited for the authorities to come and pick him up. When the prisoner finally left the farm he was still trying to fathom the British war mentality. To be first ignored and then given chocolate was beyond his comprehension."

Unfortunately, Stanley Randall did not name the Rippers employee involved.

Cyril Martin, a commercial traveller who later became manager of the London office

Winifred Martin adding up cash in the wages office in 1923

Archie Ross, retired sawmill manager riding his bicycle in 1969 aged 99 years

Jack Hart with a 'Ripper Woodwork' timber lorry used for hauling large trees

The directors and employees of Rippers Limited at the works in 1922 in four sections

First Section

Second Section

Third Section

Fourth Section

The directors and employees of Rippers Limited at the works in February 1926 in four sections

First Section

Second Section

Third Section

Fourth Section

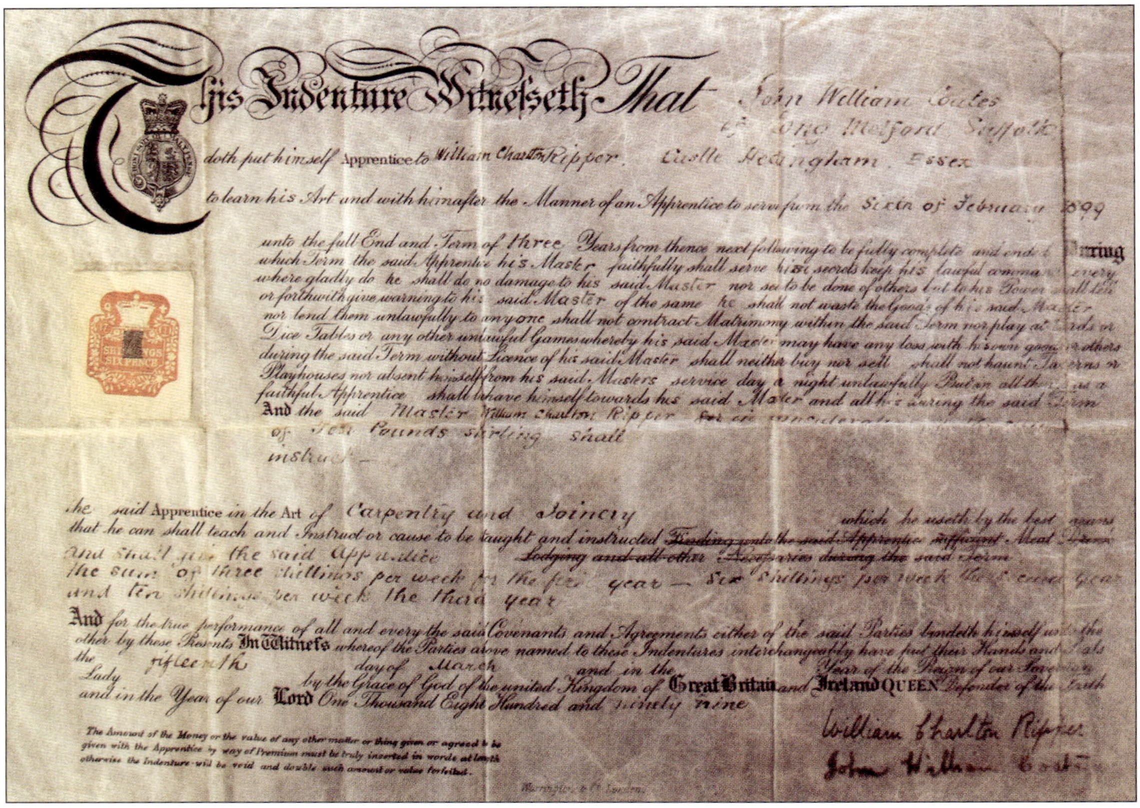

This Indenture Witnesseth That John William Coates of Long Melford Suffolk doth put himself Apprentice to William Charlton Ripper Castle Hedingham Essex to learn his Art and with him after the Manner of an Apprentice to serve from the Sixth of February 1899 unto the full End and Term of three Years from thence next following to be fully complete and ended During which Term the said Apprentice his Master faithfully shall serve his secrets keep his lawful commands everywhere gladly do he shall do no damage to his said Master nor see to be done of others but to his Power shall let or forthwith give warning to his said Master of the same he shall not waste the Goods of his said Master nor lend them unlawfully to any one shall not contract Matrimony within the said Term nor play at Cards or Dice Tables or any other unlawful Games whereby his said Master may have any loss with his own goods or others during the said Term without Licence of his said Master shall neither buy nor sell shall not haunt Taverns or Playhouses nor absent himself from his said Masters service day or night unlawfully But in all things as a faithful Apprentice shall behave himself towards his said Master and all his during the said Term And the said Master William Charlton Ripper for in consideration [illegible] of Ten Pounds sterling shall instruct the said Apprentice in the Art of Carpentry and Joinery which he useth by the best means that he can shall teach and Instruct or cause to be taught and instructed ~~Finding unto the said Apprentice sufficient Meat Drink Lodging and all other Necessaries during the said Term~~ And shall pay the said Apprentice the sum of three shillings per week for the first year — Six shillings per week the second year and ten shillings per week the third year

And for the true performance of all and every the said Covenants and Agreements either of the said Parties bindeth himself unto the other by these Presents In Witness whereof the Parties above named to these Indentures interchangeably have put their Hands and Seals the fifteenth day of March and in the [illegible] Year of the Reign of our Sovereign Lady [illegible] by the Grace of God of the united Kingdom of Great Britain and Ireland QUEEN Defender of the Faith and in the Year of our Lord One Thousand Eight Hundred and ninety nine

William Charlton Ripper
John William Coates

The Amount of the Money or the value of any other matter or thing given or agreed to be given with the Apprentice by way of Premium must be truly inserted in words at length otherwise the Indenture will be void and double such amount or value forfeited.

Apprenticeship indenture of John (Jack) Coates to William Charlton Ripper dated 15th March 1899. This was for a three year apprenticeship for carpentry and joinery commencing 6th February 1899. Jack Coates was paid three shillings a week for the first year, six shillings for the second year and ten shillings for the third year. Fifty years later he was included in the following photograph.

Long serving employees in front of the main entrance to the canteen in 1949
Left to right, back row: Jack Coates, B. Drury, William Calver, Alec Yerbury and E. Cox
Front row: Charles Drury, Percy Harris and J. Springett

Long serving employees, left to right: Jim Redgewell (carpenter and later an engineer), Bill Theobald, Dick Hunwick (manager) and R. Underwood

William ('Buller') Drury in the timber yard 1930s

Cyril Smith and Alf Eves sitting on planks "in stick" in the timber yard in 1932

Timber yard personnel in 1937
Left to right: Mr. Twitchett, Bill Hazelwood, Tom Mourne, Fred Noble, Bert Miller, Frank Happe, Bill Ditton, Bill Mansfield, Capt. Peachy, Jim Drury and Walter Honeywood. On 15th May 1940 Walter Honeywood was engaged measuring timber on railway trucks in Rippers sidings when he fell from a truck and sustained serious injury. He was taken to Essex County Hospital at Colchester where he died the following evening. At the inquest held on 20th May a verdict of accidental death was returned. He was 44 years old and had been employed by Rippers as a labourer for fifteen years.

John Moles and Stephen Ripper in 1974
In the background is the extended Cutting Out Department, Sawmill Gantry and new Maltings

Stair case assembly in Stair Shop in "S" Mill Workshop c1958
Left to right: Fred Lewis, Peter Cracknell, Allan Dowsett and Maurice Wiseman

Stair case assembly
Left to right: Kathy Stewart, Derek Bunton and Mick Brown

Four fitters moving and fitting a machine, two unknown, Ben Cox standing on right and Jock McCulloch kneeling in front

A staff outing to Great Yarmouth during the early 1970s
Left to right: Jim Ripper, Eric Symonds, Mac Smith, Eric Judd and Monty Boreham

Chapter 18

Work and Play

This chapter features a miscellany of information relating to Rippers and its employees, including numbers of staff, wages, advertisements and social events.

Work

The number of employees at Rippers fluctuated over the years but unfortunately figures are not available for every year. However the following is a selection for a few years:

1896	12
1899	38
1900	48
1901	75
1909	85
1922	207
1926	550
1931	About 500
1933	About 600
1959	696 including 110 staff
1960	639 including 110 staff
1961	655 including 115 staff
1962	636 including 115 staff
1963	676 including 115 staff
1964	668 including 120 staff
1965	684 including 120 staff
1966	653 including 120 staff
1967	597 including 120 staff
1968	586 including 130 staff
1969	563 including 130 staff
1970	600 including 135 staff
1971	607 including 135 staff
1972	640 including 140 staff
1973	627 including 120 staff

In July 1973 Rippers was taken over by Bowater and the following year saw a significant reduction in the number of employees.

1974	451 including 111 staff
2009	110 employed by Premdor upon closure

On 1st October 1907 a 'Lock Out' took place when men who arrived late for work were locked out. A photograph of these men was taken at the main entrance to the works at the side of the workmen's cottages in Station Road. Approximately 80 men were employed at the time of which 60 were locked out, which represented about three quarters of the workforce. Following this action, workmen arrived on time for work in future.

During the First World War, many young employees served King and Country and therefore older men were employed together with women for the first time. Following the end of the First World War there was difficulty finding enough work for employees and short time was introduced to avoid as much unemployment as possible but overtime was worked whenever there was sufficient work to make up the loss.

'Lock Out' 1907
Men in the photograph include: Ted Beadle, Lewis Boorer, Frank Boreham, Bertie Corder, Ted Corder, Ernie Gepp, Billie Letch, William Letch, George Ruffle, George Springett, Jim Springett, Fred Toswell and Alfred Underwood

John Fuller checking time cards at the clocking in and out machine for the yard labour force in 1929. One of the 'huts' is on the left.

During the Second World War, women were again employed in many departments to help the war effort. The workforce increased to a reputed one thousand employees. Following VJ Day there was a gradual return of ex-service personnel and normal work was resumed.

Wages

The following is an example of the wages paid to the Ripper Brothers and their workmen for the week ending 18th January 1896.

Name	Hours worked	Hourly rate	Weekly Pay £.	S.	d.
E. J. T. Ripper (Ted)	71	7d	2	1	5
H. T. Ripper (Tucker)	68½	7d	1	19	11½
W. C. Ripper (Charlton)	48½	7d	1	8	3½
J. Clark	52	5½d	1	3	10
W. Smith	51½	5d	1	1	5½
J. Ridgewell	60	4d	1	0	0
A. Westrop	53½	2½d		11	2
W. Shelly	49½	5d	1	0	7
H. Jaggard	49½	3d		12	4
W. Everitt	49½	3d		12	4
B. Staines	31½	2½d		6	6½
Total			11	18	0½

In 1926 the hourly rate for craftsmen was 1s 2½d, labourers 10d and the boy apprentices earned 2d an hour.

Examples of craftsmen and labourers' wages and increases they received between 1945 and 1955.

Date		Increase	Old Wage		New Wage
1945	craftsmen	1d	1/11d	to	2/0d
	labourers	¾ d	1/6½d	to	1/7¼d
1947	craftsmen	3d	2/5d	to	2/8d
	labourers	2½d	1/11¼d	to	2/1¾d
	female (craftswomen)	2d	1/9d	to	1/11d
	female (labourers)	1½d	1/5½d	to	1/7d
1949	craftsmen	½d	2/8½d	to	2/9d
	labourers	½d	2/2d	to	2/2½d
	females	½d	1/11½d	to	2/0d
1951	craftsmen	2½d	2/10½d	to	3/1d
	labourers	2½d	2/5d	to	2/7½d
1953	craftsmen	2d	3/4d	to	3/6d
	labourers	2d	2/10½d	to	3/0½d
1955	craftsmen	½d	3/8½d	to	3/9d
	labourers	½d	3/3d	to	3/3½d

Newspaper reports and miscellany

Chelmsford Chronicle, Friday 19th March 1909

'A meeting in support of the Territorial Army was held at the Bell Hotel Assembly Room, Castle Hedingham. Mr. Ripper, the proprietor of the joinery works in Hedingham told him (Mr. Taylor presiding), that his firm would put no obstacle in the way of his men joining the Territorial Army'.

Chelmsford Chronicle, Friday 22 March 1918
"Bricklayers, for urgent Government work, good money; long job. Ripper Saw Mills, Castle Hedingham."

Praising work done by apprentices. On the 22nd November 1949, W.J. Jay (Bill) sent the following memo to Stephen Ripper, Estimating Department.
"Re: Mr. D.L. Bloom, Builder,
5 St. John's Road, Ipswich, Suffolk
<u>RE: Oak Gates.</u>
With reference to the oak gates recently supplied to the above, you will be interested to know that Mr. Bloom was highly delighted with the general construction and finish of these gates. I mentioned that they were made by our young apprentices which more than ever pleased him, as a result he ordered a further 12 gates with the remark that perhaps he would again give them these to make. Please pass this on to Mr. Finch as it is a pleasure to pass on compliments so often given for the high standard which we maintain in the Ipswich district".

Newspaper advertisements for school leavers, apprentices and staff vacancies.
Chelmsford Chronicle, Friday 25th February 1938 *"Wages Clerk (female) age 25 to 30 required immediately; permanent position for suitable applicant with experience of modern wages methods. Write stating age, experience and salary required to Accountant, Rippers Ltd., Castle Hedingham".*

Chelmsford Chronicle, Friday 2 August 1946
"Rippers Ltd., Castle Hedingham, have vacancies for Female Operatives; light, interesting work; good canteen and rest room; hours 44 per week, starting at 1s 3d per hour, rising to 1s 9d after 3 months training. Applicants must be not less than 17 years of age, and must be willing to work an additional 4 hours overtime when necessary, for which time and a quarter will be paid. There are also a few vacancies for part-time work".

In the 1960s there were plenty of opportunities for apprentices at Rippers, as the following article shows: *"Opportunities exist for boys leaving school to serve apprenticeships at Rippers Ltd., Joinery and Cabinet Manufacturers, with a view to becoming either joiners or wood cutting machinists. The works employs approximately 600 people and have every facility, including a large canteen and a surgery with a nurse in attendance. A boy upon joining the company undergoes a trial period, after which, if satisfactory, he serves a five year apprenticeship, during which he is required to attend Technical College for one day each week in order to acquire further knowledge. A wide range of wood products is manufactured at Castle Hedingham. These products include stock size windows and door frames, staircases and kitchen fittings for general house building, in addition to specialist-made joinery such as bank and office fittings; also radio and television cabinets, furniture and the like. A worth-while future is assured for the boy by virtue of the fact that he has every chance to develop into a first-class tradesman".* (Obviously before equal opportunities for boys and girls)!

Essex County Standard and Halstead Gazette February 1970
"Rippers Ltd., Castle Hedingham urgently require Females for joinery assembly. At age 19 yrs. or over the starting rate is £14 6s 8d rising to £15 16s 8d after 6 months for a 40 hr. 5 day week. For girls aged 16, 17 and 18 yrs. the rates are 3/4½d, 5/- and 6/- per hr. respectively. Good working conditions and canteen facilities available. The Personnel Office will be open for interviews until 9 p.m. on Tuesdays and Thursdays for the next two weeks".

Essex County Standard and Halstead Gazette September 18 1970
"Urgently required for our Maintenance Department Centre, Lathe Turner and Fitter who should be able to service, maintain and repair woodworking machinery, preferably with previous experience in the woodworking trade. Also a Pipe Fitter with experience of steam and air lines, compressed air tools, spray painting gear and oil fired heating systems. Hours from 7.30 a.m. to 12.30 p.m. and 1.30 p.m. to 4.30 p.m. for a 40-hour 5-day week. Wages linked to productivity. Good canteen facilities available. Please apply to Personnel Services Manager, Rippers Ltd".

Essex County Standard and Halstead Gazette, September 24th 1971
"Rippers Ltd., require a Secretary for the sales director. Previous experience essential and must be able to work on own initiative. Please apply to the Personnel Manager, Rippers Ltd".

1972 –*"Rippers Manufacturers of Standard and Special Windows, Staircases and Kitchen Units offer 4-year Apprenticeships to 16-year-old school leavers who would like to become Joiners or Woodworking Machinists. First-class tuition given and day release allowed to Braintree and Colchester Technical Colleges respectively. Call or write for full details Rippers Limited".*

Circa 1971/2. *"Wanted Urgently! Rippers of Castle Hedingham, Joinery Manufacturers urgently need men and women as: Machinists, Joiners, Female Assemblers, Painters and Sprayers, and Labourers. We have lots of work and have taken steps to make sure that this work load is maintained and expanded in the future. Conditions in our factory are good; canteen serves excellent meals for only 2/-. Come and talk to our Director of Personnel Services, Mr. Jim Ripper. For those of you who can't come during the day, he stays in his office until 9 p.m. every Tuesday and Thursday. His office is located at the main office entrance in Station Road".*

Halstead Gazette, Friday October 4th 1974
"We have a vacancy for a Post girl, preferably a School Leaver. Duties include sorting and distributing internal post, dealing with all outgoing mail, operating and printing machines and the Addressograph. Hours 8.30am to 5.00pm. Excellent Canteen facilities. Please apply to: The Personnel Manager, Rippers Ltd.".

During the early 1970s Michael Ripper, managing director, devised an advertising campaign to encourage people to join the work force at Rippers. Five employees, each from a different department in the factory posed with Michael for a photograph which was taken by the Halstead Gazette. Each employee was paid 10/6d for appearing in the advertisement.

Come and join us!
Left to right: Derek Smith-French polisher, Hazel Shipperley - office, Leslie Pilgrim - carpenter, Michael Ripper - managing director, Bill Edwards - machinist and Dennis Brunner - labourer

Peter West, who was a sports commentator and television personality, opened a new kitchen showroom at the works in 1971. Here home buyers, architects and developers could see two complete kitchen layouts, and also see the interesting range of colours, finishes and sizes available. The showroom was open to the public from Mondays to Fridays 8.30 to 12.30 and 1.30 to 5.00. Visitors were requested to ask for A. Codling or John Marsh who would be pleased to show them round the displays.

Keith Hopkins was Rippers 'pin up boy' in 1973, and his photograph appeared in local newspapers when advertising for employees to join Rippers Limited. Under the headline, "Local Boy Makes Good, and if you live round our way – so can you!" Rippers set about recruiting joiners, painters, labourers, wood machinists, apprentices and girls. Keith had joined Rippers straight from school in 1964 as an apprentice joiner, completed his apprenticeship and started in Production Planning in 1969. He gained 8 certificates covering all aspects of building and joinery, and by 1973 had been promoted to Production Manager.

In April 1973 Keith and three other employees flew out of London Airport to visit the Alco Company at Goslar, near Hanover, West Germany. The one week trip was for the men to train in the manufacture of Alco Ripper timber and aluminium windows.

Keith Hopkins, Paul Cook, Stuart Boreham and Graham Hume setting out on their training trip to the Alco Company

Play

On Saturday 11th February 1899 the Essex County Standard stated that employees of Ripper's Steam Joinery Works, numbering 34, were entertained to supper in the British Schoolroom. Several Ripper family members were present and included Edward and Louisa, Tucker and Edith, Ted and Lizzie and Charlton, as well as Mrs Alice Drury and Miss E. Amey. After supper 'tobacco' was distributed and an informal meeting was held. This was followed by some first rate entertainment; The Reverend George Monson gave a reading 'Turning Points', George Springett recited 'The Twins' and the Ripper gentlemen contributed to the entertainment with some songs. Lizzie Ripper sang 'Molly Darling', Mr. J. Clark 'Cockles and Mussels', Mr. A. Underwood 'Hearts of Oak' and Mr. A. Mulley 'Jim, the Carter's Lad'. Edward and Tucker Ripper played their violins, Charlton his flute and Ted the cello. Mr. J. Stammers on the bassoon and Edith Ripper on the piano. At the end of the evening George Springett proposed a vote of thanks to the ladies for making the arrangements. The evening ended with the singing of the 'National Anthem' and 'Auld Lang Syne'.

In July 1899 it was reported that the employees of Ripper's Joinery Works had their annual excursion on Saturday 1st July to Yarmouth, Norfolk. It was an early start for the workers who joined the Halstead excursion train to Yarmouth because they arrived in the seaside town at 8am! The morning was spent at leisure with everyone meeting at 'Foulshams' (Restaurant) for "Dinner". The return journey commenced at 7.50 pm and ended at midnight. In 1900 the employee's excursion took them to London for the day.

The Essex Chronicle reported on Friday 8th March 1901: *"Upwards of 70 employees of the Joinery Works of Mr. William (Charlton) Ripper partook of Dinner in the British Schoolroom on Friday 1st July. A capital repast was served by Mrs. Tucker Ripper. Several happy speeches, full of good feeling, were afterwards made by the employer and employed"*.

1935 saw plenty of celebrations to mark the Royal Silver Jubilee. One evening men and youths took part in various sports at Hedingham Castle, which saw Rippers tug of war team beat A. T. Mortimer's grocers and drapers shop team.

During 'The Hedinghams War Weapons Week' held in July 1941 one of the events included 'a mile of pennies'. Pennies were to be laid, starting at both Sible and Castle Hedingham Post Offices, meeting at Ripper's Works. With numerous other events taking part during the week it was hoped that £15,000 would be raised.

In 1944 a 'mock' auction in connection with the 'Salute the Soldier' week was held at Rippers Canteen and the sum of £6,897 was raised.

During the 1960s a cricket match was held annually at the cricket ground, Castle Hedingham between the 'Works' and the 'Reps'. Lunch for the players was served in Rippers Canteen. The sight screen at the ground was made at the works during the 1940s, at the request of Harry Ripper, who was a member of the Cricket Club Committee.

In the early 1970s over 200 hundred employees and guests enjoyed a dinner dance hosted by Rippers Limited at the Village Hall. The Tony Gilbert Trio and the Countrystyle band provided the music for the event. One lucky guest won a deep freeze; a raffle prize provided by the firm.

During May 1970, apprentice joiner, Stephen Billings of Halstead joined the 300 ton sail training schooner, Sir Winston Churchill at Hull, to take part as a trainee in an 800 mile cruise, which ended a fortnight later at Dover.

Along with 30 cadets, many of whom had never been to sea, Stephen set about learning the ropes and when they sailed to Amsterdam three days later, Stephen worked as bo'sun's mate. Unfortunately when they set sail for Bruges on the return journey they encountered a gale, and Stephen who was not feeling at all well, was assigned to assist the chef! They returned to Dover via Boulogne and the Isle of Wight. This was the first time that Rippers had sponsored a trainee to sail on the ship, and they were confident that it would become an annual event.

Stephen Billings

The sailing schooner Sir Winston Churchill

Jim and Stephen Ripper were both very involved with the Hedingham carnival for a number of years and Rippers, Cousins and Tanners lorries were used for the floats. Other members of the Ripper family were also involved with the carnival, and when Linda Crichton with Jacqueline Pilgrim and Eileen Vigar, were chosen as carnival queen and attendants, Jane Ripper, Michael's wife, was one of the judges, while Michael presented each of the winners with a bouquet.

Rippers tug of war team early 1950's
Left to right back row: Maurice Halls, Jack Hart, Tom Fraser, Sparky Cornell and Jim Westrop
Front row: Cecil Ruffle, Wilfred Collar, George Hedges and Alec Tait

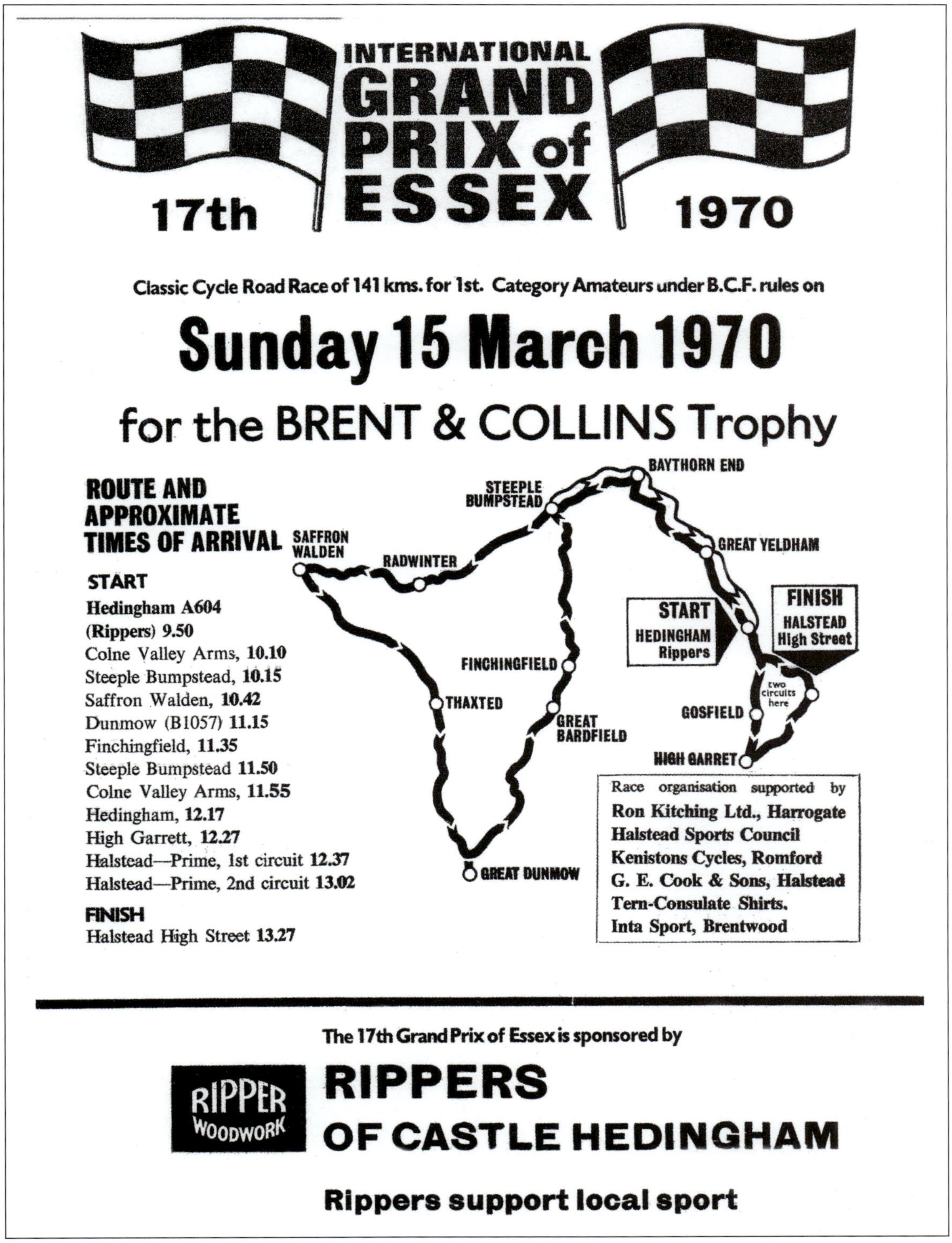

The 17th Grand Prix of Essex cycle race was sponsored by Rippers Limited

A field of nearly sixty top class cyclists started off from outside Rippers and followed a route around North Essex finishing in Halstead High Street. The race was won by Phil Carnall, of Kirkby Cycling Club who completed the course in 28 minutes and 28 seconds. He was presented with the trophy by Christine Fenner, an employee of Rippers.

Directors of Rippers and Evans Bellhouse during the Second World War
Left to right: Dennis Ripper, Harry Ripper, Stanley Finch, Kenneth Ripper, Donald Ripper and Ashley Ripper

Long serving employees at Rippers Limited photographed about 1949
Back row left to right: Alfred Ambrose, Herbert Partridge, Harry Scott, Harry Cansell, Sid Garwood, Tucker Ripper, Ernest Chatten, Stanley Ambrose, Albert Turner and Herbert Schooling
Front row: Ernest Gepp, Ernie Farrant, George Howard, Lewis Boorer, Frank Westrop, Edward Beadle, Albert Amey, Alec Yerbury and William Beadle

Chapter 19

Long Service and Retirement Awards

Long service awards were presented to the following employees in 1976 and 1977

Long service awards were presented to the following employees in December 1976

Key to numbers:

1.	L. Broyd	2.	G. Faiers	3.	C. Reeve
4.	E. Judd	5.	E. Drury	6.	A. Coe
7.	E. Boreham	8.	M. Boreham	9.	H. G. Cansell
10.	G. Hilsden	11.	W. Ambrose	12.	M. Wiseman
13.	C. Boorer	14.	?	15.	B. Ruffle
16.	C. Smith	17.	T. Wells	18.	C. Rippingale
19.	B. Edwards	20.	H. Springett	21.	J. Reeve

22. P. Pannell	23. A. King	24. ?
25 B. Wilding	26. S. Letch	27. E. Corder
28. A. Stockdale	29. J. Jarman	30. D. Beadle
31. L. Turner	32. W. Alliston	33. D. Sparke
34. A. Dowsett	35. R. Coe	36. H. Jay
37. B. Bickers		

Those who received gold watches were:
38 years: Ernest Ashton.
40 years: Maurice Borehan, Alfred Debenham, Gordon Faiers, Maurice Wiseman. William Wilding.
41 years: Cyril Reeve, Dennis Sparke.
42 years: William Alliston, William Ambrose, Leonard Broyd, Alfred Coe, Harry Springett, Albert Stockdale, Leslie Turner.
43 years: Edward Corder, Alan Dowsett, William Ruffle.
44 years: Stanley Letch.
45 years: Frederick Cobbold, Douglas Hasler, Percy Pannell.
46 years: Leonard Cansell, William Edwards, Jack Reeve, Charles Rippingale, Cyril Smith, Walter Smith, Thomas Wells.
47 years: Joseph Carder.
48 years: Albert Cross, Harry Jay
49 years: Albert Bickers, Ernest Boreham, George Hilsden, William Wilkin.
50 years: Cecil Boorer, George Cansell, John Jarman.

Long service awards were presented to the following employees in December 1977

All smiles after the presentations.

Key to numbers:

1. Reginald Brian Staines
2. John Marsh
3. L. C. Ellis.
4. R. Cocks.
5. Cecil E. Chatten.
6. R. D. Laver.
7. Harold Hume.
8. F. R. Earey.
9. A. Neville Beckwith.
10. A. C. Sutton.
11. M. B. Halls
12. D. F. Baggaley.
13. R. E. Harper.
14. Gordon Faiers.
15. ?
16. D. R. Beadle.
17. G. A. J. Nicholls.
18. V. L. Clarke.
19. Ken Abbott.
20. Peter Cracknell.
21. Alec Tait.
22. William R. Slee.
23. C. R. Everitt.
24. L. G. Pilgrim.
25. Ben Cox.
26. J. W. Smith.
27. Frank Ralph Dowsett.
28. C. R. Everitt.
29. D. M. McCulloch.
30. J. Boreham.
31. Derek Pratt.
32. Aubrey W. K. Ince.
33. P. Cook.
34. D. J. Nichols.
35. ?
36. H. Hewitt.
37. G. F. Brown.
38. J. T. Andrews.
39. S. D. Pilgrim.
40. C. Smith.
41. ?
42. Miss Ruby F Gepp.
43. J. H. Reynolds
44. Maurice Nash.
45. K. R. Fellows
46. Mrs. K. F. Ruggles.
47. L. G. Hart
48. Mrs. K. Stephniewska.
49. H. S. G. Williams.
50. ?
51. S. Stephniewska.
52. C. Williams.
53. C. J. Westrop.
54. Mrs. M. J. Brooks.
55. R. C. Raymond.
56. C. E. Williams.
57. Miss Olive Raymond.
58. Mrs. D. M. Tracey.
59. P. Cocks.
60. R. Pilgrim.
61. F. Wells.
62. Stan Ellis.
63. Jim McAleese.
64. S. M. Hale.
65. B. G. Duce.
66. ?
67. Mrs E. Muncey.
68. Mrs. M. C. Black.

Those who received gold watches were:
25 years: K. Abbott, P. P. M. Blackwell, D. V. Briner, R. R. Everitt, J. W. Kendall, L. G. Hart.
26 years: J. T. Andrews, J. Boreham, C. E. Chatten, M. B. Halls, T. Ross, C. J. Westrop, Mrs. C. Black.
27 years: C. L. Coe, P. Cock, D. J. Mickley, W. R. Slee, W. T. Smith, R. B. Staines, K. Stepniewska, Mrs. D. M. Tracey.
28 years: G. F. Brown, D. A. C. Diss, H. F. Moules, D. W. S. Pratt, R. C. Raymond, Miss. O. Raymond,
29 years: A. N. Beckwith, G. R. Clarke, A. B. Cox, F. R. Dowsett, S. H. Hale, T. Hussey, D. M. McCulloch
29 years: J. H. Twiggins, S. Stepniewska.
30 years: S. Ellis, C. R. Everitt, H. Hewitt, H. G. Hume, R. D. A. Laver, A. C. Sutton, J. McAleese.
31 years: V. L. Clarke, H. A. Fellows, G. A. J. Nicholls, S. D. Pilgrim, A. Tait.
32 years: P. W. Cook, B. G. Duce, D. J. Nichols, A. H. Pilgrim, Mrs. M. J. Brooks, J. Marsh.
33 years: P. Cracknell, Mrs. K. F. Ruggles.
34 years: L. G. Pilgrim.
35 years: W. W. Smith, M. B. Nash, H. S. G. Williams.
36 years: J. W. Smith, P. Smith.
37 years: R. E. Harper, B. H. Kendall, C. J. North, R. Cocks, J. H. Reynolds, F. Wells.
38 years: I. C. Johnson.
39 years: D. A. Beadle, A. W. K. Ince.
40 years: D. F. Baggaley, F. A. Earey, L. C. Ellis, R. C. Hardy, P. Rayner, Miss. R. F. Gepp, Mrs. I. E. Muncey.
44 years: V. A. Everitt.

Retirements

In January 1970 William Jay (Billy), who was one of the first 'reps' to take to the road retired from Rippers after travelling about 1½ million miles while working for the company; for the first 7 years he travelled around East Anglia visiting prospective clients on a motorcycle!

Billy Jay (right) receives his gold watch from Norman Ripper, a director of the company

During the Second World War when house building was at a stand-still Billy travelled around the country buying timber for the company. A native of Castle Hedingham he had played football, cricket and tennis for the village teams and was the first to play on the new Castle Hedingham tennis courts. He was also a member of the Hedingham Choral Society. For the last 38 years

Billy lived in Chelmsford and was a keen supporter of Chelmsford Football Club and a member of the Essex County Cricket Club. He was also a member of the Chelmsford Orpheus Choir and a chorister and deacon of the London Road Congregational Church.

A luncheon party was held in London to mark Billy's retirement after 52 years service. He received a gold watch from the company and a reproduction of a Constable painting from his fellow representatives which was presented to him by Jim McAleese. Several directors of Rippers were present including, Norman, Jim, Stephen and Michael Ripper, as well as John Moles and many representatives.

In 1970 two joiners, Percy Ralph Bareham of Sible Hedingham, known as Ralph and Clifford Potter of Glemsford, Suffolk retired after more than forty years service with the company. They were both presented with watches by Michael Ripper, the managing director.

Ralph Bareham receiving his watch from Michael Ripper

Ralph Bareham lived in a Rippers built house, at 156 Swan Street. He played football for Hedinghams United and was a member of the local Tennis Club. A native of Castle Hedingham, he sang in the Congregational Church choir and was choir master at the Baptist Chapel for twenty years. He played with the old Hedingham Brass Band and the Legion Band, as leading cornet and assistant bandmaster.

Clifford Potter receiving his watch from Michael Ripper

Clifford Potter who was a native of Long Melford played football for the local village team and was a member of the cricket club. After he stopped playing cricket Clifford maintained his interest in the sport as he took on the role of umpiring until 1969. He was also a member of Long Melford choir and a keen gardener.

Archie Wright retired at the end of July 1970 in his 50th year with Rippers. He was born in Castle Hedingham in 1905 and completed a joinery apprenticeship after starting with Rippers in 1921. Before the Second World War, Archie played cricket for the Castle Hedingham village team.

Archie Wright (right) receiving his gold watch from Michael Ripper

Two more employees retired in 1970, Leonard Arthur John Guilding, known as Jack and Len Day who were presented with Omega watches by Michael Ripper. Jack Guilding who lived in Castle Hedingham retired after working in the timber yard. During the Second World War Jack was a member of the Observer Corps at the Castle Hedingham Post.

Len Day was a well known figure at Rippers as he was on the maintenance staff and had been a member of the works fire brigade during the war. Len later joined the Hedingham Fire Brigade and retired on his 65th birthday. He was the landlord of The Oak Public House, High Street, Great Yeldham.

Jack Guilding who retired after 44 years with the company

Len Day (right) receives his watch from Michael Ripper

Robert Ross retired after working for Rippers for nearly 50 years. He received a gold watch from the company and a golf trolley and bag from his colleagues. Alma Hardy retired in 1971 and received a gold watch from Rippers and a teasmade from the staff, presented by Tom Wells of "D" department.

Robert Ross (left) being presented with a gold watch by Michael Ripper

Alma Hardy (right) receiving a teasmade from Tom Wells

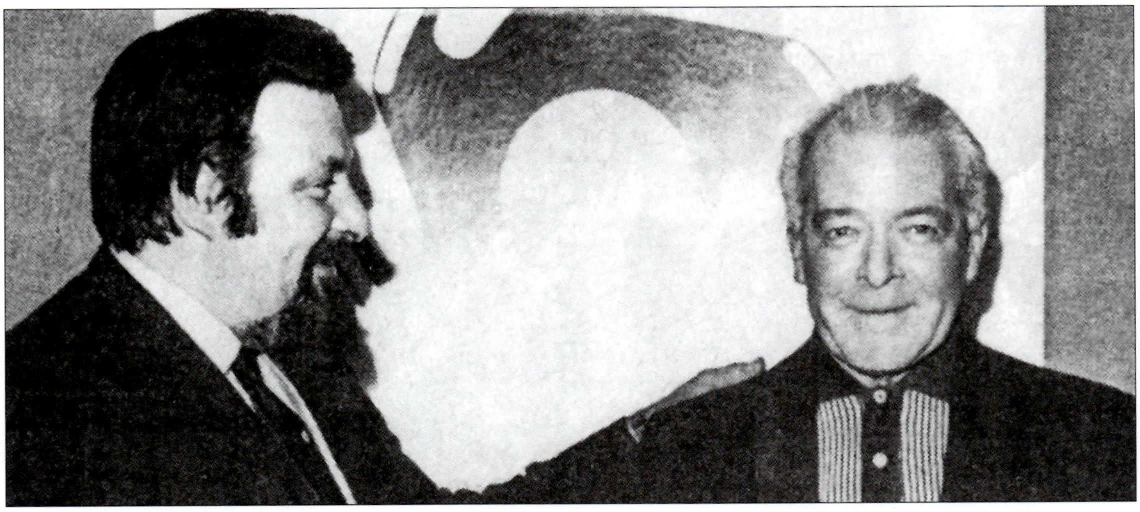

Charlie Berry receiving his cheque from Michael Ripper in February 1974 having worked for the company for 33 years

Jim Ripper (right) receives his retirement gifts from Maurice Nash, company secretary

Jim Ripper the personnel director retired in September 1974 having joined the company in 1939. Jim received a print of John Constable's "Haywain" and a silver plated tankard from the staff.

Other employees known to have received retirement presentations from 1970:

September 1970, after 51 years with Rippers, Oscar Robert Brett (Charlie) had worked for Rippers for 51 years and received a gold watch from Michael Ripper and a clock from his workmates when he retired. The clock was presented to Charlie by Doug Smith.

February 1974, Alfie Deal of Alexandra Road, retired after 27 years and was presented with a cheque by Eric Judd, the production manager.

September 1974, Dick Read of Yeldham Road, completed 48 years service with the company when he retired and was also presented with a cheque from Eric Judd.

September 1974, Bill Turner of Alderford Street, completed 26 years service as a company car driver, having joined Rippers in 1948. He was presented with a cheque by Michael Ripper.

January 1980, after 50 years with the company Len Cansell of Alexandra Road, retired and received a cheque from Malcolm Whitton, the personnel executive of Bowater Ripper Limited. (Len had previously received a gold watch, at the long service award presentations in 1976)

1992. Maurice Nash of Castle Hedingham retired after more than fifty years service which was spent at Rippers and successor companies. His colleagues held a surprise party and Maurice was presented with a garden chair, specially made for him in the factory, a decanter, sherry glasses and wine.

Long service awards 1998. Back row, left to right: Tony Andrews, Colin Westrop and Alan Sibley. Front row: Sid Berry, Derek Pratt and Dick Raymond. After forty years service, the above gentlemen amassed a total of two hundred and seventy years in the joinery business and almost half of that time was with Rippers. When they left, the men worked for Premdor Crosby.

Chapter 20

Unions and Friendly Societies

The Workers Union

Some labourers employed by Rippers were members of The Workers Union during the 1910s.

Amalgamated Society of Woodworkers

A number of woodworkers were members of The Amalgamated Society of Carpenters and Joiners, which was established in 1860 and continued until the end of 1920. In 1917 a difference arose between Rippers and members of both the Unions. The Unions on behalf of the employees applied for an advance in wages. The issue was heard before Charles Doughty, sitting at Colchester on 12th September 1917, as a single Arbitrator under the provisions of the Munitions of War Acts 1915 and 1917. Tucker Ripper appeared on behalf of his company. The application on behalf of the joiners and machinists was for an advance of 1d per hour and on behalf of the labourers for 2d per hour. The Award made on 14th September 1917 was for an advance of 1d per hour for joiners and machinists as war wages and 1d per hour for labourers, also as war wages. It was further awarded that no able bodied man over 18 years of age be paid less than 5d per hour plus the war wage of 1d an hour and the war bonus of 3/6d a week making 31/6d for a week of 56 hours. The Award was to be paid from 16th July 1917.

The Amalgamated Society of Woodworkers (ASW) was established on 1st January 1921 when it incorporated the following:
General Union of Carpenters and Joiners, established 1827
Amalgamated Union of Cabinetmakers, established 1833
Amalgamated Society of Carpenters and Joiners, established 1860
Associated Carpenters and Joiners of Scotland, established 1861
The ASW later incorporated the Amalgamated Society of Painters and Decorators. The primary object of the ASW was the raising of the status of the artisans engaged in the trades of carpenters, joiners, cabinetmakers, painters and decorators and generally to improve the social conditions under which they worked.

Many employees of Rippers were members of the Castle Hedingham branch of the ASW. The earliest known member was Stanley Underwood who was a woodworker and joined the predecessor of the ASW on 19th July 1916. In 1919, following the end of the First World War three more members joined namely William Dan Corder (1886-1970), Reginald Rayner (1903-1982) and Frank Woodcock (1883-1981). Among the later branch secretaries were Frank Woodcock, W. G. Ellis, Ronald Mallott and Bill Lynch.

In 1969 William Corder completed fifty years as a member of the ASW. As a veteran trade unionist he was presented with his fifty-year membership badge and a cheque at a special evening at the White Horse Inn, Church Street, Sible Hedingham on 22nd October 1969. Bill Corder was apprenticed as a carpenter and joiner on 16th June 1902 to Harry Gooch, a joiner and builder in Swan Street, Sible Hedingham. He completed his apprenticeship on 16th June 1906 and later joined Rippers where he worked until April 1959, with the exception of army service during the First World War. He did not retire from Rippers until he was seventy-two.

Reginald Rayner was employed for fifty-three years having started work at Rippers on 21st May 1919 at the age of sixteen. At one time he lived in a Ripper's house at 10 Yeldham Road. Frank Woodcock started at Rippers on 16th July 1919 at the age of thirty-five. He lived in one of Ripper's huts (a wooden bungalow) and later moved into another Ripper's house at 15 Brook Terrace. He was employed by the company for thirty-eight years, initially as a joiner and later in the Setting Out Department. He was labour officer for the ASW for thirteen years and also secretary for seventeen years. Reginald and Frank were presented with fifty-year membership badges and cheques in 1969.

The presentation was made by Thomas Vale, president of the local branch of the ASW. Thomas joined Rippers and the ASW in December 1920 at the age of twenty-eight, following service in the First World War and completed his own fifty-year membership in 1970.

The ASW eventually became the Union of Construction, Allied Trades and Technicians (UCAT) and the Castle Hedingham branch secretary was John Blanden who lived at 3 Parkfields, Sible Hedingham.

William Corder (left) being presented with his fifty-year badge by Thomas Vale in October 1969

From 1969 Presentation Evenings were held at the White Horse Inn until the early 1980s. Presentations were made by the Regional Council Officers of fifty-year badges, tankards and free cards. Whilst later presentations were made during the Bowater Ripper era, all recipients had been employed by Rippers Limited for many years prior to the takeover.

The 1976 Presentation
Left to right: Les Ambrose, George Cansell, Dave Hardy and Bernard Abraham

George Harry Cansell (1911-1988) joined Rippers and the ASW on 10th November 1926 aged just fifteen years. He appears on the 1926 photograph of the employees at the extreme left of the front row. His brother Leonard William Cansell (1915-1981) completed fifty years with Rippers working from 1930 to 1980, including war service with the Royal Engineers. They were sons of Harry Cansell (1885-1950) who is in the 1949 photograph of Tucker Ripper with the long standing employees. The collective service of these three members of the Cansell family was one hundred and fifty years.

The Transport and General Workers Union

Employees of Rippers and The Sible Hedingham Red Brick Company Limited, were members of the Castle Hedingham Branch of the Transport and General Workers Union. Ripper's employees included Harry Cansell, F. King and E. Wilding and brick company employee, Albert Redgewell, who fired the kilns from 1938 to 1953.

Society of Woodcutting Machinists Union

Some employees were members of the Society of Woodcutting Machinists Union such as A. Ambrose, D. Beadle, H. G. Britton, C. Reeve and V. H. Smith.

The Hedingham Joinery Works Benefit Society

The Hedingham Joinery Works Benefit Society consisted of all the male employees of Rippers, who appointed their own officers with the exception of the treasurer and secretary. Its object was to raise funds by subscription for rendering assistance to members who were sick and unable to follow their employment and also benefits for funerals. ' Sick' visitors were appointed to visit sick members and pay their allowance every Saturday before eight in the evening. In 1958 contributions, were deducted from wages at the rate of 1s 3d per week and the sick benefit was

£1 1s 3d for the first eight weeks and 11s 3d for the next eight weeks. For boys under eighteen the rate of subscription and benefit was half that of men. In 1946 the officers were Harry Ripper, treasurer and John Wilkin Porkess, secretary. In 1958 the officers were Ashley Ripper, secretary, Maurice Nash, treasurer and George Anderson, claims secretary.

Loyal Webster Lodge of Oddfellows

A number of Rippers employees were members of the Loyal Webster Lodge of Oddfellows based in Sible Hedingham. Many of them were previously employed in the brickmaking industry and continued as members of the Oddfellows when they were later employed by Rippers. (A detailed history of the Loyal Webster Lodge of Oddfellows is included in the book, 'Our Ancestors were Brickmakers and Potters – A History of the Corder and related families in the clayworking industries', by Adrian Corder-Birch, 2010, pages 139 to 141) Among former brickmakers who were later employed by Rippers and continued their membership with the Oddfellows were Fred Corder, Walter Corder and William Raynham, D.C.M.

Pension and Life Assurance Scheme

In 1948 Rippers Limited entered into a special arrangement with the Legal and General Assurance Society Limited of 188 Fleet Street, London for the benefit of certain employees. These arrangements, which were made by William Heap & Son Limited, incorporated insurance brokers of 78 King Street, Manchester, provided pensions and benefits, which were supplementary to the National Insurance Scheme. The cost was shared between the company and its employees and included male administrative and clerical staff, foremen and managers over 21 and under 60 years of age and female administrative and clerical staff over 25 and under 59 years of age.

Presentation to Ernie Drury (1913-2013) Harry Jay (left) and Clifford Potter (right) in 1979. Ernie, third from the left, joined Rippers and the ASW at the age of 16 years on 25th September 1929

The National Federation of Building Trade Operatives
A. Kibble and R. Paynter.

The Amalgamated Engineering Union
Established in 1920 and in 1948 admitted Horace Reeve as one of its members.

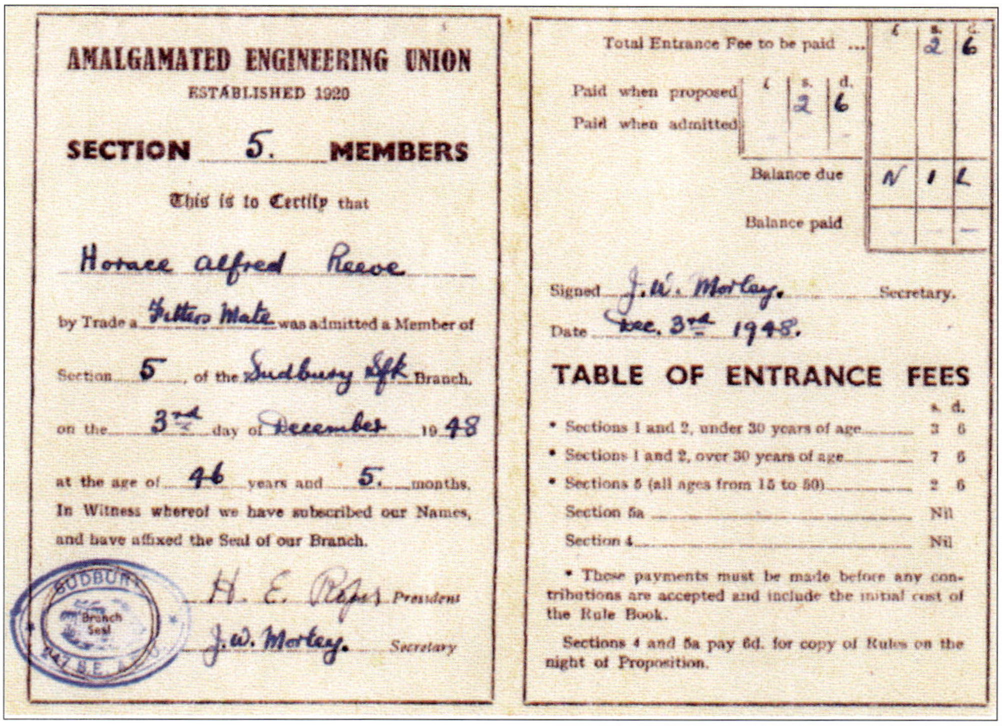
AMALGAMATED ENGINEERING UNION
ESTABLISHED 1920

SECTION 5. MEMBERS

This is to Certify that

Horace alfred Reeve

by Trade a Fitters Mate was admitted a Member of Section 5 of the Sudbury Sfk Branch, on the 3rd day of December 1948 at the age of 46 years and 5. months. In Witness whereof we have subscribed our Names, and have affixed the Seal of our Branch.

H. E. Ripper President

J. W. Morley. Secretary

	£	s.	d.
Total Entrance Fee to be paid ...		2	6
Paid when proposed / Paid when admitted		2	6
Balance due	N	I	L
Balance paid		–	–

Signed J. W. Morley. Secretary.
Date Dec. 3rd 1948.

TABLE OF ENTRANCE FEES

	s.	d.
• Sections 1 and 2, under 30 years of age	3	6
• Sections 1 and 2, over 30 years of age	7	6
• Sections 5 (all ages from 15 to 50)	2	6
Section 5a	Nil	
Section 4	Nil	

• These payments must be made before any contributions are accepted and include the initial cost of the Rule Book.

Sections 4 and 5a pay 6d. for copy of Rules on the night of Proposition.

Horace Reeve's membership card for the Amalgamated Engineering Union

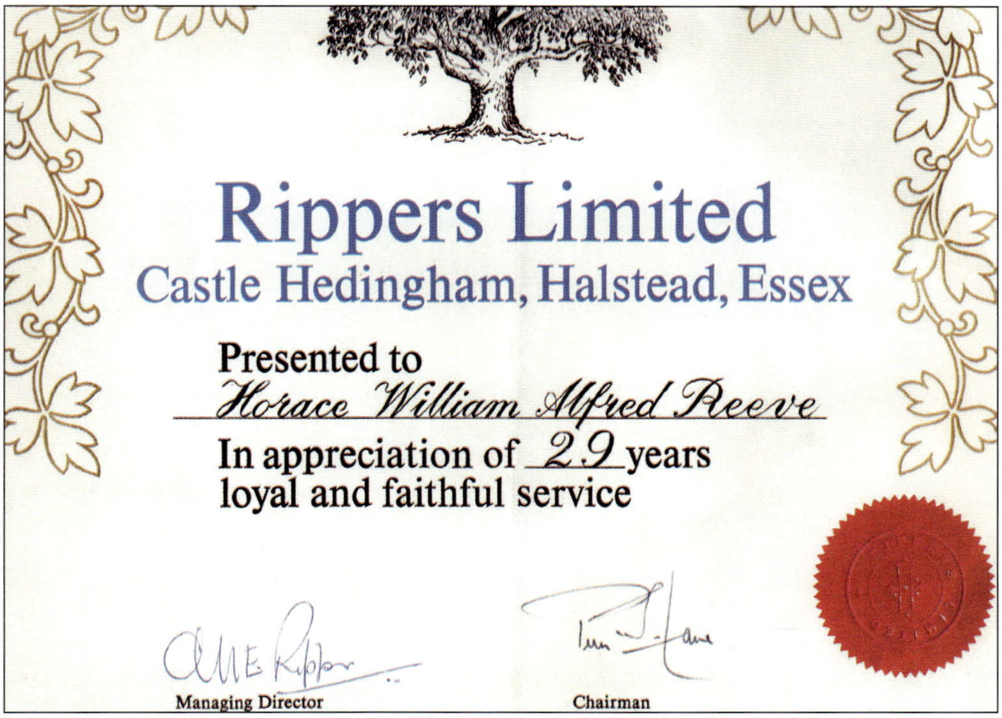
Rippers Limited
Castle Hedingham, Halstead, Essex

Presented to
Horace William Alfred Reeve
In appreciation of 29 years
loyal and faithful service

Managing Director

Chairman

Certificate, which accompanied a gold watch, presented to Horace Reeve in 1971 and signed by Michael Ripper (managing director) and Peter Lane (chairman)

Arthur King's membership certificate for The Amalgamated Society of Millsawyers & Woodcutting Machinists dated 19th October 1918. He worked for Rippers all his working life.

Chapter 21

George Evans & Sons Limited, later Evans Bellhouse Limited

In 1922 Rippers Limited acquired a controlling interest in George Evans & Sons Limited, (which was established in 1837) and Tucker Ripper sent his two younger sons, Donald aged 23 and Dennis aged 21 to Newton Heath, Manchester, where the company was based, to run the business. Tucker also spent two days a week in Manchester and two days in Hedingham; making contacts in London, on his way through. Donald and Dennis were later joined by their cousin Ken and they all remained in the area for the rest of their lives. During the 1920s the company employed about 200 personnel.

In 1928 a complete remodelling of the power plant was undertaken, but unfortunately just before the new gas engines were fitted to the machinery, a fire occurred and the new power plant was completely destroyed. Although the new plant was covered by insurance it was many months before normal work was resumed.

On 1st January 1931 George Evans & Sons Limited took over J. & W. Bellhouse Limited, (which was established in 1792), and the name of the company was changed to Evans Bellhouse Limited. This amalgamation gave the Manchester works the opportunity to widen its range of products. The parent company of John and William Bellhouse was formally liquidated in February 1932. By 1934 Rippers Limited owned all the shares in Evans Bellhouse.

Aerial view of Evans Bellhouse, circa 1950s/1960s

By 1936, £40,000 had been spent by the company on additions, improvements to land, buildings, plant and machinery and for over three years the company had been earning satisfactory profits. On 27th April 1936 Evans Bellhouse Limited was incorporated under the Companies Act 1929 to acquire and take over as a going concern the private company of the same name. The principal objects were timber importers and merchants, box-makers and joinery manufacturers. The executive directors were, Donald, Dennis and Kenneth Ripper and Michael Bellhouse.

The other directors were Tucker, Charlton, Harry and Ashley Ripper, John Wilkin Porkess, senior and Stanley Finch.

On 1st May 1936 Donald Ripper was appointed as managing director for an initial period of six years. The chairman was Tucker Ripper, the company secretary was John Robert Oakley and the registered office was at Newton Heath Saw Mills, Manchester. This was the principal works, situated about three miles from the centre of Manchester. It occupied a site of 9¾ acres and was well equipped with modern machinery and adequate storage and transport facilities. The company also had a factory at City Road, Manchester, which was engaged in the production of crates, cases and boxes for various trades and shaped boards for textile manufacturers. The total employees of the company then exceeded four hundred. The company offered 50,000 6 per cent Cumulative Preference shares of £1 each at 12 shillings per share and 100,000 Ordinary shares of 10 shillings per share in a bid to raise capital.

In 1937 Norman Ripper and John Wilkin Porkess, junior, were appointed as directors. That year the company made a trading profit of £25,802. Operations at Evans Bellhouse included merchanting of all descriptions of English and foreign timber, both wholesale and retail. Sawmilling and planing to the trade; the manufacture of wooden goods for the electrical storage battery trade and the manufacture of all kinds of packing cases.

The three Ripper directors of Evans Bellhouse who relocated to Manchester
Left to right: Kenneth, Donald and Dennis.

In April 1940 Tucker Ripper (chairman) delivered a speech at the fourth annual general meeting of the company. In it he referred to the wartime conditions and the many shipments of timber imports, which were cancelled, especially those from European sources. An exception was timber imports made by the Timber Control branch of the Ministry of Supply, where Evans Bellhouse acted as wharfingers for the Ministry. To overcome the shortage of foreign timber, Evans Bellhouse purchased considerable quantities of home-grown timber. A great deal of work and expense was caused by the provision of A.R.P. protection for all the factories.

A number of staff joined H.M. Forces, as did Michael Bellhouse, a director and manager of the City Road factory. The company was faced with depleted staff and conditions in the house building industry were little short of chaotic. Nevertheless the company remained busy in all departments and sought an increase in staff. Evans Bellhouse made many products to help the war effort. This included the production of aircraft components and battery separators to packing aircraft parts and vehicles ready for transportation to the front line. By 1945 they employed 1000 staff who worked day and night, 7 days a week.

Michael Bellhouse returned safely from active service but left the company in 1947. Donald Ripper died in 1949 and Ken and Dennis became joint managing directors until Dennis died in 1955. Dennis's two sons, Tony and David, worked periodically for the company following their father's death. Tony joined Evans Bellhouse in 1945 to gain experience in the various departments of the business. He left in 1946 to complete his compulsory National Service, and re-joined the company again in 1948. Tony's employment with Evans Bellhouse was for a short time only as he joined F. J. Gibson (Builder) Limited at Wilmslow. Following Donald's death Tony returned to Evans Bellhouse in 1950 as assistant manager of the joinery department. By 1955 he was in charge of the manufactured woodwork division of the company. Tony joined the board of Evans Bellhouse in 1958. On 3rd November 1965 whilst still with Evans Bellhouse, Tony was granted a patent for "Double sash windows and operating mechanism thereof".

From left: Tony Ripper with his wife Nora, and Peter Ripper taking part in a Timber Trades car rally circa 1957/1958

Peter Claybourn Ripper, Donald's son who trained at William Evans of Widnes before his father's death, returned to Evans Bellhouse as a soft wood buyer and became the director of soft wood imports in 1955. Peter also oversaw all the saw milling operations and gradually took on responsibility for sales of milled timber and was in charge of a number of salesmen. At this time he was very involved in various 'timber trade associations' and held a number of different offices through the 1950s and 1960s. Peter also played a leading role in the introduction of revolutionary new methods of import and trans-shipment of softwood timber as a pre-packaged product in the United Kingdom. The arrival of a second shipment in 1963 saw part of it received by William

Evans and Company (Manchester) Limited, an associate company of Evans Bellhouse. In 1954 Evans Bellhouse agreed to supply Ferranti of Moston, Manchester with 4020 cabinets for their model14T4 table television and 2000 cabinets for their model 045 table radio. The radio cabinets were sold to Ferranti for £2 18s 0d and both orders were to be completed and supplied by mid February 1955.

Towards the end of the 1960s Evans Bellhouse lorries travelled to Salford Docks to empty timber direct from the hull of ships from Poland and Russia. The timber would be stacked onto trailers and taken directly to Newton Heath where it was deposited in the 'Ranch' area, before it was milled, planed and entered the production area.

During the 1950s and early 1960s, Evans Bellhouse made products primarily for the building trade with occasional special joinery, such as kitchen fittings, roof trusses and wooden casings for electrical goods. Wood wool moulded packs were specially pre-shaped to fit a product and supplied with cartons. They could be used for fragile items as they were shockproof and therefore suitable for overseas destinations. The 'KEB' (Kays Evans Bellhouse) packs, as they were known, were approved by the Ministry of Supply for packing batteries and air blast cooled pentodes. KEB also supplied cases for typewriters, cameras and many other products.

In the late 1960s a small section for retail trade was set up, which sold greenhouses and sheds. In 1969 the company offered 'individually styled' kitchens for around £250. Ken Ripper had equipped several millionaire's homes in the Bahamas and Seychelles, with these kitchens, before he launched them in the United Kingdom.

Business at Evans Bellhouse began to decline during the late 1960s when there was a reduction in the workload of some departments. Competition from other companies got tougher, new products appeared in the market place and competitors operated out of more modern and efficient premises.

By 1971 the directors of Evans Bellhouse Limited were Ken Ripper (managing director), Stanley Finch, Jack Porkess, Norman Ripper, G. W. Graham, Peter Ripper, Thomas Mears and Anthony Ripper. Rippers Limited, the majority shareholders with 44.9 per cent of the capital, wanted to sell out and in June 1971 Tower Assets Limited acquired the shareholding of Rippers Limited in Evans Bellhouse for 85p a share. The board of Evans Bellhouse advised their other shareholders to accept the Tower bid. Tower Assets was an investment holding company with trading subsidiaries operating in the manufacture of kitchen furniture and the importing of timber, which were fields allied to Evans Bellhouse. The existing timber interests of Tower Assets Limited were carried on by David Roberts, Son & Co. (Bootle) Limited and its subsidiary Mallinson & Eckersley Limited and manufacturing interests through Bowker Bros. (Clitheroe) Limited. The directors of Evans Bellhouse were invited to continue in office, with Ken Ripper as managing director. He was also invited to join the board of Tower Assets.

Following the takeover, all the joinery and construction side carried out at Evans Bellhouse at Newton Heath was abandoned, and the softwood importing section went to David Roberts, Son and Co. (Bootle) Limited, based in north Liverpool. The overall company became known as Tower Timber Group Limited. Peter Ripper was adamant that the name of Evans Bellhouse was retained; this was agreed and he became a director of a successor company Evans Bellhouse (Timber) Limited, importing softwoods.

Shortly before the takeover the following personnel worked for Evans Bellhouse Limited under Peter **Ripper, Timber Director:**

Salesmen

A. J. Callard, W. Dermody, S. Higginson, A. S. K. Cronshaw, D. A. Emsley, C. B. Smith, P. J. Rimmer, M. Stanton.

Buyer	**D. Lathom**	
Shipping Clerk	G. Blomeley	
Typist and Purchase Clerk	Mrs. Gwyneth Morrice	
Timber Sales	**W. J. Burke**	
Timber Sales	S. Campbell	plus a school leaver
Timber Yard Manager	**F. Horrocks**	
Yard Foreman	A. Ward	plus 1 charge hand and 22 labourers
Yard Office Clerk	G. Thomas	
Timber Office Clerks	R. J. Allen and S. Muirhead	
Typist & Delivery Notes	Anne Edwards	
Sawmill Foreman	**F. Farmer**	plus 1 charge hand and 15 males
Tool Room	**A. Hall**	plus 3 males
Transport Manager	**F. Hall**	plus 21 males
Retail Salesman	R. P. Dale	
Salesman (Newton Heath)	F. Mycock	plus 9 labourers & 1 part time
Salesman (City Road)		J. Bradbury
Peter and Kenneth Ripper:		
T. B. Stewart	Managing Director James Stewart (Joinery) Limited	
Representative	C. C. Menzies	
Inside Manager	J. L. Wilson	
Storeman	S. McNally	
Lorry Driver	James Crawford	

Ken continued as managing director of Evans Bellhouse Limited until he retired in 1971 at the time of the takeover by the Tower Group. Both Tony and David had left the company several years earlier. In February 1972 Tower Assets were selling the buildings at Evans Bellhouse with a 35 year lease on the factory. Three months later there was a severe fire in the timber yard.

The Evans Bellhouse site on Oldham Road, Newton Heath disappeared a long time ago, and today nothing remains of this once, prosperous joinery manufacturers.

Non Ripper family directors of Evans Bellhouse Limited:
Michael Alexander Hamilton Bellhouse
Michael Bellhouse was born in 1906, the son of Walter and Mary Winifred Bellhouse, formerly McNab. Walter died in 1927 and Michael joined J.&W. Bellhouse Limited in 1928 when he had just completed his Bachelor of Arts Degree and remained a director of Evans Bellhouse Limited until 1947. As a timber importer and merchant he travelled to South America, United States of America and Canada.

Michael married Ruth Lamb in 1930 and they had two daughters. He served in the Royal Air Force during the Second World War and, in 1943 was a Wing Commander who worked for the Ministry of Aircraft Production. Michael married secondly Joyce Finlay in 1945 and they had a son. After the war he joined the Press Steel Company, an independent car body manufacturer and eventually became its deputy chairman. Shortly before Michael's death in 1968 the company was taken over by the British Motor Corporation and became part of the Rover Group.

Michael Bellhouse

G. W. Graham

George(?) Graham was educated at Ducie Avenue Central School in Manchester. He left School in 1913 and was employed for three years in the accountant's office of the City Treasurer, Manchester before joining J.B. Wrigley and Company, a prominent firm of accountants in the city. George left in 1942 and joined Evans Bellhouse as the cost accountant. When John Oakley retired as company secretary, George took over the position. He was appointed a director in 1958.

Thomas W. Mears

Thomas Mears originated from Fifeshire, Scotland. Following his education at Madras College, St. Andrews Thomas served an apprenticeship at D. and R. B. Scott, Engineers, and shortly after finishing joined James Donaldson and Sons Limited at their Tayport sawmills. In 1939 he joined Evans Bellhouse as their chief engineer and at the start of the Second World War had the responsibility of converting the works to war requirements. When the War ended he restored the factory to peace time activities. In 1950 Thomas designed the machinery which was installed in the packaging department. In early 1958 he was appointed general manger of the department and later that year a director.

Three new directors appointed to the board of Evans Bellhouse 1958
Left to right: George(?) Graham, Tony Ripper and Thomas Mears.

Chapter 22

William Kay (Bolton) Limited

From at least 1891 William Kay ran a timber merchant's business at Bark Street, Bolton. He lived at Chorley New Road with his wife Gillis, two daughters and a son; Gillis Stuart who was born in 1877, Ada Elizabeth in 1886 and William Stuart, known as Billy, who was born in December 1881.

By April 1901 when he was 19 years old Billy had joined his father at the sawmill and worked as a timber merchant.

Billy Kay married Constance Dutton, a daughter of James Dutton, a solicitor, and his wife Jane in 1910, and they lived at Dobson Road, Bolton. Billy continued to work for his father and in 1911 he was the manager at the timber yard and sawmills. Following his father's death in 1913, Billy continued to operate as a timber merchant and was a director of William Kay (Bolton) Limited.

In October 1920 Billy travelled to Quebec as a Congress party delegate and toured Canada and the United States of America. By 1922 he was trading with merchants in Germany.

In December 1928 Billy, now at Park House, Chorley New Road, obtained his Great Britain Royal Aero Club Aviation Certificate. He took his test in an Avro Alpha 80 hp at Lancashire Aero Club. William and Constance later moved to Barncroft, Heston, Bolton.

A photograph of William Stuart Kay (Billy) taken in 1928 when he obtained his pilot's licence

Kays was well known in Bolton, not least because it had a prominent chimney displaying the words: Kays for Timber. When Billy wanted to retire, with no family to take on his business he approached Evans Bellhouse, and in spring 1943 his company was taken over by them. On 21st May 1943 William Kay sold 24,349 ordinary shares for £34,197 0s 7d and Constance Kay sold 6,000 ordinary shares for £8,437 10s 0d to Evans Bellhouse Limited. The common seal of Evans Bellhouse Limited on the share transfer documents were witnessed by Tucker Ripper and Kenneth Ripper, directors and John Oakley, company secretary. Billy died in 1958 and Constance in 1966.

During the Second World War, The Loyal Regiment (North Lancashire) recruited men primarily from the towns of central Lancashire including Bolton, Chorley, Preston and Wigan including many of Kays employees. The regiment was present at the fall of Singapore when large numbers of men were taken prisoner by the Japanese. Following the surrender of Japan several of Kays employees returned, but were very traumatised.

Jack Porkess who had worked for Rippers took over as managing director of Kays in 1945 after his demobilisation. With his wife Betty and young children, Elizabeth Jill, known as Jill born in 1940 and Roger John Edward born in 1943, the family left the Essex countryside and moved to Bolton.

Jack Porkess with his son Roger and daughter Jill

Jack Porkess

It was a tough time for Jack to take on a new business role with post-war austerity. The north of England was also subjected to two bitterly cold winters in 1947-1948, and 1948-1949 which eventually forced Kays to close for a fortnight when it became too cold to work, therefore losing valuable production time.

Kays bought and sold timber with most of it being imported from abroad including Russia, when annual negotiations with Russian officials would take place. One year a very likeable Russian negotiator visited Kays and the staff hoped to meet him again the following year, alas this was not to be, as he was shot by his own people for being too accommodating!

During the war Jack received a first class education in engineering, and this had a profound influence on the direction of Kays work over the following years.

However, it was in fabricated goods that Kays began to excel. Jack was an inventor and designed and built machines working on compressed air, which automated the production of ladder making.

Advertisement for William Kay, timber merchants and sawmillers - 1947

The company also developed an expertise in roof trusses, and one of Jack's innovative designs was the K-beam. As glue technology advanced it became possible to laminate timber and this allowed roofs to be made with futuristic shapes, such as hyperbolic paraboloids. Kays were one of just a handful of companies in the country that could undertake such work.

Jack Porkess took out three patents, one for Evans Bellhouse Limited and two for William Kay (Bolton) Limited as follows:

August 1953 – (EB) Improvements in moulded packing units for the protection of goods in transport and when stored. A moulded packing unit which was resilient and permeable by air was made of lightly compressed wood wool, wood shavings, shredded wood, cereal straw, hay, dried grass, or flax rug which was flax mechanically broken down, or a mixture of two or more of those materials, held together by a thermosetting.

June 1955 – (Kays) Improvements in television and wireless aerials.
A television or wireless aerial assembly comprising lengths of flexible conductor attached together by means of an insulator and having their outer ends attached to insulators.

August 1956 - (Kays) Improvements relating to wooden beams or girders.
A wooden beam or truss, comprising a timber frame formed of laminated lower and upper members.

Advertising the timber yard

Two photographs of the yards at William Kay (Bolton) Limited showing logs and sawn timber

William Kay (Bolton) Limited remained a wholly owned subsidiary of Evans Bellhouse Limited until the latter's takeover by Tower Assets Limited in 1971. Jack retired on 30th March 1972 when two of the last directors of Kays were W. J. Johnson and A. J. Bewick. With just 100 employees on the payroll, Kays was a close knit company and it was a bitter disappointment when Tower Assets Limited closed the company down and sold the assets, not long after Jack's departure.

Chapter 23

Bowater Ripper Limited and subsequent companies

Bowater Ripper Limited

By April 1973 Rippers Limited was in negotiations, which led to an offer being made in July 1973 to being taken over by the Bowater Corporation of Bowater House, Knightsbridge, London. A 1.78 million bid was agreed and the works became Bowater Ripper Limited. Bowater continued and expanded the business of Rippers in conjunction with F. Hills & Sons, an existing joinery manufacturing subsidiary. An associate company was formed in April 1975 which then operated simultaneously from Castle Hedingham. This was Bowater Building Products Limited, which provided sales and technical advice in the south of England and also had a northern office at Norton Road, Stockton-on-Tees, Cleveland.

Rippers – still a family atmosphere

The following article appeared in the Suffolk Free Press, September 8th 1977.

"Take a walk around Rippers factory blindfolded and you'd still be in no doubt about the material they work with. The atmosphere is filled with the tangy smell of wood. The scream of the saws bombards your ears (workers wear ear muffs). Asking someone their name requires the voice box of a town crier – but everyone smiles indulgently until you make yourself understood.

Rippers, is no longer the family concern it used to be, although there is still Clive Ripper there. He is in charge of the timber buying department.

The giant Bowater Corporation took over four years ago, but the personal touch down to the gold watches for local employees, remains. Possibly the greatest change the local people will see is when the factory's giant chimney comes down. It used to belch smoke when it was used as a power house, burning up sawdust and woodchips. Rippers now use electricity – and 25 tons of all that sawing made each week is sold for curing bacon.

Inside, work is geared to an ever expanding market. Ripper's door frames, window frames, kitchen units and stairs are literally sold all over the world. To say Bowaters have many connections in world markets is a bit of an understatement. It is a multi-million pound corporation involved in everything from paper to packaging, cotton in Sudan to forests in Canada, jewellery in the United States, insurance and furniture in the U.K., wine and cognac shipping in France, rubber in the Far East, leather in Germany and the list goes on. Rippers meanwhile are working hard on building markets at home and abroad.

As Chief Executive John Alexander explains, the distressed state of the building industry in Britain means that to suppliers like Rippers, exports are the best guarantee of a rosy future. While production is at full pelt, plans for the future are well on the way. The design team is always busy on new and better lines.

Rippers are particularly proud of their newly-launched standard range of Philippine mahogany window frames. They come in all shapes and sizes, are interchangeable, and can be used in combinations that give architects a great choice of designs. The kitchen unit trade is booming too, and a new range of high gloss units is waiting in the wings for an autumn launch.

Since Rippers moved to their present site at the turn of the century, more and more huge workshops and stores have been added. Doubtless they will still grow. Currently plans are afoot to bring in even more up to date machinery – and the company is always on the lookout for skilled wood machinists and joiners. Years ago, the main trouble with wood was that it rotted. Householders were faced with disconcerting occurrences of their windows finally dropping out of their rotting frames. All that, is now over. All the wood that comes to Rippers – most of it soft wood from Sweden – is plunged into a bath of anti-rot treatment before anything else happens to it.

By the way, as you'd imagine with all that wood around, there is a regulation for workers which is vital. Nobody smokes at work. Safety is something else the company is very concerned about. The 'occupational hazard' of the old days – losing the odd finger – is something they naturally take every precaution against. In fact, Rippers workers and executives don't just make sure they obey Government safety regulations – they help make them. Production heads don't just read through the pages of new-at-work legislation. They make sure new laws are a two-way process by constantly keeping in touch, sending comments, making suggestions".

A photograph of the power house chimney being dismantled in 1977

The chimney was 120 foot high and thought to contain some 400 tons of bricks. It was erected in the 1920s as part of the power house system by which power was generated from wood chips. At one time the possibility of 'blasting' the chimney down was considered, but the idea was rejected as there was the possibility of damaging underground services.

The red brick facade of Ripper's old offices being demolished in June 1981

A Ripper's lorry being loaded with products outside "B" Mill after the takeover by Bowater

Senior directors and managers, during the Bowater Ripper era. Left to right: Brian Donner (National Sales Executive), Dale Bluemink (Export Sales Manager), David Hicks (Managing Director), Roy Wakeman (Sales and Marketing Director) and Mark Robbins (Marketing Executive)

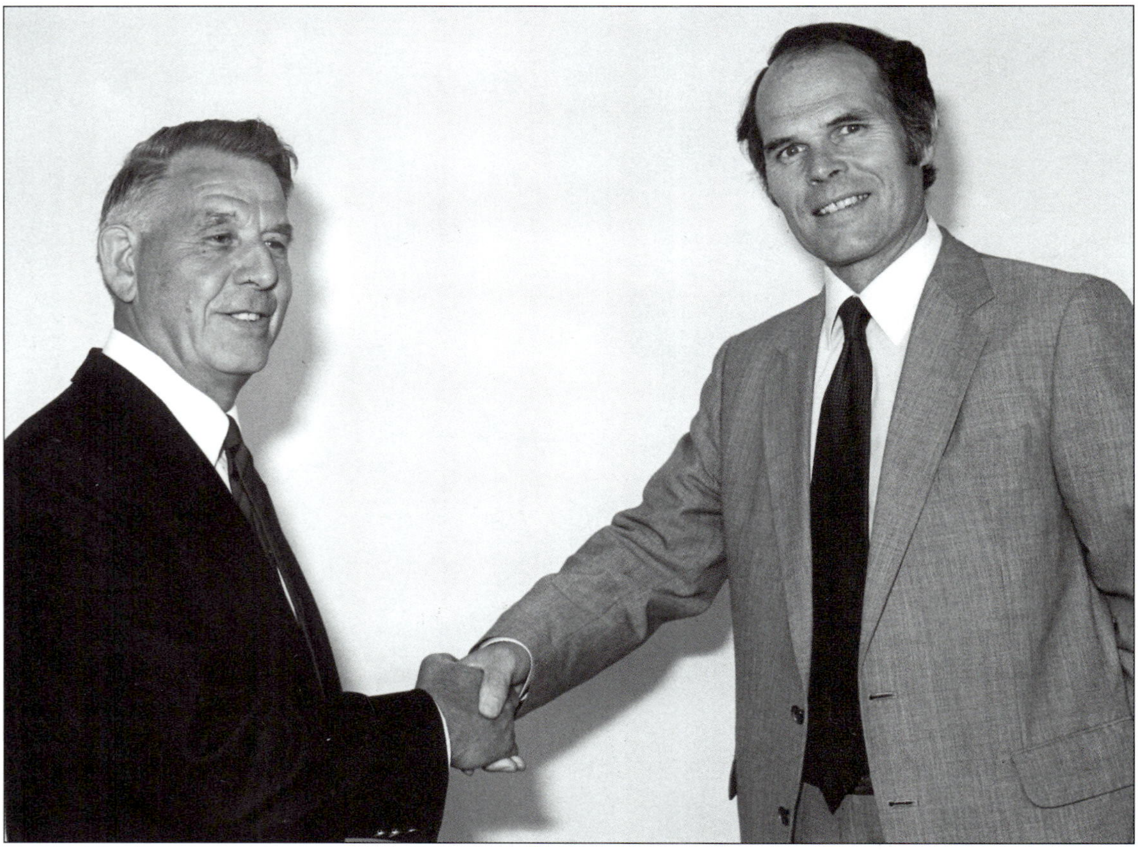

Mark Robbins (right) giving a farewell handshake to Edward Corder (left) upon his retirement in July 1983 after fifty years including war service with REME. He was presented with a cheque by David Hicks and a carriage clock and gift token from his colleagues.

Bowater Ripper apprentice machinists and instructors in 1976. Left to right: David Young, Peter Blake, David Munson, Nigel Palmer, unknown instructor, Pete Leader, Ted Rodgers (instructor), Terry Faux, Roget Lloyd (instructor), Andy Holloway, Tim Back, Peter O'Halloran, Steve Dennis, unknown and unknown. A few of these apprentices remained with the following successor companies.

Sarek Joinery Limited

Sarek Joinery Limited was in existence in the late 1980s and was part of Sarek Wood AB, a major Swedish wood producing group. They described windows manufactured by them at Castle Hedingham as 'Ripper Windows' and it was pleasing to see the Ripper name continued under their ownership.

Crosby Sarek Limited

Crosby Sarek Limited was operating the 'Hedingham' works during the early 1990s until 1995.

Norcros Limited

Norcros Limited of Ladyfield House, Station Road, Wilmslow, owned the site from August 1995. The Crittall companies of Braintree, Silver End and Witham were subsidiaries of the Norcros Group.

Premdor Crosby Limited

By 1998 Sible Hedingham was one of five sites operated by Barnsley based Premdor. It also had sites at Bridgwater, Middlesborough and Swindon. Their factory at Swan Street, Sible Hedingham continued to manufacture a variety of door frames and windows. Interior and exterior doors were made at Swindon and cubicles and washroom systems at Middlesborough. The Barnsley factory was the main distribution facility. Unfortunately the Sible Hedingham site closed in 2009 when the remaining employees, some of whom had originally been employed by Rippers, were made redundant. In February 2010 an online auction of 623 lots of the woodworking machinery, factory equipment, dust extraction, paint spray line, demountable buildings and stock took place. Interestingly some of the machinery dated back to the Rippers era. In 2013 planning permission was granted for development of the site, including 193 dwellings and land allocated for a new Doctor's Surgery and Medical Centre for the Hedinghams. Demolition of the majority of factory buildings commenced towards the end of 2013 and continued during early 2014 following which the construction of dwellings by Bloor Homes commenced.

The Rockways site
The former Maltings site, later known as Crosby Sarek Works, 23-25 Station Road, Sible Hedingham has been occupied by Rockways Limited, manufacturers of water features for over twenty years. The company still occupies the building known as the Maltings, which was built by Rippers during early 1963. The Premdor and Rockways sites were designated as one regeneration area by Braintree District Council. At the time of writing pre application plans are being considered for residential development on the Rockways part of this regeneration area.

The Ripper Legacy
The Ripper name continued with Rippers Court, which are commercial premises, comprising a mixture of offices and workshops, now owned by Braintree District Council and let to small businesses. They occupy the former 'brick' workshops parallel to Crosspath, which were erected by Rippers in 1917 and now known as Enterprise House. A small residential development at the junction of Swan Street and Station Road is named Charlton Close after William Charlton Ripper, whose beautiful red brick Edwardian house, which he built in 1905, named 'Willowbrook' stood on this site until it was demolished in 2006.

In order to further retain a legacy of the Rippers era a number of street names relating to the history of the site were agreed in 2010 between Premdor Crosby Limited, Braintree District Council and Sible Hedingham Parish Council, following public consultation. From an original list of sixteen names, eight were shortlisted namely: Ashley, Edward, Finch, Hogarth, Norman, Osier, Westrop and Woodpecker. In 2013 a ninth name was agreed namely 'Taylor' after Vero William Taylor, who owned extensive maltings in the Hedinghams including the Halfway Malting in Station Road, which was later purchased by Rippers and converted into workshops. The former bank building adjacent to Brook House will be retained and the adjoining land fronting Swan Street will become a public open space, principally gardens, and in the centre will be erected a steel sculpture of an industrial chimney containing panels depicting scenes from the history of Sible Hedingham including Rippers.

JSR Joinery Limited
When Jim and Stephen Ripper left Bowater Ripper Limited following the Bowater takeover in 1973, they together with work colleague John Moles set up a new specialist joinery company called JSR Joinery Limited at Woodpecker Court, Poole Street, Great Yeldham. This was in premises previously owned by George Argent, whose business of builder and funeral director was incorporated into the new company. The directors were Jim and Stephen Ripper and John Moles. They were joined by a number of former Ripper's employees including Cyril Bishop, Mick Brown, Reg Harrington, Anthony Ince and Graham Ince. In addition Mary Hart, another former employee, looked after the accounts. The business operated successfully for several years and when the directors approached retirement it was sold to John Townrow.

C. R. Timber Limited
This company was incorporated on 9th October 1982 with Clive Ripper as managing director, a position he held until his death on 25th June 2006. It specialised in wooden roof trusses and operated from the former airfield at Earls Colne, starting in an old wartime Nissan hut and gradually expanding. On 24th July 1991 Norman Ripper became a director and company secretary. He resigned as company secretary on 6th March 2006 but remained as a director until his death on 18th November 2006. Clive's wife Sandra and his sons Nicholas and William became directors for a short time until 2008.

Amalgamated Society of Woodworkers incorporating Amalgamated Society of Painters and Decorators – Castle Hedingham Branch – Members 1916 to 1970s

C.H. = Castle Hedingham and S.H. = Sible Hedingham

Name	age	Date of Entrance	Trade	Address
Ambrose, Ronald	16.5	21.01.25	Woodworker	112 Nunnery Street, C.H.
Ambrose, Victor Donald	15.3	06.01.26	Woodworker	36 Alexandra Road, S.H.
Abraham, Bernard	16	02.03.27	Woodworker	1 Station Road, S.H.
Ambrose, Leslie	19.4	08.06.24	Woodworker	Hillview,LambLane,S.H.
Alliston, William George	22	02.05.34	Woodworker	24 Brook Terrace, S.H.
Ambrose, William Alfred	16	21.08.35	Woodworker	19 Station Road, S.H.
Ambrose, Bert	16	05.01.38	Woodworker	40 Brook Meadow, S.H.
Anderson, Peter George	16	22.09.48	Woodworker	13 Yeldham Road, S.H.
Archer, John H.	16	24.11.65	Woodworker	23 New Park, C.H.
Archer, Thomas Edwin		22.09.72	Painter	Flat 13 Abels Road, Hal.
Acres, Nigel	20.8	30.11.73	Painter	8a Holmes Road, Halstead.
Austin, Brian	23.2	24.07.73	Woodworker	Cornhall Cottage, Bures.
Andrews, Derek	19.4	18.03.76	Woodworker	52 Cherry Garden Road, Great Waltham.
Boreham, Ernest J.	16.5	09.06.26	Woodworker	116 Nunnery Street, C.H.
Boorer, Cecil Lewis	15	05.01.27	Woodworker	28 Yeldham Road, C.H.
Brown, Albert George	15.4	11.05.27	Woodworker	10 Pye Corner, C.H.
Bareham, Percy Ralph	22.6	28.09.27	Woodworker	156 Swan Street, S.H.
Boreham, Ernest Arthur	15.5	05.12.28	Woodworker	14 Yeldham Road, S.H.
Blamire, Robert	21.6	17.07.29	Woodworker	13 Brook Terrace, S.H.
Barber, Charles Arthur	16	08.10.30	Woodworker	Prayors Hill Cottage, S.H.
Bacon, William Harry	16.1	18.03.36	Woodworker	18 Alexandra Road, S.H.
Broyd, Leonard David	16.1	15.04.36	Woodworker	9 Saffron Gardens, Wethersfield.
Boreham, William Edward	35	19.09.45	Woodworker	8 Yeldham Road, S.H.
Beales, Alfred	46	04.09.46	Woodworker	Hilldon, Hall Street, Long Melford.
Bishop, Anthony	16	01.09.54	Woodworker	5 Brook Terrace, S.H.
Blanden, John Frederick	16.5	29.11.56	Woodworker	3 Parkfields, S.H.
Bowyer, C.	60	30.06.69	Painter	27 Belle Vue Terrace, Halstead
Boreham, Robert	16	28.07.71	Woodworker	56 Oxford Meadow, S.H.
Butcher, Vincent		22.09.72	Woodworker	Church Cottages, Toppesfield
Boreham, Stuart John		10.01.73	Woodworker	29 Church Street, Lavenham.
Bowles, Gregory	16.5	14.08.73	Woodworker	10 Ronald Road, Halstead.
Bezzant, Peter John	16.2	21.09.73	Woodworker	129 Rosemary Avenue, Braintree.
Chatten, Ernest		19.06.20	Painter	11 The Bungalows, S.H.
Clarke, Albert	17.11	10.07.20	Woodworker	19 Cherry Gardens, Sawbridgeworth, Herts.
Cook, Donald F.	22.10	22.09.21	Woodworker	Yeldham Road, S.H.
Clarke, Charles Thomas	15.6	06.01.26	Woodworker	7 Yeldham Road, S.H.
Cansell, George Harry	15.0	10.11.26	Woodworker	20 Leather Lane, Great Yeldham.

Chatten, Cecil	15.5	28.08.29	Woodworker	154 Swan Street, S.H.
Carder, Joseph		15.07.33	Painter	168 Swan Street, S.H.
Coe, Ronald	16.1	27.05.36	Woodworker	Chiltonia, Moat Street, Gestingthorpe.
Coe, Alfred	16.0	03.03.37	Woodworker	46 Nunnery St, C.H.
Cook, Peter	22.0	19.09.45	Woodworker	19 Church Fields, Great Yeldham.
Chambers, Ronald	21.0	19.05.48	Woodworker	Vignall, Parsonage Street, Halstead.
Crissell, Percy	42.0	10.03.58	Painter	5 Brook Street, Glemsford.
Cook, Paul		29.01.69	Woodworker	31 Ronald Road, Halstead.
Cousins, Paul		17.11.71	Woodworker	Shearing Cottages, Belchamp St. Paul.
Clark, Michael John	19.10	18.09.71	Painter	6 Church Lane, C.H.
Chipp, Terrance	25.0	22.07.76	Woodworker	9 Albert Close, Wood Green, London.
Drury, Ernest F.	16.0	25.09.29	Woodworker	Pye Corner, C.H.
Dace, Aubrey	31.0	21.02.45	Woodworker	28 Station Road, S.H.
Duce, Bernard	41.0	25.02.46	Woodworker	14 Brook Terrace, S.H.
Debenham, Reuben	20.0	16.07.47	Woodworker	63 Alexandra Road, S.H.
Dowsett, Francis	33.0	08.09.48	Woodworker	48 Nunnery Street, C.H.
Dyson, Samuel Robert	28.0	26.01.49	Woodworker	32 Station Road, S.H.
Deal, Albert Victor	40.0	23.05.56	Woodworker	19 Leather Lane, Great Yeldham.
Dyer, Raymond		20.06.72	Woodworker	1 Church Road, Great Yeldham.
Drury, Roy Henry	47.4	07.09.73	Painter	20 Oxford Meadow, S.H.
Dixon, Peter	33.10	04.03.75	Woodworker	10 Hawkwood Road, S.H.
Dickason, Walter	58.2	18.03.76	Painter	45 Barryfields, Shalford.
Everitt, Victor	16.0	25.07.34	Woodworker	The Causeway, Toppesfield.
Earey, Harold John	16.0	10.03.36	Woodworker	1 Christmas Field, S.H.
Everitt, P.	26.0	16.07.47	Woodworker	19 Church Lane, Toppesfield.
Everitt, Ian	16.0	15.04.64	Woodworker	2 The Causeway, Toppesfield.
Everitt, Glen	16.0	19.11.69	Woodworker	2 Council Houses, Toppesfield.
Earey, Kenneth		25.03.70	Woodworker	41 Brook Meadow, S.H.
Ellis, James	56	05.09.73	Painter	"Langthorne", Wethersfield Road, S.H.
Edwards, Timothy John	16.6	21.09.73	Woodworker	11 Gilchrist Way, Braintree.
Faiers, Gordon	16.2	27.10.37	Woodworker	30 Brook Meadow, S.H.
Foxley, Trevor S.	16.0	28.09.66	Woodworker	138 South Street, Braintree.
Fuller, James	16.2	12.01.72	Woodworker	32 Monksdown Road, Coggeshall.
Fletcher, S.	16.1	23.08.72	Woodworker	9 Cedars, Church Road, Gosfield.
Fryer, Ian James	16.4	02.10.74	Woodworker	41 Stephenson Road, Braintree.
Frost, Nigel	18.9	18.03.76	Trainee	1 Crepping Hall Cottages, Wakes Colne.
Foxley, Trevor (re-admitted)	26.1	02.09.76	Woodworker	8 St. Peter's Close, Bocking End, Braintree.

Gould, Reginald H.	32.1	25.06.35	Woodworker	43 Station Road, S.H.
Girvan, Hugh	43.0	06.01.40	Woodworker	(from Northern Ireland)
Gwy, Derrick	35.5	18.03.76	Painter	22 Mill Hill, Haverhill.
Harrington, Reginald J.	15.4	15.04.25	Woodworker	10 Toppesfield Road, Great Yeldham.
Hilsden, George Stanley	15.5	14.09.27	Woodworker	16 Brook Terrace, S. H.
Hardy, H.	44.0	02.08.52	Painter	13 Park Lane, Toppesfield.
Halls, Douglas	37.0	20.06.56	Woodworker	9 Church Road, Stambourne.
Harrington, Rex	26.0	11.09.57	Woodworker	119 Swan Street, S.H.
Hoadley, Malcolm	16.0	22.07.64	Woodworker	Berwick Hall Cottages, Toppesfield.
Hume, Graham	16.0	02.02.66	Woodworker	Hillcrest, Halstead Rd, S.H.
Harrison, J. S.		10.08.70	Woodworker	4 Moat Road, Birdbrook.
Harper, D.		23.09.70	Woodworker	2 New Park, C.H.
Hardy, L.		16.08.71	Woodworker	11 New Park, C.H.
Harris, Michael F.	27.11	06.03.74	Woodworker	9 Tawneys Ride, Bures.
Jay, Harry Edward	16.1	30.07.30	Woodworker	20 Yeldham Road, S.H.
Jones, Edward	36.11	14.11.60	Painter	"Starcrest", Seven Star Green, Aldham.
Jones, Bernard William		12.08.70	Woodworker	The Manse, Parsonage Street, Halstead.
Jones, Trevor John	20.11	22.11.73	Improver	42 Brook Meadow, S.H.
Kendall, Frederick	35.0	26.07.47	Painter	53 Brook Meadow, S.H.
Keefe, James Frederick	16.0	15.04.64	Woodworker	George Lane, Glemsford.
Leathers, Jack D.	38	19.09.45	Woodworker	New Park, C.H.
Letch, Stanley	16	15.11.33	Woodworker	43 Brook Meadow, S.H.
Lowe, Alan Patrick	22	03.12.69	Woodworker	2 Egypt Cottages, Little Maplestead.
Lynch, William			Painter	11 Brook Meadow, S.H.
Lee, Michael Anthony		22.09.72	Woodworker	10 Currants Farm Road, Braintree.
Mallott, Ronald A.	27	20.02.24	Woodworker	182 Swan Street, S.H.
Moore, Robert John	25	23.10.40	Woodworker	Elm Villa, High Street, Great Yeldham.
Millidge, John Edward	16.3	08.03.50	Woodworker	26 Rowan Rd, Rodbourne Cheney, Swindon, Wilts.
Mills, Robert S.		19.01.53	Woodworker	"Walnut Tree", 8 Church Street, Colne Engaine.
Metson, Keith Alec	15.0	02.05.62	Woodworker	The Windmill, Braintree. Road, S.H.
Metson, Colin		01.03.67	Woodworker	ditto
Marsala, Tony	16.7	11.08.71	Woodworker	85 Rosemary Avenue, Braintree.
Millar, Paul		16.08.71	Woodworker	21 Ashen Road, Ridgewell
Moules, Horace		22.03.72	Painter	10 Church Lane, C.H.
Morton, Mrs. Elsie		31.03.54		
McAndrew, John	50	30.11.59	Painter	29 Ridgewell Road, Great Yeldham.
Nicholls, Dick J.	21.4	20.04.26	Woodworker	39 Station Road, S.H.
North, Cecil	25	08.05.40	Woodworker	11 Alderford Street, S.H.
Nicholls, Dennis J.	16.2	09.01.46	Woodworker	47 Station Road, S.H.
Newton, Aubrey Harry	55	19.04.50	Woodworker	C.H.
Needham, George	52	15.10.52	Woodworker	15 Brook Terrace, S.H.
Orbell, David Roy	16	08.10.58	Woodworker	

Ogden, G.M.			Painter	54 High Garrett, Bocking
Owen, Stephen	17.3	21.03.73	Woodworker	4 Church Fields, Great Yeldham.
O'Hara, Paul	16.3	02.10.74	Woodworker	North Waver, Belchamp Walter.
Orbell, David Roy (re-admitted)	33.6	30.10.75	Woodworker	50 Nunnery Street, C.H.
Paynter, R. F.	18.0	11.11.22	Woodworker	9 Station Road, S.H.
Potter, Clifford	22.0	09.10.29	Woodworker	"High Bank", Flax Lane, Glemsford.
Piper, Raymond J.	16.0	19.05.43	Woodworker	75 Oxford Meadow, S.H.
Pilgrim, Leslie G.	16.3	24.01.45	Woodworker	48 Oxford Meadow, S.H.
Pannell, E. J.	25.2.	12.03.46	Woodworker	12 Parkfields, S.H.
Pannell, Percy	28.0	04.09.46	Woodworker	114 Coggeshall Road, Bradwell.
Partridge, J.	48.0	16.09.50	Painter	16 Market Hill, Clare.
Pledger, Leslie James	43.0	08.06.55	Woodworker	62 Swan Street, S.H.
Perkins, J. D.		14.01.70	Woodworker	Catley Cross, Wickham St. Paul.
Peacock, Arthur Victor	18.11	13.06.73	Woodworker	3 Lock Road, Halstead.
Plumb, A.	16.0	30.08.73	Woodworker	9 Bakers Road, Belchamp St. Paul.
Peacock, Gordon William	16.2	21.09.73	Woodworker	3 Lock Road, Halstead.
Pickering, Harry		19.04.72	Painter	10 The Croft, Gt. Yeldham.
Rayner, Reginald F.	16.0	21.05.19	Woodworker	10 Yeldham Road, S.H.
Rayner, Leslie H.	15.2	15.04.25	Woodworker	27 Christmas Field, S.H.
Read, Dick	19.0	06.01.26	Woodworker	9 Yeldham Road, S.H.
Ruffle, William	16.1	27.11.35	Woodworker	3 New Park, C.H.
Reeve, Cyril John	16.0	03.03.37	Woodworker	The Lodge, Gestingthorpe.
Raymond, Richard Charles	16.0	08.03.50	Woodworker	Shanklin, Gestingthorpe.
Ruffle, Arthur Richard	33.0	17.02.54	Woodworker	115 Swan Street, S.H.
Ruffle, Stephen Frederick	34.0	10.11.54	Woodworker	11 Station Road, S.H.
Robinson, Basil	30.0	01.02.56	Woodworker	7 The Croft, Gt. Yeldham.
Rulton, Anthony Alex	22.0	15.02.56	Woodworker	6 New Park, C.H.
Robinson, Glyn	16.0	27.10.65	Woodworker	7 The Croft, Gt. Yeldham.
Reeve, Derek Cyril	15.7	15.03.67	Woodworker	Crouch House Cottage, Gestingthorpe.
Robinson, Neil		14.07.69	Painter	7 The Croft, Gt. Yeldham.
Rash, Raymond Charles	37.0	21.11.73	Section	7 Mill Lane, Great Maplestead
Rayner, Robert Charles	30.0	25.11.73	Painter	13 Grange Close, Halstead.
Robinson, Roy	16.7	02.10.74	Woodworker	7 The Croft, Gt. Yeldham.
Staines, Sydney	17.4	17.09.24	Woodworker	Rose Cot., Gt. Maplestead.
Smee, Thomas William	15.9	07.07.26	Woodworker	12 Leather Lane, Great Yeldham.
Springett, Cecil	16.0	16.02.27	Woodworker	Woodview, Cut Maple, SH
Smith, Arthur	16.7	15.05.28	Woodworker	18 Sarcel, Stisted.
Stockdale, Albert	16.0	23.09.31	Woodworker	10 Brook Terrace, S.H.
Smith, Walter Frank	16.1	18.03.36	Woodworker	1 Brook Terrace, S.H.
Smith, John W.	26.0	27.01.43	Woodworker	Sunny Dene, Curds Road, Earls Colne.
Smith, William Walter	16.1	19.04.44	Woodworker	9 Wethersfield Road, S.H.
Stoker, Joseph M.	26.0	14.04.54	Woodworker	24 Ridgewell Road, Great Yeldham.
Staines, Bert	31.5	01.04.39	Woodworker	15 Recreation Road, S.H.

Smith, Cecil George	32.0	08.02.61	Woodworker	1 Parker Way, Halstead.
Smith, Derek	28.0	01.10.62	Painter	7 Lock Road, Halstead.
Stewart, Malvin Alan	15.0	22.01.63	Woodworker	21 Duddery Hill, Haverhill.
Skeggs, A.	50.0	15.12.53	Painter	Cambridge Avenue, S.H.
Shinner, John Peter	16.0	19.11.69	Woodworker	106 Rosemary Avenue, Braintree.
Shipperley, Paul		12.08.70	Woodworker	15 School Road, S.H.
Sable, J.		23.08.72	Woodworker	4 Milton Ave, Braintree.
Sears, Leslie	51.7	04.03.76	Painter	Mandaville Cot., Audley End, Gestingthorpe.
Stewart, William	39.1	01.04.76	Painter	14 Kersey Avenue, Great Cornard.
Sullivan, George	36.8	01.04.76	Painter	12 Harvey St., Halstead.
Turner, Leslie E.	20.0	16.05.34	Woodworker	13 Recreation Road, S.H.
Taylor, Frederick James	23.0	26.01.49		16 Brook Meadow, S.H.
Turner, Allan James	16.0	27.10.65	Woodworker	6 Yeldham Road, C.H.
Tarbin, John Charles	22.0	11.03.70	Woodworker	55 Highfields, Gt Yeldham.
Thomas, Stanley	29.2	22.07.76	Woodworker	16 Spenser Road, Herne Hill, London SE24.
Turner, Bertram		24.06.76	Painter	1 Harvey St, Halstead.
Underwood, Stanley	22.6	19.07.16	Woodworker	12 Cambridge Ave, S.H.
Vale, Thomas M.	28.8	06.12.20	Woodworker	81 Alexandra Road, S.H.
Woodcock, Frank	35.6	16.07.19	Woodworker	Shirley, Croydon, CR0 8QQ.
Wilkin, William	15.4	26.10.27	Woodworker	Old Oaks, Leather Lane, Great Yeldham.
Wells, Thomas Richard	15.9	19.10.32	Woodworker	7 Station Road, S.H.
Wiseman, Maurice W.	16.1	11.11.36	Woodworker	Alexandra Road, S.H.
Wilding, William Ernest	16.2	28.04.37	Woodworker	High Street Green, S.H.
Wells, William A.	16.2	27.10.37	Woodworker	143 Colchester Road, Halstead.
Walters, Samuel	32.0	24.11.45	Woodworker	13 Station Road, S.H.
Wiseman, Ray Albert	15.0	20.01.54	Woodworker	52 Brook Meadow, S.H.
Walden, James	43.7	25.06.55	Painter	5 Yeldham Road, C.H.
Williams, Frederick	52.0	21.08.61	Painter	190 Swan Street, S.H.
Wiffen, Thomas Edward	25.5	02.09.63	Painter	8 Helions Park Grove, Haverhill.
Watkinson, Trevor	16.0	11.08.71	Woodworker	8 Ronald Road, Halstead.
Woods, D.		09.02.72	Painter	50 Oxford Meadow, S.H.
Whiting, Geoffrey Jordon	36.0	12.02.74		Lilacs, 30 Yeldham Rd C.H.
Winch, Peter Graham	16.2	02.10.74	Woodworker	1 Kitchen Farm Cottage, Bulmer.
Wilding, Roy	52.9	27.05.76	Bricklayer	5 Brook Meadow, S.H.

Another member of the ASW not listed above was W. W. Beadle.

Appendix Two

List of buildings where Rippers supplied the woodwork

Most of the buildings are featured in 'Ripper Woodwork Advertising Catalogues'. The exact dates of work are given where known. (For the majority of Essex buildings please see chapter 11).

	Building	**Joinery work if specified**
(1902)	Westminster Cathedral Hall, London.	Staircase and hall.
(1909)	Selfridges, Oxford Street, London.	Wall fittings.
(1910)	Longstowe Hall, Cambridge.	The gallery arcading.
(1923)	Cox's Bank, Waterloo Place, London.	Now Sofitel Hotel, St. James Hotel.
(1934)	Chartered Insurance Institute, Aldermanbury, London.	Staircase.
(1934)	Arlington House, St. James, London.	Oak staircase and continuous handrail.

Circa 1922

	New Infirmary, Christchurch.	Hygienic flush doors.
	Dr. Elsie Inglis Memorial Hospital.	

Catalogue circa late 1920s

(1923)	Adelaide House, London Bridge.	Now offices for Berwin Leighton Paisner, (Solicitors).
(1924)	Liberty & Co., Great Marlborough Street, London.	The main staircase.
	Almemar Golders Green Synagogue, London	
	Pensions Office, Acton, London.	Now flats – Bromyard House.
(1928)	Melbury Court, High Street Kensington, London.	
(1928)	Firestone Factory, Brentford.	Demolished 1980.
(1928)	Carreras New Factory, Camden Town, London.	Now offices.
(c1924)	Blanchards Club, Beak Street, London.	
	Ipswich Co-operative Society, Suffolk.	Lift doors.

Catalogue circa early 1930s

	Shell-Mex House, London.	All the joinery was supplied by Rippers.
(1929)	London Fruit & Wool Exchange, Spitalfields, London.	Auction room - Oak paneling and rostrum.
	Westfield School, Ham Common.	New dining hall.
(1930)	First Clubland Church, Camberwell, London.	Paneling, altar rails, pulpit and other joinery.
	Private house, Guildford.	Paneling, doors and staircase.
	Moreton Hall, Warwickshire.	Doors and paneling.
(1932)	Prudential Assurance, Holborn, London.	Directors' luncheon room – Austrian Wainscott oak. Manager's luncheon room – Teak with figured Teak veneered dado. Committee room – Gabon Mahogany.
	Henekeys, Bromley.	Staircase, entrance doors and other features – Oak.
(1929)	Burwood House, Caxton Street, London.	Cuban Mahogany doors.

(1930)	Cloth Fair, Smithfield, London.	
(1930)	Orchard Court, Portman Square, London.	Paneling in Indian Laurel.
(1932)	Harvey Nichols and Co. Ltd., Knightsbridge, London.	Internal joinery.
(1934)	Chartered Insurance Institute, Aldermanbury, London.	Staircase

Other buildings

(1934)	Kent and Sussex Hospital, Tunbridge Wells, Kent.	
(1934)	Mount Royal Flats, Oxford Street, London, (now the Thistle Hotel).	All the joinery, including built-in wardrobes and kitchen fittings.
(1934)	Watford Joint Isolation Hospital.	Extension.
(1937)	West London Hospital, Hammersmith Road, London.	New extension.
	Bristol Baths.	
	'Daily Sketch', London.	
	London Midland and Scottish Railway.	
	Flats in Hendon, Finchley and Ealing, London.	
(1950s - 1960s)	The New towns of Harlow, Haverhill and Stevenage.	
(1960s)	The Worth Estate, Crawley.	
	Cooper Estates Limited.	Door, windows and staircases.

Catalogue 1967
All the external windows/infill panels were supplied on the following contracts:
1. Greater London Council, Draper Street, Southwark, London.
2. London County Council, Warwick Crescent, Paddington, London.
(625 Flats in 5 – 21 Storey Blocks).
3. London Borough of Waltham Forest Housing – Leyton.
(300 Flats in 3 – 21 Storey Blocks.)

(1967) Greater London Council, Housing: Trellick Tower, North Kensington, London.
(1970) Greater London Council, Housing: Carradale House, Poplar, London.
(1970) Joinery was supplied for 195 old people's dwellings at Thamesmead for the G.L.C.,
(1973) Sites supplied with Standard Ripper Woodwork:
Chequers Estate, Crowborough Estate at Lancing.
Feering Mount Estate.
Estate at Beckenham.

Special joinery:
1. 1413 Easiform and Storiform Dwellings, New Addington, Croydon, for the London Borough of Croydon.
2. & 3. Houses, Flats and Maisonettes, Basingstoke town expansion, Hampshire.
Constructed with prefabricated timber infill panels to front and rear elevations.

1700 Central pivoted teak windows supplied to the Fleet Building for the Post Office (Ministry of Works).

The twenty five storey tower block at Samuda's Wharf, Tower Hamlets Development, Isle of Dogs. The total contract consisted of the tower block and eleven low blocks providing a total of 500 flats.

Appendix Three

Machinery

The majority of the machinery at the works was of a highly specialised character. The following is a description of some of the machinery and equipment designed and installed by Bertram Hogarth, which existed in 1971 and meticulously recorded and photographed by him. The location, uses and production processes are included.

Special equipment for stock joinery: (1) Four sash presses, (2) Vestibule frame press, (3) Sash hanging jigs, (4) Door frame press, (5) Stock door press and (6) Sash locating jig.

Special assembly equipment for stock windows: (1) Four light window assembly jig, (2) Three light jig, (3) Two light jig, (4) One light standard jig, (5) One light narrow jig, (6) Bay window assembly jig, (7) Double vent assembly press.

Universal horizontal drilling machine.

Internal door frame jig.

Automatic tenon chipper.

Double wheel sash comb joint gluing machine.

Pivot sash assembly press.

Special equipment for kitchen fittings: Vertical drilling machine for kitchen units and other products including compressed air multi head vertical drilling machine.

Three universal presses for the assembly of special joinery particularly wall panels. Construction of the presses allowed for either the assembly of one panel up to 12 ft. long or two panels of smaller size. The largest press in the works was used on special joinery in "C" department to take joinery 16 ft. by 9 ft. A universal assembly jig that could take wall units and panels up to 12 ft. by 6 ft. was installed in 'The Maltings'. There were also numerous other assembly jigs around the works to take various sizes for the assembly of internal doors and fan (window) frames, panels and hatches.

Staircase assembly plant also included presses.

Panel painting system: When units arrived in the paint shop, they were lifted onto hooks and knotted. Each unit was run into a spray booth on an overhead track, a section of which descended and lowered the unit into a pit for painting the top of the unit. The units were then run out of the booth and left untouched until dry. One man could spray 80 units per day.

Sash dipping plant, which comprised two conveyors, holding approximately 1300 sashes.

Protim dipping plant number one: A cage of joinery parts was run onto the dripping plant platform and the cage lid and front were closed by air power. The cage was immersed in protim for three minutes and rose automatically from the tank at the end of the set time. The plant was designed to take random lengths of special joinery parts up to 12 ft. long. Protim dipping plant number two: This plant was designed to take pallets of machined parts, as stacked in the machine shop and immersed in the dripping tank without disturbing the load. The pallets and parts were lifted onto powered rollers by a "Forklift" and moved and sunk into the protim tank, which was 6 ft. deep. The capacity was 80 loads per day.

Glossary

Carpenter	A craftsman who works with wood especially for houses
Carpenter and Joiner	Fully qualified tradesman. Carpenters are usually also trained as joiners but follow one trade or the other (see joiner)
Chisel	Hand tool with stout blade for cutting mortices
Drying kilns	For drying timber to extract moisture and making it strong and hard
EJMA	English Joinery Manufacturers' Association
Hyperbolic paraboloid	A geometric shape similar to a saddle
Improver	One who works at trade for low wage or no wage to improve his skill
Joiner	Craftsman who makes joinery mainly at a bench in the than that of a carpenter who often works outside
Litany desk	A moveable desk for the Minister to kneel whilst reading
Logs in stick	Logs sawn into planks with sticks inserted in between to allow seasoning or the drying of green timber to reducethe moisture content. This air drying could take from one to three years
Mortice	A slot cut in wood
Morticer or morticing machine	A woodworking machine for making a hole in wood to receive the end of another piece of wood
Paterae	Flat circular ornaments representing a classical saucer
Pentodes	Thermionic valve having five electrodes
Piece work	System by which a worker was paid by the 'piece' rather than by a regular wage
Protim	Manufactured wood preservative and coatings for timber
Reredos	Screen at the back of an altar
Saw Doctor's Shop	Was a workshop for setting and sharpening saw blades
Scantlings	Either square-sawn softwood between 47mm and 100mm thick and between 50mm and 125mm wide or square-sawn hardwood of non-standard size
Spoil	Earth, etc., thrown up or brought up in excavating or dredging
Wharfinger	Wharf owner

A Pictorial History of Sible Hedingham	Adrian Corder-Birch	1988
Advertising catalogues	Rippers Limited	various dates
Anecdotes of a Country Boy and I told you so in letters to the press	Arthur John Andrews	undated
Bolton Museum and Archive Service	Share certificates of William Kay (Bolton) Limited: ZZ/462/1	1913-1946
Bricks, Buildings and Transport A history of Mark Gentry, the Hedingham red brick industry, buildings, road and rail transport	Adrian Corder-Birch	2013
Bryan Saunders (1893-1973) Ecclesiastical Master Wood-Carver	Dodo Rose	1995
Carved in Wood – Country Practice the business of Ernest Beckwith 1872-1952	Noel Riley & Andrew Beckwith	2000
Chelmsford Chronicle newspapers		various dates
Classic Dictionary of Architecture	J. Henry Parker, F.S.A., M.A.,	1986
Commonwealth War Graves Commission records		various dates
Craftsmanship in Woodwork	Rippers Limited	c1920s
Dictionary of Building	James H. Maclean and John S. Scott	1995
Essex County Standard newspapers		various dates
Essex Directories		various dates
Essex Record Office documents	Archibald Ross D/DU 1935/5	1969
	Building plans: D/RH Pb1/1	1921
	D/RH Pb1/36	1923
	D/RH Pb1/113	1920-1928
	D/RH Pb1/146	1927
	D/RH Pb1/208	1929
	D/RH Pb1/584	1936
	D/RH Pb1/743	1939
	Congregational Church, Parsonage Street, Halstead D/NC 60/3/8	1939
	Vehicle registration documents: C/DF	various dates
From Construction to Destruction An Authentic History of the Colne Valley and Halstead Railway	Edward P. Willingham	1989
Halstead Gazette newspapers		various dates
Heritage Commercials		May 2008

Industrial Housing in Essex	Tony Crosby, Adam Garwood and Adrian Corder-Birch	2006
'Old Glory' magazines, vintage restoration		January and April 1994
Our Ancestors were Brickmakers and Potters – A history of the Corder and related families in the clayworking Industries	Adrian Corder-Birch	2010
People at Work in Halstead and District	Doreen Potts (with Foreword by Stephen Ripper)	1993
Pictures from the Past Castle Hedingham in old photographs	Charles James Bird	1990
Recollections of an Old Woodpecker	Harry Tucker Ripper	1948
Rippers Limited – An Enterprising Manufacturing Firm	The Timber Trades Journal Annual Issue	1922
Ripper Woodwork	Rippers Limited	1929
Sale particulars of Brook Farm, Sible Hedingham		1901
Standard Joinery	Rippers Limited	c1920s
Suffolk Free Press		8th September 1977
The Architect and Building News		24th December 1926
The Catalogue of Standard Woodwork	Rippers Limited	c1920s
The History of Law and Order in North Hinckford (North Essex)	Frederick W. Pawsey, D.F.C., J.P.	1991
The Timber Trades Journal & Saw Mill Advertiser		June 1947
The Timber Trades Journal		1970
With Chisel, Saw and Plane	Harry Tucker Ripper (with additions by Sheila Ripper, B.A., Dip. L.D.,)	Unpublished
Wood Magazine – Forestry, Marketing, Application		September 1938
Workers' Housing in Essex	Tony Crosby, Adam Garwood and Adrian Corder-Birch Industrial Archaeology Review	2008

Index

Note: This index does not include major parts of chapters 8, 17, 19 or appendix one, where details of employees can be found mainly in alphabetical order.

About the authors

Pam Corder-Birch
Pam born in Lancashire has spent most of her life in the south east of England. After living and working for many years in London, Pam returned to Essex where she met and married Adrian. As a member of the Halstead and District Local History Society, Pam shares Adrian's interest in the history of north Essex. She is also a member of the committee of the Essex Industrial Archaeology Group and a member of the Essex, Bradford, Lancashire and Sussex Family History Societies, enjoying all aspects of genealogy. A keen interest in her family's history led to her writing her first book about William Woodhouse, an artist with a family connection. As a keen gardener, much of her spare time is spent working in the garden. However Pam enjoys researching and always has a local history project on the go!

Books written by Pam:
Accolade to an Artist – The Life and Work of William Woodhouse 1857 – 1939
(A Lancashire artist who was renowned for painting animals especially horses and dogs, as well as land and seascapes). £12.95

The Howe Estate Halstead – Its History, Inhabitants and their Families 1750 to 1960 £14.95

Remittance in English Pounds Sterling should be made payable to Pamela Corder-Birch. Please add £2.30 for Accolade to an Artist and £3.30 for The Howe Estate to cover the cost of postage and packing.

Adrian Corder-Birch, D.L.,
Adrian was born in Stambourne and has also lived in Little Yeldham and Halstead. Following thirty six years in the legal profession, he, semi retired and is now employed part time in local government. In 2013 he was appointed as a Deputy Lieutenant of Essex.

He is a member of The Association for Industrial Archaeology and Vice Chairman of the Essex Industrial Archaeology Group. He has been a member of the British Brick Society since 1978 and its Hon. Auditor since 1989. He is a life member of the British Archaeological Association, the National Trust and English Heritage. His long standing membership, of Halstead and District Local History Society, included fifteen years as Chairman and Secretary until elected as Patron. Among other positions he is a Past President of Essex Archaeological and Historical Congress and Chairman of the Editorial Board of Essex Journal to which he is a contributor of articles about local history and industrial archaeology.

Books written by Adrian:
Our Ancestors were Brickmakers and Potters - A history of the Corder and related families in the clay working industries £14.95

Bricks, Buildings and Transport – A history of Mark Gentry, the Hedingham red brick industry, buildings, road and rail transport £14.95

Remittances in English Pounds Sterling should be payable to: Adrian Corder-Birch. Please add £2.60 for each book for postage and packing.

Enquiries and orders for any of the above books should please be sent to: Rustlings, Howe Drive, Halstead, Essex CO9 2QL. Email address: corder-birch@lineone.net